Across the humanities and the social sciences, disciplinary boundaries have come into question as scholars have acknowledged their common preoccupations with cultural phenomena ranging from rituals and ceremonies to texts and discourse. Literary critics, for example, have turned to history for a deepening of their notion of cultural products; some of them now read historical documents in the same way that they previously read "great" texts. Anthropologists have turned to the history of their own discipline in order to better understand the ways in which disciplinary authority was constructed. As historians have begun to participate in this ferment, they have moved away from their earlier focus on social theoretical models of historical development (such as Marxism and modernization theory) toward concepts taken from cultural anthropology and literary criticism.

Much of the most exciting work in history recently has been affiliated with this wide-ranging effort to write history that is essentially a history of culture. The essays presented here provide an introduction to this movement within the discipline of history. The essays in Part One trace the influence of the most important models for the new cultural history, models ranging from the pathbreaking work of the French cultural critic Michel Foucault and the American anthropologist Clifford Geertz to the imaginative efforts of such contemporary historians as Natalie Davis and E. P. Thompson, as well as the more controversial theories of Hayden White and Dominick LaCapra. The essays in Part Two are exemplary of the most

THE NEW CULTURAL HISTORY

Studies on the History of Society and Culture
Victoria E. Bonnell and Lynn Hunt, Editors

THE
NEW CULTURAL
HISTORY

EDITED AND WITH AN INTRODUCTION BY
LYNN HUNT

ESSAYS BY
ALETTA BIERSACK, ROGER CHARTIER,
SUZANNE DESAN, LLOYD S. KRAMER,
THOMAS W. LAQUEUR, PATRICIA O'BRIEN,
MARY RYAN, AND RANDOLPH STARN

UNIVERSITY OF CALIFORNIA PRESS
BERKELEY   LOS ANGELES   LONDON

University of California Press
Berkeley and Los Angeles, California

University of California Press, Ltd.
London, England

© 1989 by
The Regents of the University of California

Library of Congress Cataloging-in-Publication Data

The New cultural history: essays by Aletta Biersack . . . [et
al.] / edited and with an introduction by Lynn Hunt.
    p.   cm.—(Studies on the history of society and culture)
    Includes index.
    Contents: Michel Foucault's History of culture / Patricia
O'Brien — Crowds, community, and ritual in the work of
E. P. Thompson and Natalie Davis / Suzanne Desan —
Local knowledge, local history: Geertz and beyond / Aletta
Biersack — Literature, criticism, and historical imagination:
the literary challenge of Hayden White and Dominick
LaCapra / Lloyd S. Kramer — The American parade: repre-
sentations of the nineteenth-century social order / Mary
Ryan — Texts, printing, readings / Roger Chartier —
Bodies, details, and the humanitarian narrative / Thomas
W. Laqueur—Seeing culture in a room for a Renaissance
prince / Randolph Starn.
    ISBN 0-520-06428-3 (alk. paper). ISBN 0-520-06429-1 (pbk.:
alk. paper)
    1. Social history—Historiography.   2. Culture—Histo-
riography.   I. Biersack, Aletta.   II. Hunt, Lynn Avery.
III. Series.
HN13.N48   1989
306'.09—dc19   88-19889
                                                        CIP

Printed in the United States of America
1 2 3 4 5 6 7 8 9

To Natalie Zemon Davis,
inspiration to us all

Contents

Acknowledgments

The idea for this book originally took shape at a conference, "French History: Texts and Culture," held at the University of California, Berkeley on April 11, 1987, on the occasion of a month-long visit by Roger Chartier to Berkeley during the spring semester of that year. Although the project eventually expanded to take in work in other national fields of history, all the contributors to this volume were present at the original meeting, and that collective experience was decisive in helping us to look for common themes and understandings about the history of culture. The conference was organized by the French Studies Program at the University of California, Berkeley, and it was funded by the Florence J. Gould Foundation and the Georges Lurcy Charitable and Educational Trust. We are very grateful to these two foundations and to the University of California, Berkeley for making the meeting—and the meeting of minds—possible. We would also like to thank Natalie Zemon Davis, who acted as commentator at large, and the many other scholars in French history and in other fields of history who attended the conference.

Introduction:
History, Culture, and Text

LYNN HUNT

In 1961, E. H. Carr announced that "the more sociological history becomes, and the more historical sociology becomes, the better for both."[1] At the time, the pronouncement was a battle cry directed primarily at Carr's fellow historians—especially those of the English variety—whom Carr hoped to drag along, however unwillingly, into the new age of a socially oriented history. In retrospect, it seems that Carr was quite right: the cutting edge for both fields was the social-historical. Historical sociology has become one of the most important subfields of sociology, and perhaps the fastest growing; meanwhile, social history has overtaken political history as the most important area of research in history (as evidenced by the quadrupling of American doctoral dissertations in social history between 1958 and 1978, surpassing those in political history).[2]

In history, the move toward the social was fostered by the influence of two dominant paradigms of explanation: Marxism on the one hand and the "Annales" school on the other. Although Marxism was hardly new in the 1950s and 1960s, new

1. Edward Hallett Carr, *What Is History?* (New York, 1965; first published 1961), p. 84.
2. Robert Darnton, "Intellectual and Cultural History," in *The Past Before Us: Contemporary Historical Writing in the United States*, ed. Michael Kammen (Ithaca, N.Y., 1980), p. 334.

1

currents were coming to the fore within that explanatory mode that promoted historians' interest in social history. At the end of the 1950s and early in the 1960s, a group of younger Marxist historians began publishing books and articles on "history from below," including the by now canonical studies of George Rudé on the Parisian crowd, Albert Soboul on the Parisian sansculottes, and E. P. Thompson on the English working class.[3] With this inspiration, historians in the 1960s and 1970s turned from more traditional histories of political leaders and political institutions toward investigations of the social composition and daily life of workers, servants, women, ethnic groups, and the like.

The Annales school, though a more recent influence, came to prominence at the same time. The original journal, *Annales d'histoire économique et sociale*, was founded in 1929 by Marc Bloch and Lucien Febvre. It moved to Paris from Strasbourg in the 1930s, and took its current name, *Annales: Economies, Sociétés, Civilisations*, in 1946. The *Annales* became a school—or at least began to be so called—when it was institutionally affiliated with the Sixth Section of the Ecole Pratique des Hautes Etudes after World War II. Fernand Braudel provided a sense of unity and continuity by both presiding over the Sixth Section and directing the *Annales* in the 1950s and 1960s.[4] By the 1970s, the prestige of the school was international; the 1979 *International Handbook of Historical Studies* contained more index entries for the Annales school than for any other subject except Marx and Marxism.[5]

But was there really an Annales "paradigm," as Traian Stoianovich insisted in his book by that name? He claimed that the Annales school emphasized serial, functional, and structural approaches to understanding society as a total, integrated organism. "The *Annales* paradigm constitutes an inquiry into

3. George Rudé, *The Crowd in the French Revolution* (Oxford, 1959); Albert Soboul, *Les Sans-culottes parisiens en l'an II*, 2d ed. (Paris, 1962); E. P. Thompson, *The Making of the English Working Class* (London, 1963).

4. For the history of the Annales school, see Traian Stoianovich, *French Historical Method: The Annales Paradigm* (Ithaca, N.Y., 1976); and Guy Bourdé and Hervé Martin, *Les Ecoles historiques* (Paris, 1983).

5. Georg G. Iggers and Harold T. Parker, eds., *International Handbook of Historical Studies* (Westport, Conn., 1979).

how one of the systems of a society functions or how a whole collectivity functions in terms of its multiple temporal, spatial, human, social, economic, cultural, and eventmental dimensions."[6] Little is left out of this definition; consequently, in its presumed drive toward "total history" it loses all specificity.

Fernand Braudel, the central figure of the Annales school in the decades after World War II, laid out an apparently more precise model in his work on the Mediterranean world. He posited three levels of analysis that corresponded to three different units of time: the *structure* or *longue durée*, dominated by the geographical milieu; the *conjoncture* or medium term, oriented toward social life; and the fleeting "event," which included politics and all that concerned the individual. The structure or long term had priority, whereas events were likened to dust or foam on the sea.[7]

Although Braudel himself was enormously influential (thanks at least in part to his consolidation of important academic positions), his example did not inspire much specifically comparable work. Rather, French historians of the third Annales generation—men such as Emmanuel Le Roy Ladurie and Pierre Goubert—established an alternative model of total regional history, focusing not on world economic regions but on regions within France. In their work, economic and social history dominated; the *longue durée* certainly got its due, but the geographical dimension, though present, appeared only as a kind of formula at the beginning of each study, not as a guiding spirit. Still, this model of historical explanation was basically similar to Braudel's: climate, biology, and demography ruled over the long term along with economic trends; social relationships, which were more clearly subject to the fluctuations of the *conjoncture* (defined usually in units of ten, twenty, or even fifty years), constituted a second order of historical reality; and political, cultural, and intellectual life made up a third, largely dependent level of historical experience. The interaction between the first and second levels assumed primacy.

The Annales emphasis on economic and social history soon

6. Stoianovich, *French Historical Method*, p. 236.

7. Fernand Braudel, *La Méditerranée et le monde méditerranéen à l'époque de Philippe II* (Paris, 1949); English translation London, 1972–73.

spread even to the more traditional historical journals. By 1972, economic and social history had replaced biography and religious history as the largest categories after political history in the very conventional *Revue historique*.[8] The number of economic and social history articles in the U.S. journal *French Historical Studies* nearly doubled (from 24 to 46 percent) between 1965 and 1984.[9] Although I have looked carefully only at journals of French history, I suspect that the same trend can be detected in most fields. E. H. Carr was not an Annales historian, but his words express the *Annales* position well: "Since the preoccupation with economic and social ends represents a broader and more advanced stage in human development than the preoccupation with political and constitutional ends, so the economic and social interpretation of history may be said to represent a more advanced stage in history than the exclusively political interpretation."[10]

In recent years, however, the very models of explanation that contributed most significantly to the rise of social history have been undergoing a major shift in emphasis as Marxists and Annalistes alike have become increasingly interested in the history of culture. The turn toward culture in Marxist-inspired history was already present in Thompson's work on the English working class. Thompson explicitly rejected the metaphor of base/superstructure and devoted himself to the study of what he called "cultural and moral mediations"—"the way these material experiences are handled . . . in cultural ways."[11] In *The Making of the English Working Class* (p. 10), he described class consciousness as "the way in which these experiences [of productive relations] are handled in cultural terms: embodied in traditions, value-systems, ideas, and institutional forms." Al-

8. Alain Corbin, "*La Revue historique*: Analyse du contenu d'une publication rivale des *Annales*," in *Au Berceau des Annales: Le Milieu strasbourgeois, l'histoire en France au début du XXe siècle*, ed. Charles-Olivier Carbonell and Georges Livet (Toulouse, 1979), p. 136.

9. My figures are drawn from Lynn Hunt, "French History in the Last Twenty Years: The Rise and Fall of the *Annales* Paradigm," *Journal of Contemporary History* 21 (1986): 209–24.

10. Carr, *What is History?* pp. 164–65.

11. Quoted in Ellen Kay Trimberger, "E. P. Thompson: Understanding the Process of History," in *Vision and Method in Historical Sociology*, ed. Theda Skocpol (Cambridge, 1984), p. 219.

though the book provoked great controversy among Marxists, many of whom accused Thompson of a bias toward voluntarism and idealism, it nevertheless had great authority among younger historians.[12]

The most striking instance of Marxist historians' turn toward culture is their growing interest in language. In 1980, the editors of *History Workshop*, in an editorial entitled "Language and History," recognized the growing influence of what they called "structural linguistics" (a misuse of the term, but showing the influence of the interest in language). They argued that attention to language could challenge "reflective theories of knowledge" and affect the practice of "socialist historians" by focusing on the "'semiotic' functions of language."[13] William Sewell's book on the language of labor in the French working class is the best-known product of this interest within French history.[14]

Yet for all their attention to the workings of the "superstructure," most Marxist historians have done little more than fine-tune the fundamental Marxist model of historical explanation. As Thompson put it, "class experience is largely determined by the productive relations into which men are born—or enter involuntarily."[15] In a self-consciously Marxist book on history and linguistics, Régine Robin claimed that sense can be made of political discourse only with reference to an "extralinguistic" level of experience, namely the experience of the social relations of production.[16] In Marxist models, then, the social experience is, by definition, always primary.

The most noteworthy exception to this characterization of

12. Trimberger reviews many of the criticisms of Thompson in ibid.

13. *History Workshop* 10 (1980): 1–5; quotes p. 1.

14. William H. Sewell, Jr., *Work and Revolution in France: The Language of Labor from the Old Regime to 1848* (Cambridge, 1980).

15. Thompson, *Making of the English Working Class*, p. 10. Even Sewell's "dialectic of revolution," despite its emphasis on the role played by contradictions in Enlightenment thought, retains a fundamentally Marxist schema. Workers' consciousness moved forward under the impact of changes in labor organization and the political struggles of the various French revolutionary eras. For a critique of Sewell's position, see Lynn Hunt and George Sheridan, "Corporatism, Association, and the Language of Labor in France, 1750–1850," *Journal of Modern History* 58 (1986): 813–44.

16. For a discussion of Robin's position and those of other Marxist historians of French revolutionary language, see Lynn Hunt, *Politics, Culture, and Class in the French Revolution* (Berkeley and Los Angeles, 1984), p. 22.

Marxist interest in culture may prove the rule. In his path-breaking collection of essays *Languages of Class*, Gareth Stedman Jones tried to grapple with the inadequacies of the Marxist approach. In discussing the Chartist language of class, he observes: "What has not been sufficiently questioned is whether this language can simply be analysed in terms of its expression of, or correspondence to, the putative consciousness of a particular class or social or occupational group." Likewise, he criticizes Thompson for assuming "a relatively direct relationship between 'social being' and 'social consciousness' which leaves little independent space to the ideological context within which the coherence of a particular language of class can be reconstituted." Yet by showing the importance of the ideological tradition of radicalism and of the changing character and policies of the state, Stedman Jones is in effect moving away from a Marxist analysis. As he himself maintains in his introduction, "We cannot therefore decode political language to reach a primal and material expression of interest since it is the discursive structure of political language which conceives and defines interest in the first place."[17] Can such a radical displacement of the Marxist agenda still be considered Marxist?

The challenge to old models has been especially dramatic within the Annales school. Although economic, social, and demographic history have remained dominant in the *Annales* itself (accounting for more than half the articles from 1965 to 1984), intellectual and cultural history have taken a strong second place (claiming some 35 percent of the articles, as opposed to 11–14 percent on political history).[18] As the fourth generation of Annales historians have become increasingly preoccupied with what the French rather enigmatically term *mentalités*, economic and social history have receded in importance.[19] This deepening interest in *mentalités* (even among the older generation of Annales historians) has likewise led to new challenges to the Annales paradigm.

17. Gareth Stedman Jones, *Languages of Class: Studies in English Working Class History, 1832–1982* (Cambridge, 1983), pp. 94, 101, and 22.
18. Hunt, "The Last Twenty Years," table 1.
19. Volker Sellin traces the history of the word and of the concept in "Mentalität und Mentalitätsgeschichte," *Historische Zeitschrift* 241 (1985): 555–98.

Fourth-generation Annales historians such as Roger Chartier and Jacques Revel reject the characterization of *mentalités* as being part of the so-called third level of historical experience. For them, the third level is not a level at all but a primary determinant of historical reality. As Chartier claimed, "the relationship thus established is not one of dependence of the mental structures on their material determinations. The representations of the social world themselves are the constituents of social reality."[20] Economic and social relations are not prior to or determining of cultural ones; they are themselves fields of cultural practice and cultural production—which cannot be explained deductively by reference to an extracultural dimension of experience.[21]

In turning to the investigation of cultural practices, Annales historians such as Chartier and Revel have been influenced by Foucault's criticism of the fundamental assumptions of social history. Foucault demonstrated that there are no "natural" intellectual objects. As Chartier explained, "Madness, medicine, and the state are not categories that can be conceptualized in terms of universals whose contents each epoch particularizes";[22] they are historically given as "discursive objects," and since they are historically grounded and by implication always changing, they cannot provide a transcendent or universal foundation for historical method.

Certain similarities exist between Foucault and even the first- and second-generation Annales historians; all these scholars were looking for anonymous rules governing collective practices, and all participated in displacing the individual "subject" from history. Unlike the first generations of Annales historians, however, Foucault was fundamentally antipositivist. He did

20. Roger Chartier, "Intellectual History or Sociocultural History? The French Trajectories," in *Modern European Intellectual History: Reappraisals and New Perspectives*, ed. Dominick LaCapra and Steven L. Kaplan (Ithaca, N.Y., 1982), p. 30.

21. As Foucault explained in his work on discourse, he was not interested in determining the "underlying" causes of discursive formations but rather in seeing "historically how truth-effects are produced inside discourses which are not in themselves either true or false" (quoted in Mark Poster, "Foucault and History," *Social Research* 49 [1982]: 116–42; quote p. 128).

22. Chartier, "Intellectual History," p. 43.

not believe that the social sciences could be united in investigating the nature of man, precisely because he disavowed the very concept of "man" and the very possibility of method in the social sciences. Indeed, some commentators have called his "genealogies" an "antimethod."[23]

Although historians have been intrigued by Foucault's trenchant criticisms, they have not taken his method—or antimethod—as a model for their practice. Foucault refused to offer causal analysis and denied the validity of any reductive relationship between discursive formations and their sociopolitical contexts—between changes in views of madness, for example, and social and political changes in seventeenth- and eighteenth-century France. He vehemently argued against research into origins, and his "genealogies" required none of the usual grounding in economics, society, or politics. As a consequence, though his local insights into the functioning of particular institutions and types of discourse have generated considerable research (much of it aiming to correct Foucault's own often jerry-built constructions), his overall agenda remains idiosyncratic. And how could it be otherwise, when Foucault described his version of history as one that "disturbs what was previously considered immobile; . . . fragments what was thought unified; . . . shows the heterogeneity of what was imagined consistent with itself," and when he proclaimed that "I am well aware that I have never written anything but fictions"? Admittedly, he went on to say: "I do not mean to go so far as to say that fictions are beyond truth [*hors vérité*]. It seems to me that it is possible to make fiction work inside of truth."[24] Yet he never

23. For a useful discussion of Foucault's methods, see Larry Shiner, "Reading Foucault: Anti-Method and the Genealogy of Power-Knowledge," *History and Theory* 21 (1982): 382–97; and Hubert L. Dreyfus and Paul Rabinow, *Michel Foucault: Beyond Structuralism and Hermeneutics* (Chicago, 1982). The difference between the Annales school and "structuralism" is discussed in Stuart Clark, "The *Annales* Historians," in *The Return of Grand Theory in the Human Sciences*, ed. Quentin Skinner (Cambridge, 1985), pp. 177–98. Clark observes that "the structural history of Braudel and the *Annales* owes more to their hostility to any form of phenomenology than to their anticipation of structuralism" (p. 195). Braudel's determinism was based on a preference for a natural rather than a cultural account of experience (p. 192).

24. Quoted in Allan Megill, *Prophets of Extremity: Nietzsche, Heidegger, Foucault, Derrida* (Berkeley and Los Angeles, 1985), pp. 235, 234.

specifies how he can determine this "truth," or even what its epistemological status might be.

Even though Foucault may not have entirely succeeded in blazing a third path through the terrain of cultural history, beside Marxism and the Annales school, his influence on the conceptualization of the field has been undeniably tremendous. In her essay in this volume, "Michel Foucault's History of Culture" (chapter 1), Patricia O'Brien examines both Foucault's influence and his practices as a historian of culture. She argues convincingly that Foucault studied culture through the prism of the technologies of power, which he located strategically in discourse. He did not try to trace the workings of power to the state, the legislative process, or the class struggle; rather, he looked for them in "the most unpromising places"—in the operations of feelings, love, conscience, instinct, and in prison blueprints, doctors' observations, and far-reaching changes in disciplines such as biology and linguistics.

What, then, is the agenda for the "new cultural history"? Like Foucault's work, the broader history of *mentalités* has been criticized as lacking clear focus. François Furet denounced this lack of definition for fostering an "unending pursuit of new topics" whose choice was governed only by the fashion of the day.[25] Similarly, Robert Darnton has charged that, "despite a spate of prolegomena and discourses on method . . . , the French have not developed a coherent conception of *mentalités* as a field of study."[26]

The criticisms of Furet and Darnton strongly warn us against developing a cultural history defined only in terms of topics of inquiry. Just as social history sometimes moved from one group to another (workers, women, children, ethnic groups, the old, the young) without developing much sense of cohesion or interaction between topics, so too a cultural history defined topically could degenerate into an endless search for new cultural practices to describe, whether carnivals, cat massacres, or impotence trials.[27]

25. François Furet, "Beyond the *Annales,*" *Journal of Modern History* 55 (1983): 389–410; quote p. 405.

26. Darnton, "Intellectual and Cultural History," p. 346.

27. For a rather sanguine view on social history, but one that at least recognizes the existence of criticisms, see Peter N. Stearns, "Social History and

But Furet and Darnton are in some ways unfair in their criticism, not least because they themselves work in the genre they attack. Historians such as Chartier and Revel have not simply proposed a new set of topics for investigation; they have gone beyond *mentalités* to question the methods and goals of history generally (which is why their work is so filled with prolegomena on method). They have endorsed Foucault's judgment that the very topics of the human sciences—man, madness, punishment, and sexuality, for instance—are the product of historically contingent discursive formations. This radical critique has a basic problem, however, and that is its nihilistic strain. Where will we be when every practice, be it economic, intellectual, social, or political, has been shown to be culturally conditioned? To put it another way, can a history of culture work if it is shorn of all theoretical assumptions about culture's relationship to the social world—if, indeed, its agenda is conceived as the undermining of all assumptions about the relationship between culture and the social world?

The essays in this volume are devoted to an exploration of just such questions. Part One examines, critically and appreciatively, the models that have already been proposed for the history of culture. Part Two presents concrete examples of the new kinds of work that are currently under way. The reader will find little in the way of sociological theorizing in these pages because the rise of the new cultural history has been marked by a decline of intense debate over the role of sociological theory within history (at least among historians of culture in America). For this reason, the 1960s pronouncements of E. H. Carr on the subject seem very dated. Now, in place of sociology, the influential disciplines are anthropology and liter-

---

History: A Progress Report," *Journal of Social History* 19 (1985): 319–34. As Stearns himself admitted in an earlier essay, "Topical social history has an inherently centrifugal tendency. The topical approach thus not only reflects a lack of broader conceptualization but also positively hinders the development of an appropriate sociohistorical periodization" ("Toward a Wider Vision: Trends in Social History," in *The Past Before Us,* ed. Kammen, p. 224). It is noteworthy that cultural history appeared in *The Past Before Us* in tandem with intellectual history (Darnton, "Intellectual and Cultural History") rather than with social history. But of course, Darnton himself is the most social history–oriented of intellectual historians.

ary theory, fields in which social explanation is not taken for granted; nevertheless, cultural history must wrestle with new tensions within and between the models they offer. We hope that the essays in this volume will give some sense of both the prospects and the potential problems of using insights from these neighboring disciplines.

At the moment, the anthropological model reigns supreme in cultural approaches. Rituals, carnivalesque inversions, and rites of passage are being found in every country and almost every century. The quantitative study of *mentalités* as the "third level" of social experience never had many followers outside of France. The influence in Anglo-Saxon and especially American approaches to the history of culture came as much (or even more) from English and English-trained social anthropologists as from an Annales-style history of *mentalités*. In her pioneering essays in *Society and Culture in Early Modern France*, Natalie Z. Davis showed the relevance of concepts borrowed from Max Gluckman, Mary Douglas, and Victor Turner, as well as the French anthropologist Arnold Van Gennep. Her work, along with that of E. P. Thompson in "The Moral Economy of the English Crowd in the Eighteenth Century," promoted widespread interest in the motive power of "community."[28] As Davis explained in "The Reasons of Misrule," she hoped "to show that rather than being a mere 'safety valve,' deflecting attention from social reality, festive life can . . . perpetuate certain values of the community." Similarly, in interpreting rites of violence during the French religious wars, she concluded that "they can be reduced to a repertory of actions . . . intended to purify the religious community."[29] A straightforward social interpretation seemed much less fruitful than concepts introduced from the anthropological literature. In her essay in this volume, "Crowds, Community, and Ritual in the Work of E. P. Thompson and Natalie Davis" (chapter 2), Suzanne Desan explores the virtues as well as the problematic aspects of this notion of community. She concludes that historians of culture must develop a more differentiated notion of community and ritual, one more sen-

28. Thompson's seminal article is in *Past and Present* 50 (1971): 76–136.
29. Natalie Zemon Davis, *Society and Culture in Early Modern France* (Stanford, Calif., 1975), pp. 97, 178.

sitive to the ways in which different groups, including women, use ritual and community to foster their own separate positions. Violence, in her view, can transform and redefine community as much as it defines and consolidates it.

In recent years, the most visible anthropologist in cultural historical work has been Clifford Geertz. His collection of essays *The Interpretation of Cultures* has been cited by historians working in a wide variety of chronological and geographical settings.[30] In *The Great Cat Massacre and Other Episodes in French Cultural History*, for example, Robert Darnton clearly stated the advantages of Geertzian interpretive strategies. Cultural history, he announced, is "history in the ethnographic grain. . . . The anthropological mode of history . . . begins from the premise that individual expression takes place within a general idiom." As such, it is an interpretive science: its aim is to read "for meaning—the meaning inscribed by contemporaries."[31] The deciphering of meaning, then, rather than the inference of causal laws of explanation, is taken to be the central task of cultural history, just as it was posed by Geertz to be the central task of cultural anthropology.

Some of the problems associated with the Geertzian approach have been discussed by Roger Chartier in a long review in the *Journal of Modern History*. He questions the assumption that "symbolic forms are organized into a 'system' . . . [for] this would suppose coherence among them and interdependence, which in turn supposes the existence of a shared and unified symbolic universe."[32] How, in particular, can a "general idiom" be capable of accounting for all expressions of culture? In other words, Chartier questions the validity of a search for meaning in the Geertzian interpretive mode because it tends to efface differences in the appropriation or uses of cultural forms. The

30. Clifford Geertz, *The Interpretation of Cultures* (New York, 1973).

31. Robert Darnton, *The Great Cat Massacre and Other Episodes in French Cultural History* (New York, 1984), pp. 3, 6, 5.

32. Roger Chartier, "Text, Symbols, and Frenchness," *Journal of Modern History* 57 (1985): 682–95; quote p. 690. Darnton replied at length in "The Symbolic Element in History," *Journal of Modern History* 58 (1986): 218–34. See also the exchange of Pierre Bourdieu, Roger Chartier, and Robert Darnton in "Dialogue à propos de l'histoire culturelle," *Actes de la recherche en sciences sociales* 59 (1985): 86–93.

urge to see order and meaning obscures the existence of conflict and struggle.

In her essay "Local Knowledge, Local History: Geertz and Beyond" (chapter 3), Aletta Biersack echoes some of these criticisms. She suggests that a dose of Marshall Sahlins might be salutary for future work on the history of culture, given his "rethinking" of structure and event, or structure and history, in dialectical terms that rejuvenate both halves. It should be noted, however, that Geertz's own increasingly literary understanding of meaning (the construing of cultural meaning as a text to be read) has fundamentally reshaped current directions in anthropological self-reflection. In the final section of her essay, Biersack traces Geertz's influence on this textualizing move in anthropology and shows how the concerns of anthropologists are intersecting increasingly with those of historians of culture.

Chartier himself advocates "a definition of history primarily sensitive to inequalities in the appropriation of common materials or practices."[33] In proposing this reorientation away from community and toward difference, Chartier shows the influence of the French sociologist Pierre Bourdieu (also discussed in Biersack's wide-ranging essay). Bourdieu recast the Marxist explanatory model of social life by giving much more attention to culture; though he insisted that "the mode of expression characteristic of a cultural production always depends on the laws of the market in which it is offered," he directed his own work to the uncovering of the "specific logic" of "cultural goods." Central to that logic are the ways and means of appropriating cultural objects. Now that Bourdieu's most influential work, *Distinction*, has been translated into English, his influence on historians of culture will likely grow.[34]

Chartier insists that historians of culture must not replace a reductive theory of culture as reflective of social reality with an equally reductive assumption that rituals and other forms of

33. Chartier, "Texts, Symbols, and Frenchness," p. 688.
34. Bourdieu is perhaps best known for his concept of "habitus," which he defined in difficult but nonetheless influential terms as follows: "The habitus is not only a structuring structure, which organizes practices and the perception of practices, but also a structured structure: the principle of division

symbolic action simply express a central, coherent, communal meaning. Nor must they forget that the texts they work with affect the reader in varying and individual ways. Documents describing past symbolic actions are not innocent, transparent texts; they were written by authors with various intentions and strategies, and historians of culture must devise their own strategies for reading them. Historians have always been critical about their documents: therein lies the foundation of historical method. Chartier goes further by advocating a criticism of documents based on a new kind of history of reading. He offers an example, with its emphasis on difference, in his essay "Texts, Printing, Readings" (chapter 6). Taking the sixteenth-century prologue to the *Celestina* as his point of departure, Chartier shows that the meaning of texts in early modern Europe depended on a variety of factors, ranging from the age of readers to typographical innovations such as the multiplication of stage directions. His focus on the triangular relationship between the text as conceived by the author, as printed by the publisher, and as read (or heard) by the reader throws into doubt some of the canonical conceptions of the history of culture, in particular the dichotomy between popular and educated or elite culture.

Unlike Roger Chartier, most historians of culture have been relatively reluctant to use literary theory in any direct way. In his essay "Literature, Criticism, and Historical Imagination: The Literary Challenge of Hayden White and Dominick LaCapra" (chapter 4), Lloyd Kramer surveys the work of the two historians most closely associated with literary theory. His essay shows clearly how literary approaches have enabled White and LaCapra to expand the boundaries of cultural history, yet it remains sensitive to the reasons for the continued marginalization of such work. It is no accident that, in America, literary influences first emerged in intellectual history, with its

---

into logical classes which organizes the perception of the social world is itself the product of internalization of the division into social classes" (*Distinction: A Social Critique of the Judgment of Taste*, trans. Richard Nice [Cambridge, Mass., 1984], pp. xiii, 1, 170). This quote captures very well Bourdieu's relationship to Marxism: the habitus is both determined by the social world and determining of the perception of it.

focus on documents that are texts in the literary sense, but cultural historians who work with documents other than great books have not found literary theory to be especially relevant. One of the purposes of this volume is to show how a new generation of historians of culture use literary techniques and approaches to develop new materials and methods of analysis.

Kramer's essay also demonstrates the great variety of literary influences at work. The writings of White and LaCapra alone display significant divergences in emphasis—White aligns himself with Foucault and Frye, LaCapra with Bakhtin and Derrida. There are, after all, theories that emphasize the reception, or reading, of texts and those that emphasize their production, or writing, those that emphasize the unity and coherence of meaning and those that emphasize the play of difference and the ways in which texts work to subvert their apparent goals.[35] Just as Geertz and Sahlins represent two poles in anthropological writing—Geertz emphasizing unity, Sahlins difference— so too does literary criticism have its similarly dichotomized approaches: in Fredric Jameson's words, "old-fashioned 'interpretation,' which still asks the text what it *means*, and the newer kinds of analysis which . . . ask how it *works*" (that is, in particular, deconstruction, a critical approach closely associated with Jacques Derrida).[36] The former emphasizes unity; the latter, difference.

Unity is made possible in "interpretation" by what Jameson calls "an allegorical operation in which a text is systematically *rewritten* in terms of some fundamental master code or 'ultimately determining instance.'" Following this line of reasoning, we might say that in Davis and Thompson the rituals of violence are read—or rewritten—as allegories for community. It is precisely this allegorizing that Jameson finds objectionable in literary criticism. As he insists, "The discredit into which interpretation has fallen is thus at one with the disrepute visited on allegory itself."[37]

35. A brief review of literary theories currently in vogue can be found in Terry Eagleton, *Literary Theory: An Introduction* (Minneapolis, 1983).
36. Fredric Jameson, *The Political Unconscious: Narrative as a Socially Symbolic Act* (Ithaca, N.Y., 1981), p. 108.
37. Ibid., p. 58.

Yet at the same time, Jameson concludes that the tension between the analysis of what a text means and how it works is a tension inherent in language itself.[38] Unity is not possible without a sense of difference; difference is certainly not graspable without an opposing sense of unity. Thus, historians of culture really do not have to choose (or really cannot choose) between the two—between unity and difference, between meaning and working, between interpretation and deconstruction. Just as historians need not choose between sociology and anthropology or between anthropology and literary theory in conducting their investigations, neither must they choose once and for all between interpretive strategies based on uncovering meaning on the one hand and deconstructive strategies based on uncovering the text's modes of production on the other. Historians do not have to ally themselves single-mindedly with either Clifford Geertz or Pierre Bourdieu, with either Northrop Frye or Jacques Derrida.

Although there are many differences within and between anthropological and literary models, one central tendency in both seems currently to fascinate historians of culture: the use of language as metaphor. Symbolic actions such as riots or cat massacres are framed as texts to be read or languages to be decoded. In his criticism of Darnton, Chartier has drawn attention to the problems caused by the "metaphorical use of the vocabulary of linguistics": it obliterates the difference between symbolic actions and written texts, it defines symbolic forms so broadly that nothing is excluded, and it tends to consider symbols as fixed in their meaning.[39] Yet, though these warnings are certainly well taken, the use of language as metaphor or model has proved undeniably significant and, I would argue, critical to the formulation of a cultural approach to history. In short, the linguistic analogy establishes representation as a problem which historians can no longer avoid.

In both art history and literary criticism, representation has long been recognized as the central problem in the discipline:

38. Ibid., pp. 108–9. I do not have the space here to comment more extensively on Jameson's own particular variety of Marxist, poststructuralist literary criticism. Until now, it has had little influence on historical writing.

39. Chartier, "Text, Symbols, and Frenchness," p. 690.

what does a picture or novel do, and how does it do it? What is the relation between the picture or novel and the world it purports to represent? The new cultural history asks the same kinds of questions; first, though, it has to establish the objects of historical study as being like those of literature and art. An example of this endeavor can be seen in Thomas Laqueur's essay in Part Two, "Bodies, Details, and Humanitarian Narrative" (chapter 7), in which autopsy reports are shown to constitute a kind of literary canon.

I attempted a similar task in the first chapter of my recent book on the French Revolution when I claimed to treat "the diverse utterances of revolutionary politicians . . . as constituting one text."[40] The only basis for this claim was its potential fruitfulness for analysis and explanation, and the claim must stand or fall on those grounds. My aim was not to reduce revolutionary discourse to one stable system of meaning (the reflection of community, for example) but rather to show how political language could be used rhetorically to build a sense of community and at the same time to establish new fields of social, political, and cultural struggle—that is, make possible unity and difference at the same time. The point of the endeavor was to examine the ways in which linguistic practice, rather than simply reflecting social reality, could actively be an instrument of (or constitute) power. When national guardsmen asked, "Are you of the Nation?" they were not trying merely to identify their friends in troubled times; they were actually helping to create a sense of national community—and, at the same time, they were establishing new ways to oppose that sense of community. Words did not just reflect social and political reality; they were instruments for transforming reality.

Mary Ryan makes a similar point in her essay in Part Two, "The American Parade: Representations of the Nineteenth-Century Social Order" (chapter 5). This essay brings the unity-and-difference theme into sharp relief. Parades created a sense of community (pluralist democracy) in American cities precisely by expressing important lines of social and gender division. Ryan shows how critical a historical understanding of rit-

40. Hunt, *Politics, Culture, and Class*, p. 25.

ual can be by demonstrating how parading changed in function over time: whereas in the 1820s, 1830s, and 1840s the parading of differences under a unifying banner of civic pride served to foster civic unity, after mid century the parade was transformed into an ethnic festival that more exclusively emphasized differences. Ryan also points to the role of gender in these constructions of civic identity, and, like Desan in her piece on Davis and Thompson, she reminds us that gender was one of the most critical lines of differentiation in culture and society. No account of cultural unity and difference can be complete without some discussion of gender.

The importance of gender goes beyond its undeniably central positioning in social and cultural life, however; studies of women's history in the 1960s and 1970s and the more recent emphasis on gender differentiation played a significant role in the development of the methods of the history of culture more generally. In the United States in particular (and perhaps uniquely), women's history and gender studies have been at the forefront of the new cultural history. Natalie Davis, for example, relies on the distinctions between men and women to illuminate the workings of early modern culture. The work of Carroll Smith-Rosenberg, too, is exemplary of the ways in which women's or gender history can advance the history of culture as a style of investigation and writing. In the essays collected in the volume *Disorderly Conduct*, for example, Smith-Rosenberg brings to bear both anthropological and literary styles of analysis, ranging from the work of Mary Douglas to that of Roland Barthes. As she describes her project, "By tracing differences between nineteenth-century women's and men's mythic constructs, I sought to re-create the way gender channeled the impact of social change and the experience and exercise of power. The dialectic between language as social mirror and language as social agent formed the core of my analysis."[41] Here gender as a system of cultural representation that is at once social, literary, and linguistic is especially in view.

The methodological implications of the study of gender have

41. Carroll Smith-Rosenberg, *Disorderly Conduct: Visions of Gender in Victorian America* (New York, 1985), p. 45.

been most forcefully explicated by Joan Wallach Scott in her essay collection *Gender and the Politics of History* (which includes critiques of E. P. Thompson and Gareth Stedman Jones, among others).[42] Scott has been particularly influential in linking gender history with the analysis of discourse. In the work of Joan Scott, Carroll Smith-Rosenberg, and Natalie Zemon Davis, the rising influence of literary techniques of reading and literary theories can be clearly seen. Natalie Davis's most recent book, *Fiction in the Archives*, puts the "fictional" aspect of the documents at the center of the analysis. Rather than reading letters of pardon as sources reflective of contemporary social norms, she focuses on "how sixteenth-century people told stories . . . , what they thought a good story was, how they accounted for motive, and how through narrative they made sense of the unexpected and built coherence into immediate experience."[43]

The essays by Roger Chartier and Thomas Laqueur in Part Two of this volume are striking examples of the trend toward the literary. Readers will find in Chartier's essay, "Texts, Printing, Readings," a good introduction to his important new book, *The Cultural Uses of Print in Early Modern France*. No one has done more than Chartier to move the history of the book into the mainstream of cultural history. In *The Cultural Uses of Print*, Chartier reiterates his conviction that "culture is not over and above economic and social relations, nor can it be ranged beside them."[44] All practices, whether economic or cultural, depend on the representations individuals use to make sense of their world.

Laqueur's essay, "Bodies, Details, and Humanitarian Narrative," demonstrates the potential of new literary techniques in cultural history for enriching more traditional social history topics. He argues that humanitarianism depended in part on the development of a constellation of narrative forms—the realistic novel, the enquiry, and the medical case history—which created a sense of veracity and sympathy through narrative de-

---

42. Joan Wallach Scott, *Gender and the Politics of History* (New York, 1988).

43. Natalie Zemon Davis, *Fiction in the Archives: Pardon Tales and Their Tellers in Sixteenth-Century France* (Stanford, Calif., 1987), p. 4.

44. Roger Chartier, *The Cultural Uses of Print*, trans. Lydia G. Cochrane (Princeton, N.J., 1987), p. 11.

tail. By focusing on the narrative techniques of the autopsy report, Laqueur does not aim to avoid the traditional questions of class and power, nor to remove humanitarianism from the domain of social history; rather, he hopes to expand social history to include the sociology of narrative form.

The final essay, Randolph Starn's "Seeing Culture in a Room for a Renaissance Prince" (chapter 8), takes us back in time but forward into new questions about the techniques of cultural history. Although Starn's essay shows the influence of literary theory in its analysis of the fifteenth-century frescoes of Mantegna, it also takes us into the domain of "seeing" as opposed to "reading." Here, the linguistic analogy is no longer preeminent. Instead, Starn lays out a new typology of seeing that includes what he terms the glance, the measured view, and the scan. In this way Starn is able not only to show the relevance of art-historical documentation for cultural history but also, and more surprisingly, to recast the terms of art-historical debate itself. He historicizes the process of seeing by showing that even forms have historical content. This approach is tremendously exciting because it pushes cultural history beyond the stage of incorporating insights from other disciplines and into a position of refashioning adjacent disciplines in its turn.

All of the essays in Part Two are centrally concerned with the mechanics of representation. This concern almost necessarily entails a simultaneous reflection on the methods of history as new techniques of analysis are brought into use. And perhaps *methods* is too narrow a word in this context. For as historians learn to analyze their subjects' representations of their worlds, they inevitably begin to reflect on the nature of their own efforts to represent history; the practice of history is, after all, a process of text creating and of "seeing," that is, giving form to subjects. Historians of culture, in particular, are bound to become more aware of the consequences of their often unselfconscious literary and formal choices. The master narratives, or codes of unity or difference; the choice of allegories, analogies, or tropes; the structures of narrative—these have weighty consequences for the writing of history.

In the 1960s, great emphasis was placed on the identification of an author's political bias, on trying to situate oneself as a historian in the broader social and political world. The questions are now more subtle, but no less important. Historians are becoming more aware that their supposedly matter-of-fact choices of narrative techniques and analytical forms also have social and political implications. What is this introductory chapter, for example? Essays on the state of the discipline often have a canonical form all their own: first a narrative on the rise of new kinds of history, then a long moment for exploring the problems posed by new kinds of history, and finally either a jeremiad on the evils of new practices or a celebration of the potential overcoming of all obstacles. My story line is quite different from Carr's: where he saw the epic advance of social and economic history, the heroic historian marching hand in hand with the forces of progress, I tell the perpetual romance, the quest without end, the ironic doubling back over territory already presumably covered. By implication, history has been treated here as a branch of aesthetics rather than as the handmaiden of social theory.[45]

Reflection on such issues is not always pleasant for historians. As Nancy Partner said recently about the writing of history, "language-model epistemology" (as she termed it) has been "smuggled out of linguistics and philosophy departments by literary critics and free-ranging or metacritics, and lobbed like grenades into unsuspecting history departments."[46] The products of such an explosion will not fit neatly together as though preplanned, for there is no single agreed-upon method. As Clifford Geertz argued in his essay "Blurred Genres" (the very title indicating, I think, the ambiguity he felt about the situation), "The text analogy now taken up by social scientists is, in some ways, the broadest of the recent refigura-

45. The implications of this aestheticizing of history are very important, but too complex to develop in an essay of this length. See my "History Beyond Social Theory," to be published in a collection edited by David Carroll for Columbia University Press, for a fuller, but by no means definitive, discussion.

46. Nancy F. Partner, "Making Up Lost Time: Writing on the Writing of History," *Speculum* 61 (1986): 90–117; quote p. 95.

tions of social theory, the most venturesome, and the least well developed."[47]

For the moment, as this volume shows, the accent in cultural history is on close examination—of texts, of pictures, and of actions—and on open-mindedness to what those examinations will reveal, rather than on elaboration of new master narratives or social theories to replace the materialist reductionism of Marxism and the Annales school. (Are we headed here for a "comic" ending in literary terms? An ending that promises reconciliation of all contradictions and tensions in the pluralist manner most congenial to American historians?) Historians working in the cultural mode should not be discouraged by theoretical diversity, for we are just entering a remarkable new phase when the other human sciences (including especially literary studies but also anthropology and sociology) are discovering us anew. The very use of the term *new historicism* in literary studies, for example, shows this development. The emphasis on representation in literature, art history, anthropology, and sociology has caused more and more of our counterparts to be concerned with the historical webs in which their objects of study are caught. Someday soon, presumably, another E. H. Carr will announce that the more cultural historical studies become and the more historical cultural studies become, the better for both.

47. Clifford Geertz, "Blurred Genres: The Refiguration of Social Thought," in *Local Knowledge: Further Essays in Interpretive Anthropology* (New York, 1983), pp. 19–35; quote p. 30.

Part One

Models for Cultural History

One

Michel Foucault's
History of Culture

PATRICIA O'BRIEN

*For myself, I prefer to utilize [rather than comment on] the
writers I like. The only valid tribute to thought such as
Nietzsche's is precisely to use it, to deform it, to make it
groan and protest. And if the commentator says that I am
unfaithful to Nietzsche, that is of absolutely no interest.**

In 1961, Michel Foucault published his first major work, a history of madness from the sixteenth to the eighteenth centuries. *Histoire de la folie* stood outside the paradigms of the new social history. Neither Marxist nor Annaliste, Foucault's work in the intervening quarter century has been alternately praised and attacked by historians—and most often, in both cases, misunderstood. The body of Foucault's writing has seldom been recognized for what it is: an alternative model for writing the history of culture, a model that embodies a fundamental critique of Marxist and Annaliste analysis, of social history itself.

In the decade after World War II, a generation of young French historians stepped forward with new agendas and new concerns. Many of them, communist in their ideology and Marxist by training, emphasized social and economic structures in

*Michel Foucault, "Entretien sur le prison: le livre et sa méthode" (with J. J. Brochier), *Magazine littéraire* 101 (June 1975): 33.

search of a model of history compatible with their political commitments. Both the Annales school and Marxist practitioners responded to postwar needs for a history grounded in socioeconomic concerns. In 1958, three years before the appearance of *Histoire de la folie*, Albert Soboul's influential work *Les Sansculottes en l'an II* appeared; and in 1956, Fernand Braudel, author of *La Méditerranée*, assumed leadership and editorship of the *Annales*. These goliaths presided over a conquering social history that has commanded an international audience for the last thirty years. The disagreements, skirmishes, and wars between Marxist historians and Annalistes in the 1970s and 1980s have obscured their common views and shared concerns.[1]

In recent years, studies based on analysis of class have eroded under the flow of attacks of Annalistes and other historians. In turn, the history of *mentalités* has questioned assumptions of social and economic primacy and threatens to undermine the Annales paradigm from within. Thanks to the work of historians of the last twenty-five years, we now confront the challenge of a history of culture that can neither be reduced to the product of social and economic transformations nor return to a world of ideas cut free of them. Without the structural dominance of the Annales paradigm and the analytic certainty of class, historians are experimenting with new theories and models that owe little to the social scientific disciplines. Social history has brought us to the brink of a new history of culture, where society may not be primary after all and culture may not be derivative. The result is a period of confusion and perhaps crisis in the rise and fall of paradigms. Social historians have been slow to acknowledge "the general disintegration of the belief in a coherently unified interdisciplinarity."[2] The most widely articulated fear, even among the practitioners of the new cultural history, is that this post-Marxist, post-Annaliste history of culture may sink into relativism, irrelevance, antiquarianism, and political nihilism through the rejection of worldviews that no longer convince and compel.

1. André Burguière, "Annales (Ecole des)," in *Dictionnaire des sciences historiques*, ed. André Burguière (Paris, 1986), pp. 46–52.
2. Lynn Hunt, "French History in the Last Twenty Years: The Rise and Fall of the *Annales* Paradigm," *Journal of Contemporary History* 21 (1986): 215.

Foucault's controversial work stands as an alternative approach in the new history of culture. Traveling by a different route, Foucault questioned the very principle implicit in all social history: that society itself is the reality to be studied. Many of us have been influenced by one or another of Foucault's histories without perceiving the extent of his break with social-historical models.[3] Perhaps it is true that Foucault's works respond to the "now obvious problems" plaguing social and economic history.[4] If so, then a broader consideration of Foucault's challenges to historians should tell us something about the impasse or crossroads of the history of culture, as well as about the contribution of Foucault's work to historical writing.

In considering Foucault's contribution to the new cultural history, this chapter is dedicated to three main concerns: (1) Foucault's relation to and reception by members of the historical profession; (2) Foucault's achievements and failures as a historian—whether or not in method, research, and concerns he operated within the discipline; and (3) Foucault's influence on the writing of history and what the prospects are for the survival of such influence. In understanding the direction and development of Foucault's work as general history, I stand as a historian before it to ask how it is useful, how it is influential, how it is informative in conceptualizing and developing historical problems.

Michel Foucault's reception by historians has been troubled and contentious. The profession in France and this country has been slow to recognize as one of its own someone not trained in the historical discipline.[5] His rejection of positivist history, his coded language and opaque texts, his dismissal of his critics as "tiny minds" and "bureaucrats and police"[6] did nothing to

3. Foucault's approach and findings in *Discipline and Punish* have strongly influenced my own work on the intersection of the prison and culture; see Patricia O'Brien, *The Promise of Punishment: Prisons in Nineteenth-Century France* (Princeton, N.J., 1982).

4. Hunt, "French History in the Last Twenty Years," p. 222.

5. Foucault's training in philosophy and psychopathology are discussed by Alan Sheridan, *Michel Foucault: The Will to Truth* (London, 1980), pp. 1–8.

6. Michel Foucault, *The Order of Things: An Archaeology of the Human Sciences* (New York, 1973), p. xiv; and idem, *The Archaeology of Knowledge*, trans. A. M. Sheridan Smith (New York, 1972), p. 17.

bridge the gap between Foucault and academic historians. His insistence on his own innovativeness was coupled with an arrogant persistence in being misunderstood: "Do not ask me who I am and do not ask me to remain the same."[7] He countered stinging criticism with the occasional flippant denial: "I'm not a professional historian—but nobody's perfect."[8] Near the end of his life, Foucault identified his work as "studies of 'history' by reason of the domain they deal with and the references they appeal to; but," he insisted, "they are not the work of an 'historian.'"[9]

Allan Megill describes the stages of response by historians to Foucault's work as passing from what he terms "non-reception" through "confrontation" to a limited and tenuous "assimilation."[10] In spite of the positive reactions to *Histoire de la folie* in 1962 by Robert Mandrou and Fernand Braudel, Foucault was pretty well ignored by historians in the 1960s. Yet his reception outside the historical profession in this period was steadily on the rise, according to Megill's compilations from the Social Science Citation Index and the Arts and Humanities Citation Index. The historians who appear in the top ranks of these surveys are significantly "on the margins, even outside the 'generic' discipline of history."[11] None of the six historians most frequently cited, including Foucault, resided in an academic department or institute of history; none was "close to the socio-political mainstream."[12]

Foucault's perceived marginality as a historian gave way in the 1970s to a grudging recognition of the historical aspects of his work, although those who found in Foucault's approach similarities to their own often missed the intention of his work.

7. Foucault, *Archaeology of Knowledge*, p. 17.

8. In Ira Allen Chapel, University of Vermont, October 27, 1982, cited in Allan Megill, "The Reception of Foucault by Historians," *Journal of the History of Ideas* 48 (1987): 117.

9. Michel Foucault, *The History of Sexuality*, vol. 2: *The Use of Pleasure*, trans. Robert Hurley (New York, 1985), p. 9.

10. Megill, "Reception of Foucault," p. 125.

11. Megill's term *generic* instead of *conventional* is useful in its accuracy and amusing in its consumer connotations (ibid., p. 119).

12. Ibid., p. 120. The other five historians are Erwin Panofsky, art history; Ernst Gombrich, art history; Frances Yates, intellectual history/art history; Thomas S. Kuhn, history of science; and Mircea Eliade, history of religion.

For historians of *mentalités*, for example, Foucault's study of madness evoked Febvre's intentions of the 1930s. And historians on the Left recognized Foucault's histories of the clinic, the asylum, and the prison as institutional critiques demonstrating the development of social control.[13] Identification of common elements in a social-historical agenda shared by Foucault meant that apparent inconsistencies and contradictions in other aspects of his work were regarded as Foucault's failures. His work has been valued for its "local insights,"[14] but those insights were fitted into the existing agenda of social history. Where they have failed to fit, Foucault has been held accountable.

In his essay "L'Historien et le philosophe," Jacques Léonard, a social historian of nineteenth-century French medicine, somewhat self-mockingly contrasted Foucault to "the historian," a type who "must, in order to be competent, inhale over a long period the dust of manuscripts, grow old in the depositories of departmental archives, and fight with mice for morsels in rectory attics." Foucault clearly did not conduct himself as a dust-laden, aging nibbler of facts. Instead he was, Léonard tells us, "a barbarous knight," galloping across the historical terrain, recklessly abandoning in his histories of prisons, of medicine, of hospitals, careful and meticulous research. Foucault was criticized for his inattention to chronology, his oversights, his minimizations, his exaggerations. Historians of a wide range of subjects—work, the military, education, medicine—would be able, we were assured, to marshal "concrete facts" against Foucault's thesis of massive normalization. Léonard spoke for many historians uneasy with the unorthodoxy of Foucault's work. He nevertheless concluded in this introduction to a roundtable discussion of historians with Foucault that "M. Foucault is himself a historian, one who is incontestably original and whom we are interested in listening to." If he has ventured too far as "a philosopher coming to sow seeds in the field of historians, . . . his audacity," Léonard condescended, "is al-

13. Misunderstandings of Foucault's work are well treated by Jacques Revel, "Foucault, Michel, 1926–1984," in *Dictionnaire des sciences historiques*, ed. Burguière, pp. 290–92.
14. Hunt, "French History in the Last Twenty Years," p. 219.

ways seductive. . . . His work is above all a beautiful intellectual construction."[15]

Foucault understood the evaluation. His acerbic response to Léonard's damning praise is worth noting in some detail, because it is both a self-justification of Foucault as historian and a trenchant observation by Foucault of the state of historical writing. To "L'Historien et le philosophe" Foucault opposed his fablelike title "La Poussière et le nuage." He agreed with Léonard that the "stereotypical" historian has a variety of thankless roles:

the virtuous knight of accuracy ("I don't have many ideas but at least what I say is true"); the doctor of inexhaustible information ("You haven't said anything about this thing or that, or even that which I know about and you are certainly ignorant of"); the great witness of Reality ("No grand systems but life, real life, with all its contradictory riches"); the heartbroken scholar who weeps over his little piece of earth just pillaged by barbarians: just as if after Attila the grass would not grow again.

This is Foucault relishing, as an Attila, the scorched historical terrain he leaves in his wake. This is his angry response to the "dust" of the "true little facts" of history measured against the "cloud" stirred up by his "great vague ideas."[16] In railing against the narrowness, pettiness, and sterility of historians, he is not a barbarian but a reformer calling for something better, something grander. We, like Léonard, sense the audacity and hear the battle cry.

Critics have insisted and continue to insist that Foucault intended in his work to undermine the legitimacy of history, and of all disciplines, as exclusionary and limiting of knowledge. Because of Foucault's failure to employ "the usual criteria of historical scholarship," he is, as Megill observes, "antidisciplinary, standing outside all disciplines and drawing from them only in the hope of undermining them." Megill concludes that

15. Jacques Léonard, "L'Historien et le philosophe. A propos de: *Surveiller et punir; naissance de la prison,*" in *L'Impossible prison,* ed. Michelle Perrot (Paris, 1980), pp. 10, 12–13, 16, 9, 17.

16. Michel Foucault, "La Poussière et le nuage," in *L'Impossible prison,* ed. Perrot, p. 29.

"though he is not *of* the discipline, he is important *to* it."[17] Others, like Jacques Revel, acknowledge Foucault's contribution to history as an outsider. Revel asserts that "the work which has perhaps most profoundly marked French historians since the 1960s is not that of their peers, it is that of a philosopher, Michel Foucault."[18]

Those less positively disposed readily point to Foucault's deficiencies, lack of method, disregard for data, philosophical opacity, special language, oversimplifications, and abstractions as indicators of the historical invalidity of Foucault's work. Historians who are willing to admit that Foucault was writing history find it bad history, too general, too unsubstantiated, too mechanistic. No wonder, then, Foucault's piqued denials and flippant admission that "nobody's perfect."

It is possible that Foucault's view of historical discourse and of his engagement in it was more open and fluid—albeit complicated—and less destructive and corrosive than alleged. As Foucault observed in *The Discourse on Language*, "We tend to see, in an author's fertility, in the multiplicity of commentaries and in the development of a discipline so many infinite resources available for the creation of discourse. Perhaps so, but they are nonetheless principles of constraint, and it is probably impossible to appreciate their positive, multiplicatory role without first taking into consideration their restrictive, constraining role."[19] In any case, some historians have chosen to dismiss Foucault as a bad historian, or no historian. More favorably disposed commentators have chosen to see him as something other than a historian, standing on the outside, contributing as an outsider.

There can be little doubt that Foucault saw himself as an outsider, but one who intended to reshape profoundly the discipline that excluded him. In his inaugural lecture at the Collège de France, Foucault implicitly presented the "monstrosity" of his own work through a discussion of Gregor Mendel's contribution to biology. At this moment of his greatest institutional

17. Megill, "Reception of Foucault," pp. 133–34.
18. Revel, "Foucault," p. 290.
19. Michel Foucault, *The Discourse on Language* (New York, 1971), p. 224.

recognition, Foucault chose to identify with an outsider, an obscure Austrian monk, whose contributions to his discipline
were ignored until after his death. "Mendel was a true mon-
ster, so much so that science could not even properly speak of
him." His great discovery of the basic tenets of genetics could
not be contained by the science of his time: "Here was a new
object, calling for new conceptual tools, and for fresh theoretical foundations. Mendel spoke the truth, but he was not *dans le
vrai* (within the true) of contemporary biological discourse. . . .
A whole change in scale, the deployment of a totally new range
of objects in biology was required before Mendel could enter
into the true and his propositions appear, for the most part,
exact."[20] Foucault explained earlier the nature of his own, similar concerns: "What one is seeing, then, is the emergence of a
whole field of questions, some of which are already familiar, by
which this new form of history is trying to develop its own theory. . . . My aim is to uncover the principles and consequences
of an autochthonous transformation that is taking place in the
field of historical knowledge."[21]

Foucault's work denied marginalization, although he and his
critics relegate him to marginal status. Let us consider some
countervailing arguments. In creating his own title for the chair
awarded to him at the prestigious Collège de France in 1970,
Foucault chose "Chair in History of Systems of Thought." He
claimed to distance himself from such earlier works as *The
Order of Things* and *The Archaeology of Knowledge*, while at the
same time deepening his commitment to the historical inquiry
of *Madness and Civilization, The Birth of the Clinic, Discipline and
Punish*, and the multivolume *History of Sexuality*.[22] These works
are self-proclaimed histories. Yet they are not "generic" products of the historical discipline.

Foucault was attempting in his histories (as well as in his less
easily labeled historical works) to break with the conventions of
the discipline, to push out its boundaries. There was little that
was familiar in his throwing off of constraints, his questioning

20. Ibid.
21. Foucault, *Archaeology of Knowledge*, pp. 5, 15.
22. Hubert L. Dreyfus and Paul Rabinow, *Michel Foucault: Beyond Structuralism and Hermeneutics* (Chicago, 1982), p. viii.

of method, his measuring of, as he put it, the "mutations" of history, as he had done in *The Order of Things*. Yet Foucault was always single-minded and consistent, despite the counter-claims of his critics, in identifying what was wrong with the "regulatory principles" of the traditional history of ideas. In abandoning cause and effect and "the formless unity of some great evolutionary process, whether vaguely homogeneous or rigidly hierarchised," he did so in search of forms, not of new structures. "It was rather in order to establish those diverse converging, and sometimes divergent, but never autonomous series that enable us to circumscribe the 'locus' of an event, the limits to its fluidity and the conditions of its emergence."[23] Instead of consciousness and continuities, the stuff of the new social history, Foucault's new cultural history countered with discontinuities, groups of notions, series, discourses. His was primarily a methodological enterprise.

Foucault's methodological challenges nevertheless embraced one of the most traditional of historical endeavors: his collected works represent a new history of Western civilization. As a historian deeply committed to the present, he explained in *The Order of Things* that he intended to uncover the historical strata of his own culture. His works before and since represent a startling analysis of the civilization of the West in terms of normalization and discipline. Through his periodization, based on ruptures of the Renaissance, the Classical, and the modern ages, if he is not producing a *total* history, he is then producing a *general* one. As he explained in *The Archaeology of Knowledge*, total history stood for the reconciliation of the overall form of a civilization, the "laws that account for the cohesion" of all the phenomena of a period. According to total history, economic structures, social institutions and customs, mental attitudes, and political behavior are all governed by the same network of causality, by "one and the same historicity." General history dismisses the totality of Marxists and Annalistes alike, not in favor of plurality but in favor of interplays, correlations, dominances: "A total description draws all phenomena around a single centre—a principle, a meaning, a world-view, an overall

23. Foucault, *Discourse on Language*, p. 230.

shape; a general history, on the contrary, would deploy the space of dispersion."[24]

This newly deployed space is a canvas thick with bodies—bodies in hospitals, in clinics, in asylums, and in prisons. Foucault stated his own objective as "creat[ing] a *history* of the different modes by which, in our culture, human beings are made subjects" (emphasis mine).[25] In an earlier work, he described this goal somewhat differently, as the attempt "to reestablish the various systems of subjection."[26]

Fernand Braudel, leader of the *Annales* in the 1960s and 1970s, himself aiming to find a new way to look at history, understood early the breadth and ambition of Foucault's undertaking. In his assessment for the *Annales,* Braudel recognized *Madness and Civilization* as an attempt to trace "the mysterious pathways of the mental structures of civilization."[27] Lynn Hunt groups Foucault with two other professionally marginal historians, Philippe Ariès and Norbert Elias, as historians of the civilizing process. Like Lucien Febvre, they studied "long-range trends in the alteration of the structure of the psyche."[28] In examining Western culture in terms of internal values and behavior, Foucault, as a historian of "the systems of thought," differs vastly from other historians of *mentalités,* whose focus is the community, the family, the individual.

At the heart of Foucault's history of Western civilization is the organizing principle of power. Culture is studied through technologies of power—not class, not progress, not the indomitability of the human spirit.[29] Power cannot be apprehended through the study of conflict, struggle, and resistance except in the most limited manifestations. Power is not characteristic of a class (the bourgeoisie) or a ruling elite, nor is it attributable

24. Foucault, *Archaeology of Knowledge,* pp. 9–10.

25. Dreyfus and Rabinow, *Michel Foucault,* p. 208.

26. Michel Foucault, "Nietzsche, Genealogy, History," in *Language, Counter-Memory, Practice,* ed. Donald Bouchard (Ithaca, N.Y., 1977), p. 148.

27. Fernand Braudel's note to Robert Mandrou's review, "Trois clés pour comprendre la folie à l'époque classique," *Annales, E.S.C.* 17 (1962): 771–72.

28. Hunt, "French History in the Last Twenty Years," p. 217.

29. "It seems in retrospect that an analysis of power was the missing ingredient in both the *Annales* and Marxist paradigms" (ibid., p. 221). Hunt also sees Elias's work as developing the theme of power—power of value-setting elites.

to one. For Foucault, power is a strategy attributable to functions (dispositions, maneuvers, tactics, techniques). Power does not originate in either the economy or politics, and it is not grounded there. Power exists as "an infinitely complex network of 'micro-powers,' of power relations that permeate every aspect of social life."[30] Power not only represses; it also creates. Most challenging of all is the realization that power creates truth and hence its own legitimation. It is the job of the historian to recognize this truth production as a function of power.

Consistent with this view, Foucault denied that power is the power of the state. He asserted repeatedly that he had no theory, or "schema," of the state. The state itself is an effect of a multiplicity of movements (*rouages*, as in machinery). In his roundtable with historians in *L'Impossible prison*, he listed the questions with which "irritated" historians bombarded him: "What are you doing with the state? What theory are you giving us? You neglect its role say some, you see it everywhere say others." Foucault believed that his problem with historians, Marxist and non-Marxist alike, on this issue was "the absence of a schema. Nothing which resembles a schema like infra- and superstructure, like Malthusian cycle, or like opposition between civil society and the state: none of those schemas which have guaranteed, explicitly or implicitly, the smooth operations of historians for the last fifty, one hundred, or one hundred fifty years." He disdained the security of such schemas: his "game," he told us, was "different." "To make history from the 'objectification' of these elements that historians consider as objective givens (the objectification of objectivities, dare I say) is to step out of the circle that I'd like to travel in."[31]

To step into Foucault's circle, one must recognize nothing as given. "Nothing in man—not even his body—is sufficiently stable to serve as the basis for self-recognition or for understanding other men."[32] The notion of "man" itself is a "recent invention" of European culture since the sixteenth century.[33]

30. Sheridan, *Michel Foucault*, p. 139; Patricia O'Brien, "Crime and Punishment as Historical Problem," *Journal of Social History* 11 (1978): 513.

31. Foucault, "Table ronde du 20 mai 1978," in *L'Impossible prison*, ed. Perrot, pp. 54, 55.

32. Foucault, "Nietzsche, Genealogy, History," p. 153.

33. Foucault, *The Order of Things*, p. 386.

The state, the body, society, sex, the soul, the economy are not stable objects, they are discourses: "My general theme is not society, it is true/false discourse: let me say it is the correlative formation of domains, of objects, and of discourses verifiable and falsifiable which are assignable to them; it is not simply this formation which interests me but the effects of reality which are linked to it."[34]

This last passage is interesting for a variety of reasons. For one thing, it reveals the methodological centrality of discourse to Foucault's study of power. In looking for regularities in discursive formation, Foucault spoke of "rules" that govern the relations basic to discourse. Unity, distribution, and interplay of differences allow the historian to configure psychology, economics, grammar, and medicine as part of the same discursive formation. In discovering, for example, how criminality could become an object of psychiatric discourse, Foucault eschewed the goal of showing what criminality was really like in the nineteenth century (and hence searching for a reality exterior to the discourse) and instead viewed the discourse as "the ordering of objects," not merely as groups of signs but as relations of power.[35]

Foucault's fundamental commitment to this method as a means of studying power was explicitly avowed throughout his work. He devised general prescriptions for the study of power: do not study power merely as a form of repression, and do not reduce power to a consequence of legislation and social structure.[36] Foucault located power so that it could be studied: (1) one is never outside of power, there are no margins, no peripheries, as there is no center: "power is coextensive with the social body"; (2) "relations of power are interwoven with other kinds of relations (production, kinship, family, sexuality)" and can be studied through their discourses; (3) relations of power are interconnected and "their interconnections delineate general conditions of domination, . . . organizing it into a more or less coherent and unitary strategic form." Power relations can and

34. Foucault, "Table ronde," p. 55.
35. Foucault, *Archaeology of Knowledge*, pp. 48–49.
36. Arnold I. Davidson, "Archaeology, Genealogy, Ethics," in *Foucault: A Critical Reader*, ed. David C. Hoy (New York, 1986), pp. 225–26.

do historically serve economic interests but these interests cannot be taken as primary: class struggle is preserved but "rejected as the *ratio* for the exercise of power."[37] The historian must seek in "the most unpromising places"—feelings, love, conscience, instinct—the interstices of power. This is no proposal to study the origins of *mentalités*, worldviews, or sentiments related to other levels of social and economic systems. Foucault's purpose was not compatible with the dominant social-historical paradigms, in spite of the local insights and the similarities.

Foucault did not look for evolution or recurrence. At base, his method consisted in isolating differences and looking for reversals. He called his method "genealogical" and gave his own meaning to the term he derived from Nietzsche. "Genealogy is gray, meticulous, and patiently documentary. . . . It must record the singularity of events outside of any monotonous finality." Genealogy, he insisted, cannot be random. It requires erudition. The genealogist/historian looks for beginnings, *not* origins. This for Foucault was an essential distinction. Origins imply causes; beginnings imply differences. A genealogy, therefore, "will cultivate the details and accidents that accompany every beginning."[38]

How did the genealogical method operate in practice? Foucault repeatedly used the device of juxtaposition to introduce and sustain his histories. This was no mere literary device but a tool for undermining progressive assumptions about change. In *Discipline and Punish*, the reader is served up the grisly spectacle of the drawing and quartering of the regicide Damiens. This description is followed by the minutely detailed schedule of the daily routine of a nineteenth-century prisoner, equally brutal in its monotony. Foucault explained his adaptation of Nietzsche's method four years before *Discipline and Punish* appeared: "[The genealogist] must be able to recognize the events of history, its jolts, its surprises, its unsteady victories, and unpalatable defeats—the basis of all beginnings, atavisms, and

---

37. Michel Foucault, *Power/Knowledge: Selected Interviews and Other Writings, 1972–1977,* ed. Colin Gordon (New York, 1980), pp. 142, 141.
38. Foucault, "Nietzsche, Genealogy, History," pp. 139, 144.

heredities."[39] The method appears deceptively simple: recognizing and juxtaposing differences in search of the manifestations of power that permeate all social relations. Power is a complex phenomenon that challenges positivist assumptions. Foucault's method allows us to perceive how societies function. Studying power through discourse also allows us to perceive the moment when new technologies of power are introduced.

These aspects of Foucault's work are readily apparent in his study of "the birth of the prison." Foucault did not see punitive methods as simple consequences of social structures (and, by extension, he did not relate new methods of punishment to changes in the social and economic systems).[40] By looking for a common matrix in the history of penal law and the social sciences, Foucault discovered something new, a rupture: the introduction of the body/mind dichotomy into the arena of penal justice. With the injection of scientific knowledge into judicial practice, the body itself became a focus for a new kind of power relation. This shift was paralleled by changes in other (serial) institutions, including the school, the factory, the clinic, and the army, and these changes were interrelated through the strategic form of normalization. Foucault's subject is the technology of the body and how it changed with the metamorphosis of punitive methods in the modern period. By asking the question that he does, by decentering our understanding of punishment as repression, by cutting it loose from its liberal and Marxist interpretations, Foucault was able to replace repression with the concept of normalization—perhaps a concept more satisfying in explaining an enduring (functioning) system.

This is a method, not a theory. Foucault's contribution to the writing of history is not his social theory. As the Annales paradigm demonstrates, a theory of social change is not necessary for a consistent methodology. Through his study of power/knowledge/culture Foucault has, however, contributed a different methodology. Nevertheless, the counterassertion is strongly

39. Ibid., pp. 144–45.
40. Other contemporary historians of the prison have posited their studies of changes in the penal system on changes in the social structure. See Michael Ignatieff, *A Just Measure of Pain: The Penitentiary in the Industrial Revolution, 1750–1850* (New York, 1978); and Michelle Perrot, "1848. Révolutions et prisons," in *L'Impossible prison,* ed. Perrot, pp. 277–312.

established that Foucault had no method: "It is impossible to imagine Foucault's 'method' which is really the anti-method of Nietzsche and later Heidegger."[41] Or as Hunt states, "What is time-bound in discursive practice cannot provide the enduring foundation for historical method." Yet the process by which "the human sciences . . . must be historically deconstructed as the product of contingent 'micro-technologies of power'" is a method in itself.[42] At its worst, the method achieved "a mere intersection of things and words," brilliantly conceived perhaps, but not convincingly executed. Foucault was often clearer than his critics about the limitations of his work: "I would like to show that discourse is not a slender surface of contact, or confrontation, between a reality and a language (langue)."[43]

Slender as the contacts might sometimes be, Foucault sought them out in texts of all sorts—memoirs of deviants, diaries, political treatises, architectural blueprints, court records, doctors' reports—applying consistent principles of analysis in search of moments of reversal in discourse, in search of events as loci of conflict where social practices were transformed.[44] And to each discourse, text, event, he put the same questions: Where is power in this knowledge? How does this knowledge complement the technology of power?[45]

With the historian Arlette Farge, Foucault turned his attention to a body of documents well studied by historians, the *lettres de cachet* of the ancien régime.[46] He imposed his own method on the project.[47] Previously understood as indicators of the repressive and unjust monarchical system, these orders of summary arrest now provided access, not to the world of the state, but to the private worlds of parents and children, husbands and wives. For Foucault and Farge, the power of repres-

41. Megill, "Reception of Foucault," p. 134.

42. Hunt, "French History in the Last Twenty Years," p. 218.

43. Foucault, *Archaeology of Knowledge*, p. 48.

44. Charles C. Lemert and Garth Gillan, *Michel Foucault: Social Theory and Transgression* (New York, 1982), p. 132.

45. These questions are discussed in ibid., p. 136.

46. Arlette Farge and Michel Foucault, eds., *Le Désordre des familles. Lettres de cachet des archives de la Bastille au XVIIIe siècle* (Paris, 1982).

47. Arlette Farge, "Travailler avec Michel Foucault," *Le Débat*, no. 41 (1986): 164–67.

sion and creation in family relations did not originate with the
state. Their new readings of these documents necessarily transformed our understanding of the "politics" of family life on the
eve of the French Revolution and of the intersection of culture
and politics in the texts.

In reversing the historian's concerns with the *lettres de cachet*,
Foucault was collapsing the margins of power into the center,
using state documents to deny the centrality of the state. For a
similar purpose, Foucault "presented" the memoirs of a parricide, Pierre Rivière, and of a hermaphrodite, Herculine Barbin,
as individual studies of normalization in the nineteenth century.[48] Medical, legal, and political discourses were subjected to
the same methods of reversal and the same questioning. Foucault did not hesitate to have us follow the probing finger of the
medical examiner describing the internal organs of Barbin. Yet
Foucault is the absent commentator of the book, with little
more than a page of text to introduce, not Barbin's memoirs,
but the reports.[49] In the case of Rivière, Foucault likewise maintained his distance from the memoir: "Its beauty alone is sufficient justification for it today."[50]

Interpretive essays (referred to as "Notes") by Foucault and
his seminar students, present in the earlier text on the parricide, were jettisoned in the study of the hermaphrodite. Why?
One might argue that in exempting memoirs such as Rivière's
and Barbin's from analysis, Foucault attributed an authenticity
to the document that existed someplace outside of the power
relationship.[51] This seems a methodological inconsistency. As
Foucault explained, "We could hardly speak of it without in-
volving it in one of the discourses. . . . If we had done so, we
should have brought it within the power relation whose reductive effort we wished to show, and we ourselves should have
fallen into the trap it set."[52] With the diary of Herculine Barbin

48. Michel Foucault, ed., *I, Pierre Rivière, Having Slaughtered My Mother,
My Sister, and My Brother: A Case of Parricide in the Nineteenth Century*, trans.
Frank Jellinek (New York, 1975); and idem, ed., *Herculine Barbin, dite Alexina
B.* (Paris, 1978).
    49. Foucault, *Herculine Barbin*, pp. 131–32.
    50. Foucault, *Pierre Rivière*, p. 199.
    51. O'Brien, "Crime and Punishment," p. 514.
    52. Foucault, *Pierre Rivière*, p. xiii.

and the medical, legal, and press commentary surrounding his
suicide, Foucault allowed the placement of documents to carry
the entire interpretive weight. The commentator does not in-
trude except as an organizing presence. The story ends, not
with information of Herculine's suicide, but with Barbin's altered birth certificate, which changed his name and sex, *for the
record*, twenty-two years after his birth.

As a commentator from a different discipline concerned with
Foucault's intentions, David Carroll recognizes in this special
status attributed to Barbin's memoir and similar texts that "they
have served as weapons against the postulates of consciousness, reason, transcendence, continuity, totality, dialectics,
subjectivity, authorship, etc., testifying by their mere existence
to the reductive, coercive effects of the systems of thought organized according to these concepts." What might, therefore,
be characterized as an antimethodology or a methodological
contradiction is itself key to Foucault's critique of history and
constitutes "alternative discursive strategies."[53]

Foucault's method attempted to take nothing for granted.
It questioned established periodization and the need for national histories. Nevertheless, his own facility as a historian
was rooted in one country, France, and in one period, the seventeenth through nineteenth centuries. Although social historians took Foucault to task for his genealogical method, which
was too random and too sloppy, he was always ready with the
defense of a method that forgave oversights. For example, in
answer to the charge that he overlooked significant legislation
on the death penalty in 1832 crucial for understanding changing penal practices, Foucault responded that the development
of surveillance practices in eighteenth-century schools "appeared more important than the effects of the law."[54] His critics
here missed the point of his endeavor, which was certainly not
to locate the birth of the prison in legislative actions. His method
reversed assumptions and enmeshed discourse in society, institutions, and the economy, instead of twining it in on itself.

53. David Carroll, *Paraesthetics: Foucault, Lyotard, Derrida* (New York, 1987), p. 109.
54. Foucault, "La Poussière," p. 32.

Yet the problem of what to include and what to exclude continued to plague his work and trouble his critics.

His method of reversing assumptions is especially apparent
in his last project, *The History of Sexuality*. In volume two,
Foucault acknowledged that his genealogy "would carry me far
from my original project."[55] As Allan Megill put it, "Foucault
does not so much have a 'position' as a number of successive
positions. . . . There is nothing to prevent Foucault from moving off in a different direction in the future."[56] This is, of course,
the beauty of a method, any method. Foucault did not have a
fixed theory or fixed position against which all things could be
measured. In considering sexuality as "a historically singular
experience," not as a constant, Foucault was confronted with
the challenge of tracing back through successive discourses a
"long Christian tradition" inherited in the nineteenth and twentieth centuries.[57] His search for beginnings and differences led
him back to the Greeks. Foucault emphasized that sexuality
and its promise of fulfillment of the self are not liberations but
rather oppressions of a Christian tradition. Rome, in volume
three, represented a transition between ancient Greece and the
Christian world. Sex itself, as distinguished from sexuality, became a product of the discourse, not "the thing itself." This
analysis is a stunning reversal intended to highlight through
differences the shift in discourses.

All three volumes of *The History of Sexuality* lack the methodological rigor of Foucault's earlier works, and especially of *Discipline and Punish*. In fact, he had stepped into an area where he
was without expertise.

I am neither a Hellenist nor a Latinist. But it seemed to me that if I
gave enough care, patience, modesty, and attention to the task, it
would be possible to gain sufficient familiarity with the ancient Greek
and Roman texts; that is, a familiarity that would allow me—in keeping with a practice that is doubtless fundamental to Western philosophy—to examine both the difference that keeps us at a remove from a
way of thinking in which we recognize the origins of our own, and

55. Foucault, *The Use of Pleasure*, p. 6.
56. Megill, "Reception of Foucault," pp. 255–56.
57. Foucault, *The Use of Pleasure*, pp. 4–5.

the proximity that remains in spite of that distance which we never cease to explore.[58]

Whatever the problems of these last works, they are not the result of a failed commitment to his historical method.[59] In his search for "jolts" and "surprises" that took him back centuries in Western culture, he was always the genealogist at work, the "genealogist of desiring man."[60]

Yet what is new here? In 1975, Gilles Deleuze saw in Foucault's work "a theoretical revolution directed not only at bourgeois theories of the state, but also at the Marxist conception of power and its relation to the state. It is as if, at last, something has emerged since Marx. . . . Foucault is not content to say that certain notions have to be rethought; he does not even say it, he does it, and this proposes new coordinates for practice."[61] Now we must ask, since we do not have a theoretical revolution in Foucault, do we have new coordinates for practice?

Foucault jettisoned structures for forms and functions and in so doing cut himself loose from the reassuring positivist moorings of historical writing. Many of us have been drifting free of these moorings for some time. Some who are self-conscious about the drift (and Foucault included himself here) attribute it to the intellectual upheaval caused by postwar political events (1956 and 1968 are milestone dates in the chronology of dislocation) and to internal disciplinary contradictions, including the challenges of interdisciplinary history and the undermining effects of the history of *mentalités*.

Foucault's overarching concern, one shared by many postwar social historians, was cultural formation. Here lies the great promise of his work—the promise of integration in the history of culture. Power/knowledge is a facet of power/culture. The fragmentation, segmentation, "capillarity" of the work of contemporary post-Marxist cultural historians—those who study

58. Ibid., p. 7.

59. Limitations are discussed by Mark Poster, "The Tyranny of Greece," in *Foucault: A Critical Reader*, ed. Hoy, pp. 205–20.

60. Foucault, *The Use of Pleasure*, p. 12.

61. Gilles Deleuze, "Ecrivain non: un nouveau cartographe," *Critique*, no. 343 (1975): 1212.

women, villages, courts, families, prisons, adultery, odors, epi-
demics, the welfare state, and the like—can be accommodated
in his universe, in which technologies of power are rooted in
multiple serial institutions, in which subjects, sex, individuals,
the soul, Western culture itself are viewed through ruptures in
discourses.

Foucault's study of culture is a history with beginnings but
no causes. In place of the monocause or the primary cause,
Foucault gave us a game without causes. It is a universe of ruptures and breaks, but a universe nonetheless. He was no post-
structural anarchist.[62] His is a game with rules and an object.
But is it a game that more than one can play? Is Foucault's
method imitable? Only a handful of historians to date can be
considered—and consider themselves—to be following Foucault's lead.[63] One of Foucault's recognized contributions, which
a wide variety of the new cultural historians embrace, lies in
the importance he attributed to language/discourse as a means
of apprehending change. Language/discourse has had its greatest impact on the study of institutions, most notably the prison
and the asylum, but has the potential for more general application as well.

In France, teams have formed to consider problems heavily
influenced by Foucault's work. Recently, Michelle Perrot, a historian sympathetic to Foucault's endeavors but not a Foucauldian, has co-chaired with Robert Badinter a large seminar at the
Ecole des Hautes Etudes en Sciences Sociales on the "prison in
the Third Republic." Foucault is its absent presence. Recent
works on noninstitutional topics have been heavily influenced
by Foucault's methodology: François Ewald's *L'Etat providence*,
for example, and Alain Corbin's *Le Miasme et la jonquille*.[64] These
histories are vastly different in subject matter, although both

62. I put forward this view in O'Brien, "Crime and Punishment," p. 514.
Megill sees Foucault's anarchism as "one that does not assume, as the classic
anarchisms do, an underlying order that needs only to be expressed for harmony to prevail" (*Prophets of Extremity: Nietzsche, Heidegger, Foucault, Derrida*
[Berkeley and Los Angeles, 1985], p. 256).
63. Megill, "Reception of Foucault," pp. 131–32.
64. François Ewald, *L'Etat providence* (Paris, 1986); and Alain Corbin, *Le
Miasme et la jonquille* (Paris, 1982); English translation *The Foul and the Fragrant:
Odor and the French Social Imagination* (Cambridge, Mass., 1986).

are concerned with analyzing discourse (on the welfare state, on odor) in relation to other aspects of social life—politics, culture, economics, and social institutions over the long term. Both historians avowedly study technologies of power.

In the United States and Great Britain as well as France, historians have likewise been grappling with Foucault's epistemological challenges. David Rothman, Robert Nye, and Andrew Scull have all studied one or another aspect of madness, deviance, or institutional history. A new generation of historians and graduate students familiar with Foucault's work and critical of existing paradigms are committed to forging a new kind of history. The future of Foucauldian history is being decided in graduate seminars in all three countries. These institutional preserves provide a tenuous link between Foucault's histories and the historical discipline. Yet it is not at all clear how important Foucault's work will be in forging a new historical practice.

Foucault's influence is now most often identified with a range of topics rather than a method. His work on deviants, lepers, parricides, hermaphrodites, and monsters has inspired studies that some critics consider comparably eccentric and marginal. Writing in the *New York Review of Books* in 1981, Ian Hacking identified "key words in Foucault's work . . . Labour, Language, Life, Madness, Masturbation, Medicine, Military, Nietzsche, Prison, Psychiatry, Quixote, Sade, and Sex. Be neither attracted nor repelled by this adolescent list of topics."[65] But there was nothing adolescent about Foucault's intentions. He sought to undermine the assumptions of a discipline that still ghettoizes histories of women, homosexuals, and minorities, a discipline that still understands power, for the most part, as an attribute of a nation or class. Although Foucault was blind to gender as an analytic category, his method of studying power through discourse holds great promise for work in this area.

In the narrow sense of actual practitioners and in the broader sense of impact on assumptions, Foucauldian history appears an isolated practice. Much has been written about Foucault, about his inconsistency, his lack of theory. Some of us have criticized Foucault for having left human actors out of his his-

65. Ian Hacking, "The Archaeology of Foucault," in *Foucault: A Critical Reader*, ed. Hoy, p. 27.

tory of power.[66] It certainly would be true to say that biogeneticists who discovered and explored DNA were not concerned with human agency and individual human actions in their work. But such a charge would be obviously beside the point. In another sense, in fact, it would be untrue. Certainly, study of the genetic coding of human beings may not be incompatible with the study of individuality, although such study may in the long run transform or destroy previous understandings of individuality. Similarly, it can be observed that with his "microphysics of power" Foucault was constructing a history of culture that explained how subjects were constituted, although he was not at all concerned with human agency—that question was, for him, irrelevant.

Foucault saw himself as a "dealer in instruments, an inventor of recipes, a cartographer."[67] He did not claim to be a theorist or a system builder. The only way to test the utility of a method is by attempting to use it. Foucault molded Nietzsche to his own needs in studying the histories of power. Perhaps the best use of Foucault's work in writing history is, not to try to find a theory where there is none or to impose fixed boundaries where there is plasticity, but to deform his work, to make it groan and protest.

Alan Sheridan confidently asserts that "one cannot be a 'Foucauldian' in the way one can be a Marxist or a Freudian," and that is undoubtedly true.[68] Yet Foucault has left an important legacy for the reassessment of history. Not as a barbarian marauder or a breaker of systems but more like Gregor Mendel, who devised laws of heredity through his work with garden peas and experiments with hybrids, Foucault has refashioned historical understanding through practice rather than theory. In his attempt to rewrite the history of Western civilization, Michel Foucault has challenged us to question our assumptions and has provided us with the method and tools of analysis to write a new, political history of culture.

66. O'Brien, "Crime and Punishment," pp. 514–15.
67. Sheridan, *Michel Foucault*, p. 224.
68. Ibid., pp. 224–25.

Two

Crowds, Community, and Ritual in the Work of E. P. Thompson and Natalie Davis

SUZANNE DESAN

In the early 1970s, social historians struggled to expand their investigations beyond the demographic and socioeconomic analysis of lower-class life to explore popular cultural perceptions as well. Seeking to give voice and life to the peasants, workers, and artisans they studied, historians enriched their quantitative portrait by the study of *mentalités*. Two historians, E. P. Thompson and Natalie Davis, were extremely influential in providing the cultural analysis of popular behavior and attitudes with direction, validity, and method. Their work on crowd violence in particular became integral to the definition and formation of a new cultural approach to social history.

Thompson and Davis built on the work done in the late 1950s and 1960s by George Rudé and Charles Tilly, among others, who analyzed the social makeup of crowds to correct the misconception that rioters were unruly mobs who committed ran-

I have benefited greatly from the suggestions of Tom Broman, Dena Goodman, Lynn Hunt, Julie Liss, Lynn Nyhart, and the participants in the Chartier Conference at Berkeley in April 1987. I would especially like to thank Natalie Davis for her helpful comments and responses.

dom violence without rational goals and motivations.[1] In keeping with their emphasis on the power of culture, Thompson and Davis paid more attention to the ritualized and theatrical aspects of crowd action as cultural and communal expression: they focused primarily on the meaning, motivations, and means of legitimizing violent collective action. More specifically, they argued not only that rioters acted on the basis of some moral certainty and communal sense of legitimacy, but also that certain ritual patterns actually fit their violence within a coherent symbolic context and endowed their actions with legitimacy and meaning.[2] The work of Thompson and Davis on rioting has become so influential that these authors have redefined the questions most historians ask about crowds. Most people working on collective action in recent years have sought not only to probe the socioeconomic background of the crowd, if possible, but also to decode the patterns or rituals of the riot itself in order to uncover the participants' sense of its significance and validity. Thompson's and Davis's work on crowd violence has also prompted students of popular culture and community history in general to examine communal values and rituals within popular behavior broadly defined.

In this essay I will first discuss the underlying historical conceptions and agendas of the two authors as seminal figures in the development of the cultural approach. Then I will examine the most essential aspects of their work on popular activism, focusing on Davis's article "The Rites of Violence: Religious Riot in Sixteenth-Century France" and Thompson's "The Moral Economy of the English Crowd in the Eighteenth Century." I

1. Among Rudé's and Tilly's extensive writings on the crowd, seminal works include George Rudé, *The Crowd in History, 1730–1848* (New York, 1964); Charles Tilly, *The Vendée* (Cambridge, Mass., 1964); idem, *From Mobilization to Revolution* (Reading, Mass., 1978); and idem, *The Contentious French* (Cambridge, Mass., 1986). See also Robert Holton, "The Crowd in History: Some Problems of Theory and Method," *Social History* 3 (1978): 219–33; and Lynn Hunt, "Charles Tilly's Collective Action," in *Vision and Method in Historical Sociology*, ed. Theda Skocpol (Cambridge, 1984), pp. 244–75.

2. Natalie Zemon Davis, "The Rites of Violence: Religious Riot in Sixteenth-Century France," *Past and Present* 59 (1973): 51–91; reprinted in Natalie Zemon Davis, *Society and Culture in Early Modern France* (Stanford, Calif., 1975), pp. 152–87. (My citations are from the book.) E. P. Thompson, "The Moral Economy of the English Crowd in the Eighteenth Century," *Past and Present* 50 (1971): 76–136.

will assess their influence on recent crowd theory and on definitions of culture and community. Finally, I will explore how we can complement their work by broadening the cultural approach to history.

By staking out new issues and methods of inquiry, E. P. Thompson and Natalie Davis have had a tremendous impact on European history, and both well deserve their outstanding reputations. No one can now work on the Reformation without reading Davis or study the Industrial Revolution without perusing Thompson. Davis's work has widened the focus of Reformation studies beyond theological issues toward the social history of the Reformation and the examination of popular religion. Although her writing fits within the context of the Annales school, with its turn toward grassroots history and the *histoire des mentalités*, her work also complements the French approach by making greater use of symbolic anthropology and by emphasizing the crucial determining role of cultural rather than climatological, geographic, or socioeconomic factors.[3] Likewise, just as Natalie Davis left a radical mark on the study of the Reformation and of popular culture in general, E. P. Thompson transformed the study of the Industrial Revolution and critically reshaped debates over Marxist methodology. In his seminal book, *The Making of the English Working Class*, Thompson challenged the significance of the traditional quantitative debates over real wages and the measurable standard of living of the working class in nineteenth-century Britain and instead initiated a vast exploration of the cultural formation of working-class attitudes and consciousness. His study of working-class identity has had many followers, disciples, and imitators, as well as critics.[4]

3. In recent years, numerous Annalistes have shifted their point of emphasis and analysis away from long-term socioeconomic factors and toward cultural elements. On some level, the turn toward *mentalités* has even undermined the original Annales position that the critical factors were social and economic rather than cultural. See Lynn Hunt, "French History in the Last Twenty Years: The Rise and Fall of the *Annales* Paradigm," *Journal of Contemporary History* 21 (1986): 209–24, esp. p. 217. On the history of the Annales school, see Traian Stoianovich, *French Historical Method: The Annales Paradigm* (Ithaca, N.Y., 1976).

4. E. P. Thompson, *The Making of the English Working Class* (New York, 1963). On Thompson's influence, see, for example, Alan Dawley, "E. P.

As they uncovered new topics and methods of analysis, Davis and Thompson shared a common point of emphasis— the decisive role of *culture* as a driving force of historical change. They also shared a similar point of departure: in their early years as historians, both Davis and Thompson began to work within the Marxist tradition, yet each of them reacted against "traditional" Marxist interpretations that emphasized socioeconomic forces as having the primary determining role in history. They both came to reject a simple base/superstructure explanation for the formation of cultural perceptions. In the course of her doctoral research on printers and Protestants in sixteenth-century Lyon, Davis began to cross-examine the validity of the classic Marxist model of class as the most significant element in determining behavior and attitude. "The findings of the thesis itself made me rethink the significance of social class and of class conflict in religious change," she commented in an interview. "The Reformation, in its formative decades in Lyon, cut across rather than reflected class lines, but it did this for reasons that were completely understandable in socioeconomic terms."[5] Davis's later work illustrates a sensitivity to various groupings within society; these groups may fall into socioeconomic categories, or they may share different bonds, such as occupation, age, gender, confraternity membership, or loyalty to a village community. She consistently and eloquently argues for a more subtle analysis of these group dynamics and of the impact of economic forces on culture. For example, in her examination of youth abbeys and charivaris, Davis contrasts the structure of the rural village community with the more complex urban world of crafts, neighborhoods, and professions, and elucidates how these contexts influenced the organization, composition, role, and function of youth groups in different environments.[6]

Thompson and the Peculiarities of the Americans," *Radical History Review* 19 (1978–79): 33–59; Craig Calhoun, *The Question of Class Struggle* (Chicago, 1982); and Paul Slack, ed., *Rebellion, Popular Protest, and the Social Order in Early Modern England* (Cambridge, 1984).

5. Rob Harding and Judy Coffin, "Interview with Natalie Davis," in *Visions of History,* ed. Henry Abelove et al. (New York, 1983), p. 109.

6. Natalie Zemon Davis, "The Reasons of Misrule," in *Society and Culture,* pp. 97–123.

Like Natalie Davis, E. P. Thompson denies any simple correlation between economic forces and cultural constructs. Thompson's relationship with Marxism is more complicated and more
direct than is Davis's. He was an active member of the English
Communist party until 1956 and was a leading editor of the
New Left Review. He has repeatedly become engaged in debates
with other major Marxist figures, including Perry Anderson,
John Foster, and, more recently, Louis Althusser.[7] Thompson
continues to be heavily influenced by Marxism and views his
own project as a kind of rehabilitation of Marx, as a filling in of
some of the "silences" in Marx. In particular, Thompson finds
Marx silent "as to cultural and moral mediations." While he
does not deny the importance of material factors, Thompson explicitly rejects the "basis/superstructure" metaphor and seeks
to examine "the way these material experiences are handled in
cultural ways."[8]

In his use of the word *class*, for example, Thompson refutes
various "classic" Marxist views that define class according to
position within the economic structure or relationship to the
means of production. Instead, Thompson views class as a "historical category, describing people in relationship over time" in
an active "making" *process*. "We cannot understand class unless
we see it as a social and cultural formation," writes Thompson in
the introduction to *The Making of the English Working Class*.[9]
Thompson also insists that if "class" is used as a heuristic category, it "is inseparable from the notion of class-struggle."[10]
Only in the process of struggle, which leads to the gradual

7. On Thompson's relationship with other Marxists and with the Com-
munist party, see Bryan D. Palmer, *The Making of E. P. Thompson: Marxism,
Humanism, and History* (Toronto, 1981); and Ellen Kay Trimberger, "E. P.
Thompson: Understanding the Process of History," in *Vision and Method*, ed.
Skocpol, pp. 211–43. See also E. P. Thompson, *The Poverty of Theory and Other
Essays* (New York, 1978); and Perry Anderson, *Arguments Within English
Marxism* (London, 1980).

8. Michael Merrill, "Interview with E. P. Thompson," *Radical History Review* 3 (1976): 4–25; reprinted in *Visions of History*, ed. Abelove et al., pp. 3–
26; quote pp. 20–21 (my citations are from the book).

9. Thompson, *Making of the English Working Class*, p. 11. See also idem,
"Folklore, Anthropology, and Social History," *Indian Historical Review* 3 (1977):
247–66, esp. p. 264.

10. E. P. Thompson, "Eighteenth-Century English Society: Class Struggle
Without Class?" *Social History* 3 (1978): 133–65; quote p. 149.

gaining of cultural and political identity, does the class come into existence. It does not exist de facto simply because of its position within the means of production or within the economic structures more generally. Ideally, E. P. Thompson's concept of the cultural formation of class identity intends to promote subtle analysis of the dialectical interaction between economics and values, between structure and agency, between the material and cultural elements of existence. As he pursues this dialectical analysis, however, Thompson gives such marked primacy to the cultural factors in class formation that he has been repeatedly criticized for lack of adequate attention to structure, particularly in *The Making of the English Working Class*.[11]

In short, in reacting against an overly reductionist structuralist approach, both Davis and Thompson moved toward a method that emphasizes cultural elements over socioeconomic ones. Here their sources of inspiration diverge somewhat, although the end products share certain distinct similarities. Natalie Davis turned at an early stage to anthropology, first as a way of thinking about the secret rituals of early trade unions and later as a means of understanding the symbolic and dramatic elements of religious practice.[12] Her work betrays the influence of a wide range of symbolic anthropologists, including Clifford Geertz, Mary Douglas, Arnold Van Gennep, Max Gluckman, E. Evans-Pritchard, and Victor Turner. Davis expresses certain reservations about the shortcomings of anthropology and particularly criticizes its tendency to ignore change. In her own work, she consistently seeks to combine anthropological insights with a greater sensitivity to the historical dynamic. Yet Davis finds the discipline useful in helping the historian to develop a sense of the rich variety of human experience. Anthropology also provides methods for examining "informal or small-scale interactions which can express important linkages and conflicts" within the social structure.[13] While Davis

11. R. Currie and R. M. Hartwell, "The Making of the English Working Class?" *Economic History Review*, 2d ser., 18 (1965): 633–43; John Foster, *Class Struggle and the Industrial Revolution* (London, 1974); Richard Johnson, "Edward Thompson, Eugene Genovese, and Socialist Humanist History," *History Workshop* 6 (1978): 79–100; and Trimberger, "E. P. Thompson," pp. 224–25, 236.

12. Harding and Coffin, "Interview with Davis," pp. 110–11.

13. Natalie Zemon Davis, "Anthropology and History in the 1980s: The Possibilities of the Past," *Journal of Interdisciplinary History* 11 (1981): 267–75,

is by no means a strict functionalist in her anthropological approach, she assumes that various cultural events or customs, such as riots, festivals, or charivaris, have a particular function and meaning for the participants and the community. By interpreting the symbolic patterns and significance of these cultural phenomena, the historian can uncover how the social system fits together and how its participants perceive themselves and the outside world.

E. P. Thompson, in contrast, has a more ambivalent attitude toward anthropology. His early work was not directly influenced by anthropology. With a British empiricist's mistrust of "fuzzy" history, Thompson seems to have been initially reluctant to promote or rely on symbolic anthropology as a tool of analysis. Wary of cross-cultural comparisons or broad generalizations regarding symbol systems, he has, for example, criticized Alan MacFarlane's and Gareth Stedman Jones's anthropological approaches for their lack of historical specificity and for the use of abstract and ahistorical "typologies" that lack empirical rigor. At the same time, however, Thompson has recognized the possibilities of an eclectic and contextualized use of anthropological inspiration: he praised its influence in Keith Thomas's work *Religion and the Decline of Magic*.[14]

As Thompson turned his attention toward the custom-laden society of the eighteenth century, he saw increased potential for anthropology. Allying himself with Keith Thomas and Natalie Davis, he claimed in 1977: "For us the anthropological impulse is chiefly felt, not in model-building, but in locating new problems, in seeing old problems in new ways, in an emphasis upon norms or value-systems and upon rituals, in attention to expressive functions of forms of riot and disturbance, and upon

esp. pp. 269, 274–75; and idem, "Some Tasks and Themes in the Study of Popular Religion," in *The Pursuit of Holiness in Late Medieval and Renaissance Religion*, ed. Charles Trinkhaus and Heiko Oberman (Leiden, 1974), pp. 307–36. For a diachronic, anthropological approach, see Davis's "Ghosts, Kin, and Progeny: Some Features of Family Life in Early Modern France," *Daedalus* 106 (1977): 87–114. Davis is also reevaluating anthropological method in her current projects on gift giving and pleas for pardon; see her *Fiction in the Archives: Pardon Tales and Their Tellers in Sixteenth-Century France* (Stanford, Calif., 1987).

14. E. P. Thompson, "Anthropology and the Discipline of Historical Context," *Midland History* 1 (1972): 40–45, 49–53; and idem, "Folklore, Anthropology, and Social History," pp. 256–60.

symbolic expressions of authority, control and hegemony."[15] In his work on rough music, for example, Thompson makes extensive use of cross-cultural comparisons and directly addresses the anthropological question of the function of charivaris in different societies, as posed by Van Gennep, Lévi-Strauss, and Davis.[16] Yet Thompson insists that the methodology of symbolic anthropology must be reformed to take into account historical change, contextual particularity, and empirical care. Above all, it must also incorporate a Marxist awareness of class conflict. Hence, in an article on eighteenth-century class formation, Thompson notes how important it is to "decode behavior" and "disclose invisible rules of action" as an anthropologist would but still to retain the Marxist framework of class struggle. The coherence of a mental universe arises, according to Thompson, "from a particular field of force and sociological oppositions peculiar to eighteenth-century society: to be blunt, the discrete and fragmented elements of older patterns of thought become integrated by class."[17]

Thompson, then, is somewhat more cautious than Davis in adopting anthropological methods because he wishes to focus on class conflict, yet in fact he asks many of the same questions as anthropologists and shares some of their goals and assumptions. As Ellen Kay Trimberger has pointed out, his work bears some resemblance in technique and content to Geertzian "thick description."[18] Thompson repeatedly denies the possibility of subsuming historical behavior to a set of universal laws or overarching theories.[19] He does not emphasize direct causal explanations; instead he seeks to create a kind of texture of cultural

15. Thompson, "Folklore, Anthropology, and Social History," p. 248.
16. E. P. Thompson, "'Rough Music': le charivari anglais," *Annales, E.S.C.* 27 (1972): 285–312. See also Thompson's "Time, Work-Discipline, and Industrial Capitalism," *Past and Present* 38 (1967): 56–97, which, in a less direct way, reveals some anthropological thinking about changing perceptions of time. Thompson also voiced increased interest in the possibilities of anthropology in a recent interview; see Merrill, "Interview with Thompson," p. 21.
17. Thompson, "Eighteenth-Century Society," pp. 155–56.
18. Trimberger, "E. P. Thompson," pp. 226–27.
19. Thompson, *Poverty of Theory*, pp. 22–25. While Thompson specifically criticizes Althusserian theorizing, both his critique and his work betray his general mistrust of theory; see Johnson, "Thompson, Genovese, and Socialist Humanist History," pp. 82–85.

patterns of meaning and perception. Thompson has written that in the study of customary society in eighteenth-century England, the central questions "may often be concerned less with the processes and logic of change than with the recovery of past states of consciousness and the texturing of social and domestic relationships. They are concerned less with *becoming* than with *being*."[20] In short, existence and attitude rather than change and causality interest Thompson. As he delineates the formation of cultural values and views, Thompson posits a dialectical interaction between "experience" and "social consciousness." He does not define his concept of "experience" clearly in either his theoretical or his historical writing, but he seems to assume that experience is determined by "social being," that is, by one's place within the structure of human relationships in the material world. "'Social being' determines 'social consciousness,'" writes Thompson, "as experience impinges and impresses upon thought."[21]

Ultimately, through their examination of the activism, consciousness, and everyday life of the people of Reformation France and industrializing England, both Davis and Thompson seek above all to give voice to the masses of people who left few written records and whose history has for generations remained unwritten. In their emphasis on the role of culture as a mediator of social relationships and structures, Davis and Thompson express their conviction that the lower classes were not simply prey to external determining forces in history, but instead played an active and integral role in making their own history and defining their own cultural identity. Davis and Thompson both turn to the analysis of riots as an ideal arena for clarifying and exploring these historical convictions. To demonstrate the rational, autonomous, and coherent motivation of popular activists is to show in yet another crucial realm that people in the lower echelons played an important role in shaping their own history. Moreover, the analysis of a period of disturbance sheds light on the texture of communal values and relationships in more peaceful times. Finally, both Thompson

20. Thompson, "Folklore, Anthropology, and Social History," p. 251.
21. Thompson, *Poverty of Theory*, p. 25.

and Davis assume that the analysis of the political awakening of
past groups may contain clues for our own understanding of
current political situations and behavior.

As they react against interpretations that stress economic or
psychological forces, Davis and Thompson both focus on two
central questions. First, why does the crowd view its illegal and
violent activism as meaningful and *legitimate*? Second, how
does the *community* play a crucial role in defining the motivations, goals, and actions of the riot? At the core of these
questions lie two interconnecting concepts: "community" and
"legitimacy." For both scholars, these twin concepts become
critical in demonstrating the rational, indigenous nature of
crowd activism. The community's sense of identity and autonomy, as well as its shared sense of purpose and meaning, acts
as a forceful element in validating and motivating crowd behavior. Furthermore, Thompson and Davis share the methodological assumption that an analysis of the *patterns* of crowd activism will reveal its *meaning* and offer clues about community
structures. I will examine Thompson's "Moral Economy of the
English Crowd" and Davis's "Rites of Violence" to show how
their innovative focus on community autonomy and legitimacy
has strengthened recent work on collective activism, but has
also resulted in some limiting assumptions and methods.

According to Thompson, in times of dearth and high prices
eighteenth-century English food rioters believed they were justified in taking violent collective action because the community
as a whole felt that their common view of just marketing practices, or "moral economy," had been violated. Protesters found
"legitimation" for their activism because they were "informed
by the belief that they were defending traditional rights or customs; and in general, that they were supported by the wider
consensus of the community" (emphasis mine).[22] The community
at large, with a shared consensus strong enough to override
fear or deference, fought to defend the traditional "paternalist
model" as the ideal method of grain distribution. According to
the traditional model, the production, harvesting, and espe-

22. Thompson, "Moral Economy," p. 78.

cially marketing of grain and bread should be controlled to protect the interests of the community of consumers. The food rioters, who shared this "moral economy" or "paternalist model," condemned a free market economy based on the profit motive, which in theory would eventually allow grain to flow to the areas where demand was greatest. At moments of scarcity, villagers blamed grain shortages and high prices on the downfall of the paternalist model. In a disciplined and orderly fashion, they took over the role of government officials and enforced the collection and sale of grain according to the traditional moral economy by selling grain at "just" prices. While this illegal action by the rioting crowd did not necessarily bring immediate short-term success, over the long term the gentry's awareness of the threat of collective activism spurred them to forestall violence by controlling prices and maintaining some aspects of the paternalist model.

Certainly Thompson has been brilliant in arguing that a shared communal conception of moral economy, or just price, induced action and influenced the forms of crowd behavior that occurred. His insight into the motivations of the activists is especially striking because it provides a powerfully convincing model for a wide variety of forms of collective action. In Thompson's footsteps numerous analysts of uprisings have observed the provocative power of communal notions of justice and their guiding impact on the patterned actions of the rioting crowd. Historians have applied the concept of the "moral economy" not only to other food rioters—in France, for example—but also to other types of collective activism as well. Early-nineteenth-century textile workers, rebellious peasants in twentieth-century southeast Asia, and Davis's religious rioters all held some communally shared principles that legitimized their violent or illegal actions.[23]

Thompson's concept of communal consensus, however, may at times suggest a more cohesive and united community than in fact existed. He certainly does not claim uniformity of action

23. Louise Tilly, "The Food Riot as a Form of Political Conflict in France," *Journal of Interdisciplinary History* 2 (1971): 23–58, esp. pp. 45–47; James C. Scott, *The Moral Economy of the Peasant: Rebellion and Subsistence in Southeast Asia* (New Haven, Conn., 1976); and Davis, "Rites of Violence," pp. 154, 161.

by the whole community, yet he claims unanimity of conceptualization. His model fails to explain why certain groups within
the community were more likely than others to engage in riot.
Why did some people participate while others either disap-
proved or offered only unspoken and inactive approval? Admittedly, it can be extremely difficult to trace the social background
of the individual participants in an insurrection, although
Thompson himself has been quite successful in performing this
task.[24] Even if information can be found about the occupations,
gender, and income of rioters, it can still be difficult to probe
the motivations of these different groups within society. Yet the
question must nonetheless be asked: How did attitudes vary
among groups within the community so that some members
chose to riot and others did not?

Thompson mentions, for example, that women were often
leaders of the price fixing, yet he offers little real exploration of
this critical observation.[25] He notes, as have many historians,
including Davis, that because women were believed to be more
hysterical and uncontrollable by nature, they were held less re-
sponsible for criminal actions before the law; therefore, they
felt more free to commit illegal actions. Likewise, Thompson
observes that women may have been more aware of abuses of
the paternalist model because they so often were more involved
than their husbands in face-to-face marketing—but he then
drops the question of female leadership without even suggesting that it needs further probing. What he does not suggest is
that the role of women in grain riots may have given them a
certain power base or role identity within the community.[26] Because Thompson is interested in the power struggle between
the gentry and the crowd, with each group taken as representative of an emerging class, he does not adequately question

24. Thompson, "Moral Economy," pp. 115–19.
25. Ibid., pp. 115–16.
26. From the expanding literature on the role of women in riots, see Olwen
Hufton, "Women in Revolution, 1789–1796," *Past and Present* 53 (1971):
91–108; Temma Kaplan, "Female Consciousness and Collective Action: The
Case of Barcelona, 1910–1918," *Signs: Journal of Women in Culture and Society* 7
(1982): 545–66; and Susan Carol Rogers, "Female Forms of Power and Myths
of Male Dominance: A Model of Female/Male Interaction in Peasant Society,"
American Ethnologist 2 (1975): 727–56.

the tensions in authority, role, and function within the lower echelons of society. Yet the analysis of grain riots could provide clues to the structural bases for informal power for women within the village community. In short, rioting could have a transforming impact on social and political roles at the local level.

Moreover, Thompson does not seem to recognize that the "moral economy" might have different meanings or levels of significance for various members of the community.[27] For example, he points out that day laborers seemed less likely than artisans to take part in price-fixing riots, yet he does not go on to inquire into the relationship of day laborers to the community as a body social. Nor does he ask whether perhaps they had less invested in the paternalist model than did small farmers or domestic workers. Thompson also observes that in some cases a core group of leaders, such as colliers or embankers, spurred others to action.[28] One wonders about the dynamics and means by which fellow villagers were incited to act. Certainly some villagers had ambivalent or negative feelings about how worthwhile and effective violence might be as a means of guarding communal interests. Thompson himself observes that the repressive crackdown in the aftermath of an uprising could be very hard on the local community. Some community members must have anticipated this hardship and hence been wary of rioting.

Furthermore, millers and wealthy farmers within the village might well have preferred the new "laissez-faire" system, for they would benefit from a more fluid market situation. In addition, some victims of crowd violence came from within the village community itself; these "hoarding" farmers or "crafty capitalist" millers would likewise hardly favor a "communal consensus" that legitimized popular enforcement of the moral economy. Thompson bases his discussion on a polar model,

27. Calhoun, *The Question of Class Struggle*, pp. 42–43. On the exaggeration of crowd unity, see William Beik, "Searching for Popular Culture in Early Modern France," *Journal of Modern History* 49 (1977): 266–81, esp. pp. 275–77; and Robert Woods, "Individuals in the Rioting Crowd: A New Approach," *Journal of Interdisciplinary History* 14 (1983): 1–24, esp. pp. 1–2.

28. Thompson, "Moral Economy," p. 119.

which stresses the confrontation between the community and the gentry. Although he is keenly aware of the role of middlemen as both profiteers and victims, his dualistic emphasis makes it very difficult to integrate analysis of this middling group.[29] Are they destructive members of the community? Are they foreign agents? Or are they perhaps the beginnings of a group not so easily classified between crowd and gentry?

In short, Thompson never asks a crucial question: what is the power dynamic taking place *within* the village community when certain members decide to take violent, illegal action? Nor does he ask how violence may alter this dynamic and even transform the roles and functions of community members. Members of the community might consciously or unconsciously manipulate violence against outsiders, authority figures, or fellow villagers in order to redefine their own roles or gain new status and power at the local level. Here the critical role of a shared moral economy becomes bound up with issues of power, identity, and networks within the village social structure.

E. P. Thompson is not uninterested in questions of power. He does, however, seek primarily to evaluate how power of a hegemonic nature operated between the "gentry" and the "crowd." In interpreting the relationship between patricians and plebeians as emerging classes in early modern England, Thompson subtly reformulates the Gramscian model. He thinks that Gramsci overestimated the capacity of the elites to impose "cultural hegemony" on the masses and underestimated the resilient ability of the lower classes to limit and reformulate these cultural impositions. Specifically, Thompson claims that patricians and plebeians had a reciprocal relationship in the eighteenth century. The gentry used a vast repertoire of theatrical and symbolic means to assert its paternalist control and to exact deference and obedience from the crowd, but the plebeians clung to their autonomous, traditional popular culture, which enabled them to resist, redefine, and limit the hegemony of the gentry. While this behavior was not necessarily overtly political, it was not purely "unpolitical" either, for the community

29. Dale Edward Williams, "Morals, Markets, and the English Crowd in 1766," *Past and Present* 104 (1984): 56–73, esp. pp. 71–72.

acted autonomously to defend "definite, and passionately held, notions of the communal weal."[30]

Above all, in the absence of a coercive state mechanism of repression, the crowd could use riot to curtail the gentry's dominance. For example, although Thompson's grain rioters may not have been immediately successful in attaining their demands, over the long term the threat of popular violence did influence authority figures and prompted them to avoid confrontation by keeping prices down.[31] In his book *Whigs and Hunters*, Thompson makes a similar argument about the limitations of the elites' hegemonic use of the law.[32] This conceptualization of reciprocity is largely convincing, but in his concentration on the power relationship between the elites and the crowd, and in his intense desire to find autonomous, prepolitical behavior of the masses, Thompson paradoxically has failed to pay adequate attention to the power struggles within the crowd itself. The village community, like the undefined "crowd," remains an undifferentiated category in opposition to the gentry.

The fact that Thompson's portrayal of the crowd exaggerates its cohesion does not necessarily undermine the significance of his concept of the "moral economy"; analysts of crowd behavior should, however, be wary of using this term as a blanket explanation for motivations shared by the whole community. The concept of "moral economy" should be complemented and corrected by a more nuanced analysis, both of existing tensions within the community and of the impact of rioting on the community structure and polity. In part, this approach entails increased attention to the structural factors that influenced the roles and attitudes of different groups within the village. Above all, it also requires increased attention to local political dynamics of both the formal and the informal kind.

Natalie Davis's analysis of crowd action during the wars of religion in sixteenth-century France also focuses on the core

30. Thompson, "Moral Economy," p. 83.

31. Thompson, "Patrician Society, Plebeian Culture," *Journal of Social History* 7 (1973–74): 382–405; idem, "Moral Economy," pp. 125–26.

32. Thompson, *Whigs and Hunters: The Origins of the Black Act* (New York, 1976); idem, "The Crime of Anonymity," in *Albion's Fatal Tree*, ed. Douglas Hay et al. (New York, 1975), pp. 255–308.

concepts of community and legitimacy. Her article "The Rites
of Violence" first appeared in 1973, two years after Thompson's
"Moral Economy" piece, and Davis clearly shares certain aspects of Thompson's approach. Like Thompson, Davis wants to
illustrate the reasonable and autonomous nature of crowd activism; like Thompson too, she seeks to explain the "social
meaning" of religious riots and to discover how patterns of violence grew out of communal beliefs. Davis's religious rioters
drew motivation, legitimation, and patterns of activism from
expectations, traditions, and customs held by the community
at large. Whether Catholic or Protestant, these activists fought
in part to defend their communally shared notions of a pure,
unpolluted body social. The Protestants took violent action
against Catholic clergymen whose sexual and quasi-magical actions profaned God's word and contaminated the community;
they also smashed statues that, in the Huguenots' eyes, trivi-
alized and defiled the true nature of God's holiness. For their
part, Catholics attacked individual Huguenots as heretics who
were themselves "vessels of pollution," infecting the body social and ever ready in thought and action to blaspheme the
Lord, vilify churches, smash altars, and demolish images the
Catholics held as sacred.

Not only did communal values determine the nature of the
riot and the identity of its victims, but communal activities also
influenced the riot's timing, legitimacy, and ritualized quality.
Davis suggests that religious riots frequently became an extension of religious ritual: violence often stemmed from moments
of worship, and Catholic and Protestant rioters alike sometimes
based their destruction on a "repertory of actions" from the
Bible or the liturgy. Moreover, religious activists drew inspiration from traditional acts of folk justice: charivaris, which had
long been used to enforce communal norms, also provided an
ideal and "legitimate" means of humiliating an individual who
violated true doctrine and trampled the sacred. In short, community perceptions, traditions, and actions informed the goals,
legitimation, occasion, and social basis of the religious riot.

Culture and community, not economics and class, were the
critical forces that motivated religious rioters. In support of this
view, Davis convincingly refutes Janine Estèbe's argument that

rising grain prices correlated directly with religious violence and that the massacres of 1572 were in part "an expression of class hatred." Rather, Davis provides a more nuanced analysis of the participants in religious violence: she notes, for instance, that although Protestant activists came from different socioeconomic levels, a high percentage were members of the "newer or more skilled occupations" or of "occupations that had been transformed by the urban developments of the early sixteenth century." Printers and publishers, for example, as highly literate members of a new trade, were especially likely to come into contact with the printed propaganda of the new religion; people at all levels within the profession were thus more likely to convert to Protestantism. Davis also observes that certain groups, such as city women and teen-age boys, played a striking role.[33] In committing religious violence, adolescent youths carried over their traditional license to act as "the conscience of the community" and enforce social norms.

In general, Davis is much more sensitive than Thompson to the dynamics of different groups within the community, perhaps in part because she turned more definitively away from a Marxist methodology and became interested in divisions based on gender and religion. Davis has been particularly effective in illustrating the capacity of seemingly powerless groups to forge authority within the crevices or fault lines of existing social structures. She has skillfully shown, for example, how women took advantage of images of female weakness and hysteria to increase their freedom and power in various communal situations.[34]

Yet paradoxically, in "The Rites of Violence," even as she observes the distinctive roles of certain groups, Davis does not probe the fissures and varying roles within the community as

33. Davis, "Rites of Violence," pp. 175–78, 182–84; Janine Estèbe and Natalie Davis, "Debate on the Rites of Violence: Religious Riot in Sixteenth-Century France, Comment and Rejoinder," *Past and Present* 67 (1975): 127–35. On the role of youths, see "The Reasons of Misrule" and "Tasks and Themes."

34. See especially Davis's "City Women and Religious Change" and "Women on Top," in *Society and Culture*, pp. 65–96 and 124–51; idem, *The Return of Martin Guerre* (Cambridge, Mass., 1983), esp. pp. 30–34, 67–68, on the role of Bertrande; idem, "Women in the Crafts in Sixteenth-Century Lyon," *Feminist Studies* 8 (1982): 47–80.

thoroughly as she might have. Her main point of emphasis remains the idea that the religious riot had as its ultimate goal the *unity* and *purity* of the body social. She views the role of the youths, for example, essentially as supportive of community order and conscience rather than as a ritualized element within a deeply divisive power struggle. In "The Rites of Violence," for the moment she relegates her comments about the religious tendencies of members of various professions to a footnote.[35] In a sense, the unity and *cohesiveness* of the community took on even greater importance for Davis's protesters than for Thompson's activists. The religious rioters went beyond defending a shared concept of justice; they turned to violence to purge or purify the community itself and to define its boundaries against threats both foreign and internal. Perhaps Davis stresses community cohesiveness so strongly in part because she wishes clearly to delineate the contrast between Catholic and Protestant beliefs and behavior. As a result, she sacrifices more internal analysis to this broader juxtaposition of group characteristics.

The limitations in Davis's understanding of community also lie in the anthropological approach that informs and inspires, but also restricts, the kinds of questions she chooses to ask. Several influential symbolic anthropologists, such as Geertz, Sahlins, Turner, and Douglas, have defined culture primarily as a collectively held system of symbols. While these anthropologists, particularly Geertz and Sahlins, have sought to incorporate and develop a sensitivity to historical change within cultural systems, their approach ultimately stresses culture's role as a kind of subtle mechanism for the maintenance of order, meaning, and social cohesion.[36] At the risk of oversimplifying their work and its impact on historians, I would argue that

35. Davis, "Rites of Violence," pp. 177–78 n.
36. On the problems with this anthropological approach, see, for example, Ronald G. Walters, "Signs of the Times: Clifford Geertz and Historians," *Social Research* 47 (1980): 537–56, esp. pp. 553–56; William Sewell, *Work and Revolution in France: The Language of Labor from the Old Regime to 1848* (Cambridge, 1980), pp. 10–13; Johannes Fabian, *Time and the Other: How Anthropology Makes Its Object* (New York, 1983), pp. 151–52, 156; M. Greengrass, "The Anatomy of a Religious Riot at Toulouse," *Journal of Ecclesiastical History* 34 (1983): 367–91, esp. pp. 389–91.

the strong emphasis that anthropologists place on the aesthetic and conciliating function of culture has led historians to limit their points of focus accordingly. In her analysis of religious violence, Davis seeks to interpret the riot as a cultural phenomenon that, though violent, essentially had order and communal purity at its heart. Riot, as her title suggests, becomes ritual, with community unity as its goal. Davis's interpretation is compelling, and her focus on the meaning and legitimacy perceived by the crowd is original and important. But the reader might also be left with the disturbing impression that some critical questions go unasked. In particular, the emphasis on the cohesiveness of community and the forcefulness of its legitimacy leads to inadequate attention to the issues of transformation, conflict, and power.

It would in fact be possible, in probing or expanding Davis's analysis, to turn some of her arguments upside down or topsy-turvy—to use one of her favorite cultural motifs. Inverting some of Davis's points in this way should reveal new possibilities of interpretation, based on the foundation she has already laid.

First, let us take Davis's notion of community. She claims that communal self-perception legitimated the riot and influenced its form; yet one could also argue that violence actually fundamentally transformed the urban community and entirely redefined it. Rather than asserting that existing perceptions of the body social defined violence, one could say that violence over religious beliefs destroyed the existing community and tore it apart in a bloody power struggle as each group fought to draw new communal boundaries. Violence forced urban dwellers to rethink traditional definitions of community.

Indeed, Davis leaves the reader wondering to what extent Catholics and Protestants were part of the *same* community. At times the two groups seem to battle within the community for control of the sacred; at other times they act as two opposing communities at war with one another. If the two groups were in fact part of the same community and shared some aspects of their symbolic system, not to mention social space within the city, churches, municipal politics, and the urban economy, then their violence becomes part of a larger, many-layered struggle for *control* in a sometimes brutal and all-encompassing sense. While violence certainly became an integral means of defining religious identity and solidarity, the context of religious conflict also forced both Catholics and Protestants to live within an ideologically divided community. This reality had two major ramifications: over the long term it meant that both groups would eventually have to accept a new conception of the diversity and tensions possible within the urban community; in the shorter term it meant that Catholics and Protestants engaged in a very real struggle over *power* and *control,* as well as over meaning, doctrine, and definitions of the body social.

In order to understand the characteristics of this conflict that was at once religious and political, it would be helpful to know more than Davis tells us about how the Huguenot and Catholic citizens interacted in peaceful arenas, and particularly in the realm of politics. How did they relate to one another in the marketplace? Did they live in separate neighborhoods? Did they vie for positions as town magistrates? Davis probes some issues of this type in her more recent article, "The Sacred and the Body Social in Sixteenth-Century Lyon," published in 1981. In this piece, she further refines her discussion of how religious beliefs influenced Catholic and Protestant concepts of community; she also focuses on the social makeup and interactions of the two groups. Yet she leaves the political element largely unexplored. It remains for the historian of collective conflict to examine how political—as well as religious, symbolic, and social—levels of battle for municipal control interconnect.[37]

In order to explore the links between meaning and power within religious violence, we might analyze and reverse a second element of Davis's argument. She asserts that the patterns of the rioters' actions reveal their assumptions about legitimacy and their orderly, rational sense of unity and meaning; one might, however, argue that, on the contrary, these actions illustrate the activists' uncertainties about legitimacy, betray their need to forge new power, and in fact contribute to their capacity to create new roles for themselves within the city. For example, Davis asserts that the rioters felt they had a right to act in the place of civil or religious authority figures who fell short

37. Davis, "The Sacred and the Body Social," *Past and Present* 90 (1981): 40–70.

of their duty. She regards imitations of official actions, such as mock trials, as a means for religious activists to shape and reinforce their sense of legitimacy and give systematic significance to their violence. Yet Davis does not suggest the possibility that the repertoire of actions mimicking official formulas might have been a way to usurp the power of authority figures and perhaps simultaneously to mock and criticize those officials for their shortcomings. Beyond creating meaning and legitimacy, such actions may have been a deliberate means of demanding power and unprecedented authority in a very direct and explicit way.

Furthermore, they might also display the doubts of the rioters as much as their confidence. While Davis reports that some officials offered tacit approval of religious riots or even participated in them, the reader is left wondering about those officials who sought to impose tranquillity and order. What kind of dynamic existed between them and the rioters? Groups without official authority did not necessarily have communal unity and order as a priority; they might also have had particular interests to defend and have sought out techniques for doing so. In addition, it would be helpful to ask how their role as rioters perhaps lent them status or authority within the community as a byproduct of their religious leadership, just as the women or artisans who led Thompson's grain riots may have gained certain kinds of power or respect through their activism. In short, one needs to ask not only how violence reflected existing notions of community, but also how it transformed the community by endowing certain members with novel roles, power, or status.

Another fascinating, though sometimes troubling, aspect of Davis's argument that may be fruitfully questioned and even turned upside down is her position that ritual led to violence and that as a result violence somehow became rite. Davis is clearly perceptive in suggesting that religious worship became an occasion for violence and that rioting took on ritualized forms informed by biblical, liturgical, or traditional beliefs and customs. Davis notes that sixteenth-century activists may have inured themselves to the cruelty of their actions by encasing violence within ritual forms. Her analysis is subtle on this point, yet the reader may be left feeling that the author parallels the rationalization of the rioters: to say that a riot is a ritual is al-

most to smooth over its violence or to deflect attention from the
sheer power struggles involved in this killing in the streets.
Was the riot always ritual? Did it not sometimes originate in a
ritual context, then mushroom beyond ritual to take on a chaos
and brutality that can hardly be expressed within the concept
of ritual per se? For example, to stone a house where Protestants were singing psalms, to jump out of a procession to attack
a scornful spectator, or to provoke the participants in a rival
procession was not so much ritual as violence that originated in
a ritual context, and may in fact have become a distortion or
even destruction of ritual.

Use of the word *ritual* to describe patterns of violence fits
neatly within the anthropological view of culture as an aesthetic and unifying force. If violence is ritual, it seems to have
an inherent legitimacy that is somehow preordained and that
reinforces the essentially cohesive nature of community. But
the link between ritual and violence is not always so easily
made. In the first place, we need to differentiate between patterns of repeated symbolic action on the one hand and ritual on
the other.[38] Second, in those cases where violence became ritual
we need to ask how activists managed to endow violence with
ritual qualities and forge both religious legitimacy and earthly
power by transforming the nature and sometimes the meaning
of symbols themselves. In sixteenth-century France, for example, biblical and liturgical customs offered validating models of violence only if they were reinterpreted and appropriated
in certain ways. Rioters may have altered or distorted symbols
and rituals as part of their struggle for control of meaning and
authority. In sum, by recognizing that patterns of violence are
not ritual by nature but are endowed only tenuously with ritual
legitimacy through a violent and polemical struggle, the historian can reintegrate power and conflict into the interpretation
of collective activism without losing the insights gained from
anthropology.

To turn Davis's argument topsy-turvy once more, one should,
in addition to noting that religious belief shaped violence, ask
how violence in fact transformed ritual and religious percep-

38. John Skorupski, *Symbol and Theory* (Cambridge, 1976), pp. 69–75.

tions in fundamental ways. For one thing, the very context in which conflict took place expanded certain profane and political functions of ritual: ritual almost inevitably moved beyond being an expression of religiosity and of communal values. Even without turning violent, ritual became a weapon in its own right. Take, for example, a relevant case from a different era: during the radical phases of the French Revolution, some Catholics participated in illegal worship out of both political and religious motives. To dance illegally on a saint's day was not simply a religious and communal celebration; it became a politically loaded challenge as well. Similarly, in sixteenth-century France public religious devotion easily became a statement of defiance or hostility.

Davis provides many examples of hostile rituals: as the Protestant procession came to resemble an "armed parade," the psalms they sang fell like challenges and insults on Catholic ears; conversely, the Catholics in Pamiers who danced on the feast of Saint Anthony began to chant "Kill, kill!" and sparked off three days of serious fighting.[39] Davis presents such scenarios as evidence of the ritualized nature and context of violence and as proof of the strong religious motives of the rioters. But one should also ask how this particularly aggressive character of religious practice in a time of conflict had an impact on religious feelings and how religious sentiments became inextricably enmeshed with power dynamics. What did it do to the attitudes of Catholic worshipers if they knew that each procession might in fact be a provocation, that each saint's festival might become a slaughter? How did sacred and profane motives mingle when Protestants smashed icons—that is, how did religious convictions about pollution of the sacred and of the community mix with anger at a position of enforced inferiority and illegality? Religious beliefs, the defense of the true doctrine and of the religious community, were clearly sincere and important motivating factors, but in this heated atmosphere religious goals, and even religious beliefs themselves, could not be separated from issues of status, conflict, and power.

How, then, did religious violence influence and possibly

39. Davis, "Rites of Violence," pp. 73–75.

transform beliefs and the sense of communal identity? We encounter here the flip side of Davis's argument: just as communal beliefs and rites influenced and legitimated violence, so too
did violence itself tighten the boundaries of the Protestant and
Catholic communities and also influence power dynamics and
religious perceptions within each group. The Huguenot religion, for example, took shape in a caldron of opposition and
legal harassment. This opposition and the resulting conflicts
may initially have strengthened Huguenot faith, created a sense
of otherness, and lent certain characteristics to their very doc-
trines. Likewise, this era of violence could easily have influenced Catholic metaphors and spirituality. Although the concept of spirituality as a battlefield was definitely not new in the
Reformation era, perhaps its ramifications were different than
in medieval days. Furthermore, in some cases the need to fight
to defend religious doctrine or the need to practice ritual illegally could transform the form as well as the meaning of religious expression. Certainly, these questions carry us beyond
the analysis of the riot itself into the broader realm of Protestant
and Catholic spirituality, but they offer fruitful areas for examination. They also highlight the potential of violence to *transform* and not simply to reinforce communal attitudes.

By uncovering the pivotal role of the community in forging
notions of legitimacy and justice that informed popular violence in rational and meaningful ways, Natalie Davis and E. P.
Thompson have made a striking and original contribution to
the cultural interpretation of popular attitudes and activism.
Together they have salvaged the study of collective action from
its former overemphasis on economic or psychological forces.
They have decisively shown the importance of cultural and
communal factors in motivating activists and illustrated the independent and active role of rioters in making their own history. Their emphasis on worldview, ritual, and shared meaning
has had ramifications far beyond the realm of crowd study, for
they have helped shape the history of *mentalités* and popular
culture in general. Numerous historians, influenced by Davis's
and Thompson's ideas, bear witness to the significance and
timeliness of their contribution.

What we need now is not so much a return to the structural approach that Davis and Thompson sought to correct, but rather a building on the bases they have laid. We need to ask how the cultural approach to history in general and to collective activism in particular can incorporate both the anthropological emphasis on meaning and *mentalité* and a greater awareness of the dynamics of power and change. In the case of crowd activism, Davis's and Thompson's stress on the examination of community and legitimacy must be reintegrated with the analysis of power, transformation, and conflict.

First, although patterns of crowd activism can betray their meaning for the participants, these patterns are not necessarily conciliating, static, or universally interpreted in the same way. Patterns of violence, like the attitudes of villagers, may be ambiguous. We must therefore not emphasize the patterns and rituals of violence at the expense of asking how riots have a transforming impact, not only on the roles and status of community members but also on cultural attitudes and customs. Second, cultural systems may indeed reinforce the community, sustain "order," and endow various actions with legitimacy and meaning. But they can also become vehicles for creating power and sowing discord. Various members of the community have different attitudes toward symbolic systems and deliberately appropriate or manipulate symbols as part of a struggle for control.[40] We must strive to construct as nuanced an analysis of dynamics within the community as the sources will permit. Moreover, the stress on the powerful determining force of cultural factors, such as religious belief, should not cause us to ignore other motivating factors, such as political or socioeconomic conflicts and interests. Davis and Thompson have advanced the cultural approach to crowd violence by demonstrating the need to pose critical questions about communal notions of legitimacy and meaning. We need now to ask how violence contributes not only to the definition of community and meaning, but also to the transformation of symbolic systems and the realignment of power, status, and roles within the community.

40. On the various possible interpretations of symbols, see Roger Chartier, "Texts, Symbols, and Frenchness," *Journal of Modern History* 57 (1985): 685–95, esp. pp. 689–90.

Three

Local Knowledge, Local History: Geertz and Beyond

ALETTA BIERSACK

Genres are "blurring," Clifford Geertz has said.[1] For every historian who cites Braudel's summons to *la science sociale*, there is an anthropologist reminding us of Maitland's well-known dictum: that anthropology will be history or it will be nothing at all. Historians regularly acknowledge the influence of Claude Lévi-Strauss, Victor Turner, Mary Douglas, and, in particular, Clifford Geertz. And now, at the very moment when the "Annales paradigm" is most controversial,[2] Marshall Sahlins, a highly visible anthropologist, chooses to employ Braudel's term *longue durée* to mean Lévi-Strauss's "structure." For Sahlins, as will be shown, the "long run" of Hawaiian history consists in categorical rather than geographic patterns, structures in the

My thanks to Lynn Hunt for her invitation to participate in this stimulating project, and to Lynn Hunt as well as to Alexander Bolyanatz, Roger Chartier, James Clifford, Roger Keesing, Debra Kirch, George Sheridan, and the reviewers for the University of California Press for their helpful comments and suggestions on earlier versions of this piece.
    1. Clifford Geertz, *Local Knowledge: Further Essays in Interpretive Anthropology* (New York, 1983), chap. 1.
    2. Lynn Hunt, "French History in the Last Twenty Years: The Rise and Fall of the *Annales* Paradigm," *Journal of Contemporary History* 21 (1986): 209–24; see also Hunt's introduction to this volume. For a full explication of the Annales "paradigm," see Traian Stoianovich, *French Historical Method: The Annales Paradigm* (Ithaca, N.Y., 1976).

orthodox sense of the word rather than in the "geohistorical" sense of Braudel's *Mediterranean*. Nevertheless, Sahlins's salute to Braudel has its point. It serves to dramatize and charter a "paradigm shift" in anthropology, from structural anthropology, which is ahistorical, to historical anthropology.[3]

From another vantage, all roads appear to converge on literary theory. The shift from "social history" (inspired, in part, by anthropology) to a concern with historical texts and their literary properties—associated with the work of Dominick LaCapra and Hayden White (see Kramer's essay, chapter 4)—is paralleled in anthropology by a shift in focus from culture-as-text (interpretation's muse) to anthropological texts (ethnographies) and their rhetorical strategies.

The blurred genres of today are generated by a kind of post-disciplinary synergistic energy. Braudel rebaptized his geohistory "structural history" to affiliate himself with the structuralism of Lévi-Strauss. Meanwhile, Sahlins, many years later, cites Braudel to ground anthropology in history as a prelude to refashioning structuralism in historical terms. If for some anthropology should be pursued as a branch of literary studies, through the ("reflexive") critique of anthropological texts, for others literary studies entail a "new historicism"—and the very category of literature is a contested one.[4]

Each in its own way, anthropology and history have channeled the same diverse intellectual currents streaming out of Europe. Each field, mixed in its ancestry, is today a site of theoretical excitement where multiple traditions battle for hegemony or capitulate, intersect, and merge, and where key words and concepts are highly contested. These conflicts provide the fer-

3. Marshall Sahlins's principal writings on historical anthropology are *Historical Metaphors and Mythical Realities: Structure in the Early History of the Sandwich Islands Kingdom*, ASAO Special Publication no. 1 (Ann Arbor, Mich., 1981), and *Islands of History* (Chicago, 1985); the second chapter of *Historical Metaphors* is subtitled "Structures of the Long Run." Fernand Braudel delineates concisely his model of historical reality in the opening essays of *On History* (Chicago, 1980). Samuel Kinser's essay "*Annaliste* Paradigm? The Geohistorical Structuralism of Fernand Braudel," *American Historical Review* 86 (1981): 63–105, is most instructive on Braudel's language and how it changes from one edition of *The Mediterranean* to another.

4. Terry Eagleton, *Literary Theory: An Introduction* (Minneapolis, 1983), concluding chapter.

tile soil out of which each discipline is presently struggling to
create its own future. Tributaries of the same headwaters, nour-
ished by the same intellectual forces, anthropology and history
now confront the same possibilities.

In a volume exploring the "new cultural history," it is fitting
to survey the anthropologist's present terrain with an eye toward establishing its diversity and elucidating its current debates. Such a review is of necessity selective, and my choices
have been governed by the occasion. Since social history and
the study of *mentalités* mean, among other things, the employ-
ment of symbolic approaches in history, the account begins
with Clifford Geertz and his "interpretation of cultures." The
title of this essay is inspired by Geertz's own language. "Local
knowledge" refers to significant worlds and the indigenous outlooks that give them life. "Local history" (a term Geertz himself
does not use) suggests the study of local knowledge in the historical mode. Though Sahlins positions himself "beyond" Lévi-
Strauss and Braudel, his historical anthropology may profitably
be viewed as a transformation of interpretation, and I adopt
this perspective in a discussion of Sahlins's *Historical Metaphors
and Mythical Realities*. For historians debating whether to re-
sume political history—albeit less naively, out of a new cultural
awareness and in such a way as to capture center and periphery
within a single frame—Sahlins's work will prove suggestive.
Geertz is not without his critics, and I review some of the challenges to his "cultural analysis." At the close of the essay, I discuss (all too briefly) anthropology's literary turn. Here Geertz—
no longer the interpreter, but the critic—reenters as the author
of *Works and Lives*, which, like *Writing Culture*, is edited by James
Clifford and George Marcus and is a key text in the burgeoning
literature on the aesthetics and politics of anthropologizing.

In the opening essay of *The Interpretation of Cultures*, Geertz
tells us that cultural analysis involves "thick description." Se-
mantically rather than materially thick, the thickness of "thick
description" consists in its ability to distinguish a meaningless
reflex, a twitch or a blink for example, from a consciously employed communicative device, the wink. Thick description ex-

amines public behavior for what it *says* rather than what it does. It "reads" the symbolic content of action, interprets it as sign.

Nothing much in the intellectual landscape of the sixties and seventies pleases Geertz. Materialism of any kind remains an implicit target. Lévi-Strauss's structuralism is too "cerebral," as is the "savage" he conjures.[5] Ethnosemantic analysis, with its sterile taxonomic studies, is too mentalistic. Geertz's intention is "to evoke outlooks, not to anatomize codes."[6] Much of Geertz's ammunition is reserved for positivism, with its search for general explanatory laws and its naive objectivity and empiricism. Relying on a language inspired by Max Weber, among others, Geertz embraces understanding (*Verstehen*) and particularism while rejecting causal explanation. Never comparing in the ordinary sense, Geertz, by setting out similarities and dissimilarities in an effort to typologize, nonetheless does compare, if only apples and pears: he assembles cases but does not group them. His essay "'From the Native's Point of View': On the Nature of Anthropological Understanding" is a well-known example of the technique.[7]

Although Geertz's choice of text, "transient examples of shaped behavior,"[8] allows him to write of culture, there is nothing uniquely anthropological about "cultural analysis." In important ways, Geertz's "interpretation" is successor to Wilhelm Dilthey's *Geisteswissenschaften*, which treated all historical data as so many "objectifications" of the "lived experience" of the actors of the past. For R. G. Collingwood, too, experience or thought was the very stuff of history. Plainer and more homespun in his diction, Collingwood similarly envisioned historical "facts" as indices of an underlying experiential and conceptual reality.

The historian, investigating any event in the past, makes a distinction between what may be called the outside and the inside of an event. By the outside of the event I mean everything belonging to it which can

5. Clifford Geertz, *The Interpretation of Cultures* (New York, 1973), chap. 13.
6. Geertz, *Local Knowledge*, p. 183.
7. Ibid., chap. 3.
8. Ibid., p. 10.

be described in terms of thought. . . . The historian is never concerned with either of these to the exclusion of the other. He is investigating not mere events (where by a mere event I mean one which has only an outside and no inside [Geertz's blink, for example]) but actions, and an action is the unity of the outside and inside of an event.[9]

Action, Geertz would more succinctly (and hermeneutically) say, is text.

Although clear precedents for Geertz's cultural analysis exist in western historiography, Geertz has nonetheless enjoyed a relatively unmediated impact upon historians. In his introduction to *The Great Cat Massacre and Other Episodes in French Cultural History,* for example, Robert Darnton, a Princeton historian who has taught courses with Geertz, cites Geertz as his principal inspiration and dedicates his essays to "history in the ethnographic grain," to the study of "the way ordinary people make sense of the world."[10]

A more telling instance of Geertz's impact is the book *The Return of Martin Guerre.* Its author, Natalie Zemon Davis, has also taught with Geertz at Princeton (although Mary Douglas and Victor Turner influence her as well). In *The Return of Martin Guerre,* Davis uses a series of incidents from the peasant life of sixteenth-century France to probe local sentiments, motivations, values, feelings, and the lived world.

Once the objective methods of the natural sciences are abandoned, history becomes an attempt to reimagine the past while recovering it. In what does this task consist? Geertz himself addresses these matters, albeit as an anthropologist: "Anthropological writings are themselves interpretations, and second and third order ones to boot. (By definition, only a 'native' makes first order ones: it's *his* culture.) They are 'something fashioned'—the original meaning of *fictiō*—not that they are false, unfactual, or merely 'as if' thought experiments."[11] *The Return of Martin Guerre* has special value as an experiment in interpretation. As Davis was writing her history, she was also

9. R. G. Collingwood, *The Idea of History* (Oxford, 1946), p. 213.

10. Robert Darnton, *The Great Cat Massacre and Other Episodes in French Cultural History* (New York, 1984), p. 4.

11. Geertz, *The Interpretation of Cultures,* pp. 15–16.

assisting in the production of the film by the same title. More patently than her own history, the film script was an interpretation of the events of the past. Working with actors whose goals were Collingwood's—to reenact, reexperience, relive the logic and sense of a bygone era—served to pose "the problem of invention" for her.

Paradoxically, the more I savored the creation of the film the more my appetite was whetted for something beyond it. I was prompted to dig deeper into the case, to make historical sense of it. Writing for actors raised new questions about the motivations of people in the sixteenth century. . . . Watching Gérard Depardieu [the male lead] made me think about the accomplishment of the real imposter. . . . I felt I had my own historical laboratory, generating not proofs, but possibilities.

The result is a self-conscious novelization of the past in which an authorial no less than a scholarly role is assumed by Davis in her attempt to reimagine the already imagined, to use her own imagination to reconstruct the imaginations of historical subjects and their imaginings: "I did my best through other sources from the period and place to discover the world they would have seen and the reactions they might have had. What I offer you here is in part my invention, but held tightly in check by the voices of the past."[12]

Geertz, too, has written a kind of history, *Negara*, his reconstruction of the polity of nineteenth-century Bali. Geertz's object is a public ceremonial, the *negara*, at once a display of status and a dramatization of a political ideal. Underlying *negara* as a "structure of action," then, is a "structure of thought." To describe it is "to describe a constellation of enshrined ideas" and "envehicled meanings"—to read texts.[13]

As in the closing essay of *Local Knowledge*, his second collection of interpretive essays, Geertz's main effort in *Negara* is to claim for symbolic analysis a novel domain. Instead of situating the political and the symbolic in different planes or at different levels, Geertz insists on their identity.

12. Natalie Zemon Davis, *The Return of Martin Guerre* (Cambridge, Mass., 1983), pp. viii, 5.
13. Clifford Geertz, *Negara: The Theatre State in Nineteenth-Century Bali* (Princeton, N.J., 1980), p. 135.

The confinement of interpretive analysis in most of contemporary anthropology to the supposedly more "symbolic" aspect of culture is a mere prejudice, born out of the notion, also a gift of the nineteenth century, that "symbolic" opposes to "real" as fanciful to sober, figurative to literal, obscure to plain, aesthetic to practical, mystical to mundane, and decorative to substantial. To construe the expressions of the theatre state, to apprehend them as theory, this prejudice, along with the allied one that the dramaturgy of power is external to its working, must be put aside. The real is as imagined as the imaginary.

For all its materiality, the nineteenth-century Balinese polity, like the peasant life Davis describes, is rooted in the human imagination. "The dramas of the theatre state, mimetic of themselves, were, in the end, neither illusions nor lies, neither sleight of hand nor make-believe. They were what there was."[14]

Although the interpretive turn has had a strong impact inside as well as outside anthropology, anthropologists are today more acutely aware than ever of its inadequacies. Geertz's lack of methodological rigor and the epistemological quandaries of the parent framework, hermeneutics, leave cultural analysis vulnerable to skeptics who remain "allergic," as Geertz has said of them, "to anything literary or inexact."[15] Given the qualitative nature of cultural analysis, what guarantees of quality control does Geertz provide other than those of his own prodigious talent? Geertz would of course respond (without apology), none! Geertz confesses that he has never

gotten anywhere near to the bottom of anything I have written about. . . . Cultural analysis is intrinsically incomplete. And, worse than that, the more deeply it goes the less complete it is. . . . To commit oneself to a semiotic concept of culture and interpretive approach to the study of it is to commit oneself to a view of ethnographic assertion as, to borrow W. B. Gallie's by now famous phrase, "essentially contestable."[16]

Rather than putting matters to rest, such admissions—for some, begging all the questions—only fan the flames of criticism.

14. Ibid., pp. 135–36.
15. Geertz, *Local Knowledge*, p. 3.
16. Geertz, *The Interpretation of Cultures*, p. 29.

Paul Shankman writes: "The inability of interpretive theory to offer criteria for evaluating either different interpretations or different paradigms poses a formidable barrier to claims of theoretical superiority."[17] If the task of interpretation inherently lacks closure, how much interpretation is enough? How thick need description be? Talal Asad is not alone in expressing disturbing "epistemological doubts" concerning the authenticity of any one reading.[18] Vincent Crapanzano indicates his own devastating incredulity:

Despite his phenomenological-hermeneutical pretensions, there is in fact in "Deep Play" [one of Geertz's best-known essays] no understanding of the native from the native's point of view. . . . Geertz offers no specifiable evidence for his attributions of intention, his assertion of subjectivity, his declarations of experience. His constructions of constructions of constructions appear to be little more than projections, or at least blurrings, of his point of view, his subjectivity, with that of the native, or more accurately, of the constructed native.[19]

Geertz's endorsement of particularism and his rejection of explanation and generalization have also proved controversial. Instead of contributing to anthropological theory, Geertz appears to operate to one side of it, leaving his work vulnerable to accusations of triviality. The historian Ronald Walters complains:

The tendency of thick description and semiotics is to reinforce the impulse to burrow in and not to try to connect the dots. That occurs because what is an analytical strength—Geertz's attention to particularity and his orientation toward the actor's perspective—is a weakness for synthesis. Thick description leads to brilliant readings of individual situations, rituals, and institutions. It does not require saying how "cultural texts" relate to each other or to general processes of economic and social change.[20]

17. Paul Shankman, "The Thick and the Thin: On the Interpretive Theoretical Program of Clifford Geertz," *Current Anthropology* 25 (1984): 69.
18. Talal Asad, "Anthropological Conceptions of Religion: Reflections on Geertz," *Man* 18 (1983): 245.
19. Vincent Crapanzano, "Hermes' Dilemma: The Masking of Subversion in Ethnographic Description," in *Writing Culture: The Poetics and Politics of Ethnography,* ed. James Clifford and George E. Marcus (Berkeley and Los Angeles, 1986), p. 74.
20. Ronald G. Walters, "Signs of the Times: Clifford Geertz and Historians," *Social Research* 47 (1980): 551–52.

The same complaint has been lodged by Melford Spiro, an anthropologist who wishes to revive confidence in an earlier notion of anthropology's mission as a comparative science conducted in "a generalizing-explanatory mode of ethnographic research."[21]

In practice—and this may follow from Geertz's rejection of the explanatory mode and a search for causes—Geertz's cultural analysis is as static as any structuralism. Offering up a thick description of a bygone era in a far-off place, *Negara* pursues local history *qua* local knowledge. Time is merely another mode of displacement, a further estrangement. Meaning is described, never derived. The metaphors Geertz employs—thick description, text—assume new significance in this context. Instead of claiming with Dilthey that man's essence is created in time, that man is therefore inherently historical, a being that becomes,[22] Geertz asserts that "man is an animal suspended in webs of significance he himself has spun."[23] The webs, not the spinning; the culture, not the history; the text, not the process of textualizing—these attract Geertz's attention. Foucault provides an antidote in problematizing those very "webs of significance" by historicizing them and tracing their emergence over time (see O'Brien's essay, chapter 1).[24]

Though Geertz himself warns against the vices of interpretation, with its tendency to turn into "a kind of sociological aestheticism" that loses touch with "the hard surfaces of life— with the political, economic, stratificatory realities within which men are everywhere contained," thick description as Geertz actually practices it courts that danger, aestheticizing all

21. Melford E. Spiro, "Cultural Relativism and the Future of Anthropology," *Cultural Anthropology* 1 (1986): 281.

22. See Richard E. Palmer, *Hermeneutics: Interpretation Theory in Schleiermacher, Dilthey, Heidegger, and Gadamer* (Evanston, Ill., 1969), p. 116; and Theodore Plantinga, *Historical Understanding in the Thought of Wilhelm Dilthey* (Toronto, 1980), p. 132.

23. Geertz, *The Interpretation of Cultures*, p. 5.

24. Cf. Roger Chartier, "Intellectual History or Sociocultural History? The French Trajectories," in *Modern European Intellectual History: Reappraisals and New Perspectives*, ed. Dominick LaCapra and Steven L. Kaplan (Ithaca, N.Y., 1982), pp. 43–44; and Lynn Hunt, "French History in the Last Twenty Years," p. 219.

domains.[25] The language of *Negara* is indicative: "To understand the *negara* is . . . to elaborate a poetics of power, not a mechanics."[26] Walters responds:

There are dangerous and politically loaded precedents in [Geertz's] treatment of power. At one point he explicitly erases the line between its "symbolics" and its nature. [Quoting from an essay in *Local Knowledge* that replicates in part the analysis of *Negara*:] "The easy distinction between the trappings of rule," he claims, "and its substance becomes less sharp, even less real; what counts is the manner in which, a bit like mass and energy, they are transformed into each other."[27]

This transformation cuts the symbolic free from its "hard surface" moorings, liberates it from the historical and institutional settings in which it is found, and handicaps the very effort Geertz ostensibly undertakes—to provide adequate understanding. At a time when Foucault's work impresses us with the ubiquity of the political function, at a time also when Marxism, softened through a new culturalism, is enjoying a resurgence in anthropology, such claims are especially vulnerable.

Some go even further, questioning whether "local knowledge" is best understood as a symbolic realm. In a recent article, Roger Keesing wrote: "Cultures are webs of mystification as well as signification. We need to ask who *creates* and who *defines* cultural meanings, and to what ends."[28] Shankman, too, has wondered, "How does one discern whether this [Balinese] ideology reflects, represents, or otherwise expresses some symbolic principles in Balinese life or whether it masks, denies, obfuscates, or mystifies social reality?"[29] This question is all the more compelling given the feminist critique of anthropology and its androcentrism. Keesing goes on to complain that Geertz

is mainly silent on the way cultural meanings sustain power and privilege. Indeed most symbolic anthropologists, in the name of cultural relativism or interpretive detachment, have been strangely blind to

25. Geertz, *The Interpretation of Cultures*, p. 30.
26. Geertz, *Negara*, p. 123.
27. Walters, "Signs of the Times," pp. 553–54.
28. Roger M. Keesing, "Anthropology as Interpretive Quest," *Current Anthropology* 28 (1987): 161–62.
29. Shankman, "The Thick and the Thin," p. 268.

the political consequences of cultures as ideologies, their situatedness as justifications and mystifications of a local historically cumulated status quo. Where feminists and Marxists find oppression, symbolists find meaning.[30]

Examining the ideological and political character of local knowledge requires attending to the historical context in which such knowledge operates. With respect to Geertz's well-known essay "Deep Play," which thickly describes the Balinese cockfight and its "deep play" of male rivalry, William Roseberry writes:

We learn that the cockfight was outlawed by the Dutch and later by Indonesia, that it is now held in semisecret in hidden corners of the village, and that the Balinese regard the island as taking the shape of "a small, proud cock, poised, neck extended, back taut, tail raised, in eternal challenge to large, reckless, shapeless Java." Surely these matters require some interpretive attention. At the very least they suggest that the cockfight is intimately related (though not reducible) to political processes of state formation and colonialism. They also suggest that the cockfight has gone through a significant change in the past eighty years, that if it is a text it is a text that is being written as part of a profound social, political, and cultural *process*.[31]

Here Geertz is confronted with all the questions (about spinning, about textualizing) that his cultural analysis eschews.

Paralleling the criticisms of Asad, Keesing, and Shankman, Roseberry's own criticisms nevertheless raise the stakes considerably by challenging Geertz's chosen unit of analysis. An ongoing debate within anthropology—one that promises no easy solution—concerns how the units of anthropological analysis are to be defined. Are cultures islands unto themselves, to be known by placing them, as Geertz does, "in local frames of awareness"?[32] Or are they situated globally and geopolitically, within structures of domination? Inspired by dependency theory and more recently by Wallerstein's world-system theory, the political-economy framework views the locality from the per-

30. Keesing, "Anthropology as Interpretive Quest," p. 166.
31. William Roseberry, "Balinese Cockfights and the Seduction of Anthropology," *Social Research* 49 (1982): 1021.
32. Geertz, *Local Knowledge*, p. 61.

spective of a transnational, Western-dominated, capitalistic system. This perspective—a new and global holism that embraces history as its natural ally—looks "at the world as a whole, a totality, a system, instead of as a sum of self-contained societies and cultures," and unravels (in self-consciously un-Geertzian, even anti-Geertzian, fashion) "the chains of causes and effects at work in the lives of particular populations" by referring these chains to the totality and its historical development.[33]

In the extreme case, every feature of the locale is viewed as a reflex of the encompassing system and its determinants. This perspective ignores the obvious—that, though the world system is one, the outcomes of its historical impingement on the hinterland have been varied, suggesting that the history of Western imperialism depends as much on cultural mediation as on colonial and postcolonial domination for its explanation.[34] As Jean Comaroff has written of a South African tribal people, "The relationship of such a global system to local formations has to be viewed as a historical problem; it is a relationship which, while inherently contradictory and unequal, is not universally determining."[35]

None of the authors herein discussed advocate this extreme position, which is as reductionist as Geertz's. Thus, Roseberry argues that the local text is "intimately related (though not reducible) to political processes of state formation and colonialism."[36] What *is* being argued is that local and global perspectives should somehow be integrated. For example, George Marcus and Michael Fischer, critics but also admirers of Geertz, allude to "the recent call for a reconciliation between advances in the study of cultural meaning achieved by interpretive anthropology, and the concerns of ethnographers to place their subjects firmly in the flow of historic events and the long-term

33. Eric R. Wolf, *Europe and the People Without History* (Berkeley and Los Angeles, 1982), p. 385.

34. John L. Comaroff, "Dialectical Systems, History, and Anthropology: Units of Study and Questions of Theory," *Journal of Southern African Studies* 8 (1982): 145; and Sahlins, *Islands of History*, p. viii.

35. Jean Comaroff, *Body of Power, Spirit of Resistance: The Culture and History of a South African People* (Chicago, 1985), p. 155.

36. Roseberry, "Balinese Cockfights," p. 1021.

operation of world political and economic systems."[37] Such a merger would synthesize cultural and Marxist (or at least politically informed) analyses. It would also have the effect of focusing the concerns of anthropology, historical sociology, and history on a common object: the world system as a historical and heterogeneous entity consisting of plural, partially mobile, partially constrained components, within which "island" and "world," neither reducible to the other, condition each other.

In turning to Sahlins and his *Historical Metaphors and Mythical Realities,* we shift from interpretation and the surrounding controversies toward a style of analysis informed by structuralism. Searching for a bridge between history and anthropology, Sahlins seizes on Fernand Braudel (and, indirectly, the entire Annales tradition) as a precedent. He knows, for example, that, in a gesture of solidarity with Lévi-Strauss, Braudel rebaptized the "geohistory" of the first edition of *The Mediterranean* the "structural history" of the second edition.[38] Sahlins is also aware of Braudel's triadic temporal scheme and the way it replicates, albeit in other terms, the structure/event or structure/history antinomy of structuralism. Between Braudel's assertion that events (the stuff and nonsense of conventional "political history") are "delusive smoke,"[39] on the one hand, and Lévi-Strauss's like dismissal of "real time" and its events as inexplicable happenstance on the other, there is little to choose. In the abstract, the relationship between Braudel's long and short time span, between "structural history" and "political history," is the same as the relationship between Lévi-Strauss's "order of structure" and his "order of event."

Sahlins takes up the issues where Lévi-Strauss and Braudel left off. To develop the anthropology that he, after Sartre, advocates—a "structural, historical anthropology"[40]—Sahlins must rethink structure and event, structure and history, in dialectical

37. George E. Marcus and Michael J. Fischer, *Anthropology as Cultural Critique: An Experimental Moment in the Human Sciences* (Chicago, 1986), p. 44.

38. Kinser, "*Annaliste* Paradigm?," p. 83.

39. Braudel, *On History,* p. 27.

40. Sahlins, *Islands of History,* p. 72.

terms. *Historical Metaphors* reconstructs the history of early contact in Hawaii, beginning with Captain Cook's arrival in the ar-
chipelago and his eventual demise in 1779. The book opens
with a lamentation on the theoretical limitations of Ferdinand
de Saussure's structural linguistics and the "cultural structuralism" it has inspired.[41] Sahlins intends to recover event, action,
change, and the world for structural analysis. Conversely, he
intends to recover structural analysis for history.

The word *structure* in Sahlins's monograph refers to cultural
categories conceived, Saussure-like, as a conceptual grid: a system of differences, a set of categories. This grid encompasses
social statuses (chief, commoner, woman, man), the names of
divinities—in fact, the entire indigenous order in all its political,
social, and religious dimensions. How does history transform
this order, and how is history itself ordered in the process? *Historical Metaphors* is a densely argued, densely illustrated micro-
investigation into Sahlins's twin and related themes, reproduction and transformation. "The great challenge to an historical
anthropology is not merely to know how events are ordered by
culture, but how, in the process, the culture is reordered. How
does the reproduction of a structure become its transformation?" The relationship between reproduction and transformation and the dialectic on which it is predicated account for the
puzzling motto of the essay—not the structuralist's "the more
things change, the more they remain the same," but "plus c'est
la même chose, plus ça change."[42]

The first of two core chapters, "Reproduction," argues that
the events of early contact in Hawaii were "encompass[ed]
within the system as constituted." Arriving from distant parts,
Captain Cook was classified as the Hawaiian fertility god Lono,
who annually returns from Kahiki (associated with the sky and
its divinity) to participate in the Makahiki rituals celebrating
him. Feted as such, Cook was the "historical form" of a cultural
category, historical metaphor of a mythical reality. Though
space does not allow detailed recapitulation of Sahlins's nar-

41. Sahlins, *Historical Metaphors*, p. 5.
42. Ibid., pp. 8, 7.

rative, suffice it to say that even the manner of Cook's demise substantiates Sahlins's point—that insofar as events are signs, history can be "organized by structures of significance."[43]

Were Sahlins to end his analysis at this point, *Historical Metaphors* would simply corroborate the structuralist understanding of the relationship between structure and event, structure and history, claiming in effect that, however autonomously generated, events nonetheless fall subject to the determinations of structure after the fact, in the manner of Lévi-Strauss's *bricolage*. Resisting this reduction, however, Sahlins demonstrates structure's productive role in a history that, for all that, remains irreducible. "History is culturally ordered, differently so in different societies, according to meaningful schemes of things. *The converse is also true:* cultural schemes are historically ordered, since to a greater or lesser extent the meanings are revalued as they are practically enacted" (emphasis mine).[44]

In his second core chapter, "Transformation," Sahlins argues that the actual practices of historical actors introduced novelty into the Hawaiian system. Europeans brought with them exotic commercial ideologies, and their arrival created opportunities for unprecedented machinations and coalitions that were subversive of indigenous arrangements. Traditionally, for example, commoner men and women were segregated. But in these altered circumstances, the interests of commoner men and women suddenly coincided, and they began collaborating. Meanwhile, as horizontal bonds strengthened, vertical ties weakened. Traditionally the relationship between chief and commoner was phrased in the idiom of kinship to reflect the moral constraints on the bond. Chiefs, as a mark of their status, and also to allow them to accumulate surpluses for redistributive purposes, exercised the privilege of levying a taboo (*kapu*) on any item they wanted to withhold from circulation. The European presence commercially advantaged the chiefs because, through their *kapu*, they were able to control trade goods; in particular, they could exercise a monopoly over sandalwood. In a breach of the kinship ethic, Hawaiian chiefs pursued their

43. Ibid., pp. 50, 24, 8.
44. Sahlins, *Islands of History*, p. vii.

own interests at the expense of the interests of commoners, deploying the *kapu* for entrepreneurial purposes. "The historical contact with Europeans submitted the relationship between chiefs and people to unparalleled strains," Sahlins writes. The upshot of the "pragmatic improvisations" occasioned by the arrival of commercial enclaves in Hawaiian waters was a formation of classes whereby the kinship ties between commoners and chiefs were in effect abrogated.[45]

Whether discussing Hawaiian ritual and Captain Cook's fatal relation to it or the commercial use of chiefly taboo, Sahlins focuses on what he calls "signs in action": categories and values as situationally deployed. Sahlins's signs in action (Saussure's *parole*) bear one of two relationships to his "signs in place" (Saussure's *langue*). As historically used, signs may either reproduce or transform the original meaning. Cook-as-Lono (the historical event–as–mythical reality) was a sign in action that replicated the sign in place: Lono as a category of god. Other signs in action, however—other historical events—altered the meaning of the signs in place they instantiated, giving them a presence in Hawaiian history they would not otherwise have had. When Hawaiian chiefs promoted their own interests by placing signs of prohibition on sandalwood, the *kapu* sign took on an unprecedented circumstantial value. "In action, people put their concepts and categories into ostensive relations to the world. Such referential uses bring into play other determinations of the signs, besides their received sense, namely the actual world and the people concerned."[46]

The transformation on which the book centers—class formation and the origin of the state—derives from the perturbations and innovations of what Sahlins calls a "'structure of the conjuncture': a set of historical relationships that at once reproduce the traditional cultural categories and give them new values out of the pragmatic context."[47] The principal players of the structure of the conjuncture are men or women, chiefs or commoners—cultural types rather than individuals. Their practices are thus structurally situated, relationally positioned. Though particular chiefs gained leverage in the contact situation, they did

45. Ibid., p. 44.   46. Ibid., p. 149.   47. Ibid., p. 125.

so *as chiefs*, instances of the type, wielders of *kapu*. Similarly, commoners *as commoners* were disadvantaged. Inspired by the contingencies of the moment, historical action nevertheless had its structure. There was a "structure of practice" through which action—precedented but also unprecedented, conservative but also innovative—generated *principled* change. "All structural transformation involves structural reproduction, if not the other way around."

The engagement of different categories of Hawaiian society—women, men and chiefs—to the foreigners from Kahiki was traditionally motivated: the interests they severally displayed in the European shipping following from their customary relationships to each other and to the world as Hawaiians conceived it. In this sense, Hawaiian culture would reproduce itself as history. Its tendency was to encompass the advent of Europeans within the system as constituted, thus to integrate circumstance as structure and make of the event a version of itself. But in the event, the project of cultural reproduction failed. For again, the pragmatics had its own dynamics. . . . The complex of exchanges that developed between Hawaiians and Europeans, the structure of the conjuncture, brought the former into uncharacteristic conditions of internal conflict and contradiction. Their differential connections with Europeans thereby endowed their own relationships to each other with novel functional content. This is structural transformation. The values acquired in practice return to structure as new relationships between its categories.[48]

Today the *kapu* sign marks private property in a political economy that rests on class interest rather than caste privilege.

If the structures of the present are the structures of the past as modified by structurally positioned but circumstantially motivated action (the events generated by the structure of the conjuncture), then structure and event enter into dialectical relationship. Sahlins closes his monograph with the following set of claims concerning structure and history:

The dialectics of history, then, are structural throughout. Powered by disconformities between conventional values and intentional values, between intersubjective meanings and subjective interests, between

48. Sahlins, *Historical Metaphors*, pp. 68, 50.

symbolic sense and symbolic reference, the historical process unfolds as a continuous and reciprocal movement between the practice of the structure and the structure of the practice.[49]

The more things remain the same, the more they change!

In the final chapter of *Islands of History*, Sahlins takes stock of his theoretical accomplishments. Among other things, his model resolves a number of antinomies that have left their mark upon social theory. Braudel's structural versus political history, the long versus the short time span, reflects a distinction between system and action, structure and event, and the related dichotomy of society and individual, all of which have served to polarize frameworks by justifying a rift beween system- and action-oriented approaches.[50] If structure has its being *"in* history and *as* history," as Sahlins argues,[51] then these approaches become complementary perspectives on a single, intrinsically historical reality—convergent rather than divergent frameworks.

Sahlins's resolution of the structure/event antinomy is classic; it is also not unique to him. Contesting Durkheim's society/individual distinction, the British sociologist Anthony Giddens has argued in his well-known "theory of structuration" that "structure is both the medium and the outcome of . . . practices"[52]—conditioning but also conditioned—and that "the seed of change is present . . . in every act which contributes toward the reproduction of any 'ordered' form of social life."[53] In effect, Giddens's theory generalizes Sahlins's model of Hawaiian history.

49. Ibid., p. 72.
50. For a discussion of these matters, see Anthony Giddens, *Central Problems in Social Theory: Structure and Contradiction in Social Analysis* (Berkeley and Los Angeles, 1979); Ivan Karp, "Agency and Social Theory: A Review of Anthony Giddens," *American Ethnologist* 13 (1986): 131–37; and Sherry B. Ortner, "Theory in Anthropology Since the Sixties," *Comparative Studies in Society and History* 26 (1984): 126–66.
51. Sahlins, *Islands of History*, p. 145.
52. Anthony Giddens, *Profiles and Critiques in Social Theory* (Berkeley and Los Angeles, 1982), p. 10.
53. Anthony Giddens, *New Rules of Sociological Method: A Positive Critique of Interpretive Sociologies* (New York, 1976), p. 102.

The same is true of Pierre Bourdieu's "theory of practice." For Bourdieu, as for Sahlins, structure and event are inextricably linked. Bourdieu's now famous neologism, *habitus*, is psychological: "systems of durable . . . dispositions" designating "a *way of being*, a *habitual state* . . . and, in particular, *a predisposition, tendency, propensity*, or *inclination*." But habitus is also sociological. Like Sahlins's actors, Bourdieu's actors are instances of a type, members of societal segments, and as such, structurally positioned. Much as speech-performance is anchored in a more generalized speech-competence for Chomsky, action for Bourdieu is rooted in a psychological-cum-sociological (subjective-cum-objective) ground of being. Action is thus *more than* the mechanical enactment of "pre-established assemblies, 'models' or 'roles,'" *more than* pure reflex. It is an *act:* behavior shaped to a degree by the contingencies of the moment and their strategic requirements, by *practical* considerations. Grounded in habitus, action is a context for the constrained and principled invention that habitus's *"conditioned and conditional freedom"* allows—a relation, then, between convention and innovation. As in Sahlins's reformulation of the structure/event antinomy, Bourdieu argues that practice (as a conjunctive *and* generative site) can trigger structural transformation. "Objective structures are themselves products of historical practices." But historical practices are in turn "embodiments" of structure. Structure and event thus enter into dialectical relation.[54]

Within Western Marxism, there is a long-standing tradition that seeks to supplant mechanistic base/superstructure models with models in which the human subject becomes the "ever-baffled and ever-resurgent" subject of his or her own history.[55] Railing against the structural Marxism of Louis Althusser and using a less idiosyncratic language than Bourdieu or Sahlins, E. P. Thompson insists on the historical subject's ability to "make" himself or herself (see Desan's essay, chapter 2). Thompson does so fully cognizant of the historical impact of structural constraints. His agenda thus aligns with that of Sah-

---

54. Pierre Bourdieu, *Outline of a Theory of Practice*, trans. R. Nice (Cambridge, 1977), pp. 72, 214n. 1, 73, 95, 83.

55. E. P. Thompson, *The Poverty of Theory and Other Essays* (New York, 1978), p. 88.

lins and Bourdieu. The dual determinations of Sahlins's and Bourdieu's dialectic are affirmed in the famous opening paragraph of Thompson's classic, *The Making of the English Working Class:* "This book has a clumsy title, but it is one which meets its purpose. Making, because it is a study in an active process, which owes as much to agency as to conditioning [as much to action as to structure]. The working class did not rise like the sun at an appointed time. It was present at its own making."[56]

Though the language of these writers appears to be worlds apart from the language of Geertz—instead of interpretation, thick description, and cultural analysis, we hear of structure, event, and dialectics—in resolving the structure/action antinomy, the dialectical model necessarily reconciles structural with cultural analyses as well. This reconciliation is very much on the surface of Sahlins's argument. His signs in action are meaning-bearing vehicles, "objectifications," "texts." But they also exist, like Lévi-Strauss's mythemes and Saussure's *langue,* as constituents of a field of differences, a categorical scheme. In *Historical Metaphors,* Sahlins accomplishes the same intellectual feat that the philosopher Paul Ricoeur accomplishes in his essay on language, "Structure, Word, Event," which openly takes on the challenge of reconciling structuralism with hermeneutics. Here Ricoeur argues, as Sahlins does, that in being taken up in acts of speech, the word becomes exposed to the "profound dynamism" of sign usage and acquires novel meanings. The word is a "displaceable entity," situated within the structured field of signs but also within the contextual and productive field of discourse. It is (to use Sahlins's language) at once a sign in action and a sign in place. Used, laden with new meaning, the word "returns to the system" and "gives the system a history." If language "is neither structure nor event but the incessant conversion of the one into the other in discourse,"[57] the structuralism of Lévi-Strauss and the "cultural analysis" of Clifford Geertz are complementary aspects of a single argument concerning history.

56. E. P. Thompson, *The Making of the English Working Class* (New York, 1966), p. 9.

57. Paul Ricoeur, "Structure, Word, Event," in *The Conflict of Interpretations: Essays in Hermeneutics* (Evanston, Ill., 1974), pp. 84, 92, 93, 89.

Although Sahlins's express intention is to provide a correc-
tive for the shortcomings of structuralism, in reconciling Lévi-
Strauss and Geertz Sahlins also overcomes some of the dis-
abilities of cultural analysis discussed in this volume. Sahlins's
theme is not really Hawaiian history, but history itself, or rather
"historicity," the way systems tend to move. "Different cultures, different historicities"; "other times, other customs." As
he writes, "The heretofore obscure histories of remote islands
deserve a place alongside the self-contemplation of the European past—of the history of 'civilizations'—for their own remarkable contributions to our historical understanding. We
thus multiply our conceptions of history by the diversity of
structures."[58] Here, in this "structural, historical anthropology," Lévi-Strauss's distinction between hot and cold societies—the West and the rest—is dismissed, but so too is the distinction between explanation and understanding on which
cultural analysis rests. In *Historical Metaphors*, questions of gen-
esis and meaning become intertwined.

At the same time, issues of causation become far more complex. One of the most important features of Sahlins's model is
the way it combines an attention to situational pragmatics with
a focus on semantics. As historically used, the Hawaiian chief's
kapu was both signifier and instrument. Its significance had
structural roots, but its instrumentality derived from the self-
interested improvisations of the moment. Braudel's long and
short time span are thus linked as the political and the cultural, the material and the ideal, base and superstructure. Sahlins's structure of the conjuncture centers on this relation as the
source of history's dynamism. Sahlins's dialectic is thus mul-
tidimensional—which accounts for the tremendous range of
resonance of his study, from E. P. Thompson's historical materialism to Ricoeur's revisionist hermeneutics. Speaking specifically of historical materialism, but with some relevance for
other perspectives as well, Thompson succinctly captures the
necessary eclecticism of Sahlins's approach. Historical materialism, he writes, "offers to study social process in its totality;
that is, it offers to do this when it appears, not as another 'sec-

58. Sahlins, *Islands of History*, pp. x, 32, 72.

toral' history—as economic, political, intellectual history, . . . or as 'social history' defined as yet another sector—but as a total history of society, in which all other sectoral histories are convened."[59]

The title of Sahlins's collection of essays, *Islands of History*, is carefully chosen. It evokes the anthropologist's now notorious "ethnographic present," but it also alludes to the historically demonstrable points that exist beyond that present—to Captain Cook, for example. In his introduction, Sahlins identifies the unifying thread of the essays as their shared involvement with "distant encounters, South Sea incidents of the world system," encounters through which "cultural change, externally induced," nevertheless becomes "indigenously orchestrated."[60] In sum, the essays suggest that the relationship between the region and the globe is best conceived (like everything else) in dialectical terms, with respect to how each mediates the reproduction and transformation of the other. As Sahlins's colleagues at Chicago the Comaroffs have expressed the point, local history, always "the outcome of a reciprocally determining interaction of local and global forces whose logic must first be comprehended in its own terms,"[61] is best conceptualized as the reflex of a "dialectic of articulation between a local system and its encompassing context"—that is, in light of how "internal forms" and "external forces" condition each other.[62] Since the contention between those who claim the locality as a unit of analysis and those who focus on the determining power of exogenous and global forces separates those who emphasize culture from those who emphasize political economy, the shift to an islands-of-history model offers further opportunity for softening materialism through culturalist perspectives and, vice versa, for toughening the symbolic approach through an attention to the "hard surfaces of life."[63]

This synthesis does not detract from Sahlins's other point,

59. Thompson, *The Poverty of Theory*, p. 70.
60. Sahlins, *Islands of History*, p. viii.
61. Jean Comaroff, *Body of Power*, p. 144.
62. John L. Comaroff, "Dialectical Systems," p. 146.
63. Cf. Marcus and Fischer, *Anthropology as Cultural Critique*; and Ortner, "Theory in Anthropology."

that his islands are islands *of history* because systems, in their openness, move in characteristic ways. "The dynamic elements at work . . . are present everywhere in human experience. History is made the same general way within a given society as it is between societies."[64] Whether recounting the innovations of practice or Captain Cook's arrival, Sahlins is concerned to identify an Archimedean point beyond the "world" constituted by islands-of-culture, as the locus from which an unprecedented future might have its source. In Sahlins's monograph, Captain Cook becomes a historical metaphor of a theoretical reality: the world-beyond-"world," horizon-beyond-"horizon," the breach of closure that makes a future possible.

The title of Roy Wagner's book *The Invention of Culture* is intentionally ambiguous, referring to a people's invention of itself but also to the anthropologist's invention of the "other." Although "cultural analysis" or interpretation insists on the uniqueness of the natural sciences, it continues to support, albeit in weakened form, the distinction between fiction and nonfiction. In history, of course, Hayden White (see Kramer's essay, chapter 4) and R. G. Collingwood before him have challenged this distinction. But only recently, and then by a scholar trained as a historian, has the radical claim been advanced that anthropological texts are best approached as literature. Picking up where Geertz left off in *The Interpretation of Cultures,* James Clifford writes in his introduction to *Writing Culture:* "Ethnographic writings can properly be called fictions in the sense of 'something made or fashioned,' the principal burden of the word's Latin root, *fingere*. But it is important to preserve the meaning not merely of making, but also of making up, of inventing things not actually real." The anthropologist is tied first and foremost "to the worldly work of writing," to ethnography as textual production.[65] The new textualism foregrounds anthropology-as-writing rather than anthropology-as-reading (as in the interpretive framework), highlighting the way in which ethnographies are "author-saturated" rather than "author-evacuated"—as Geertz himself has put the matter in

64. Sahlins, *Islands of History*, pp. viii–ix.
65. James Clifford, "Introduction: Partial Truths," in *Writing Culture*, ed. Clifford and Marcus, p. 6.

his recent *Works and Lives*. Ethnographic texts bear what Geertz calls a "signature," evidence of "an authorial presence" within the text, and we should seek to understand them as such, by asking "how ethnographic texts are 'author-ized.'"[66] Some scholars associated with the new textualism consider Geertz "at least historically important to the trend";[67] but it is also inspired by the writings of White, LaCapra, Said, Bakhtin, Derrida, and Foucault.

Geertz's "author-izing" has a double meaning. If anthropological texts are literary, their authority rests rather fragilely on the "tropics of [their] discourse." What rhetorical strategies does an ethno-graphy employ to persuade its readers of its truthfulness? The claim that a text creates its own authority through various literary devices, by author-izing itself, casts all anthropological texts under suspicion and suggests "the partiality of cultural and historical truths."[68] This insistence on the partiality of the truths of anthropological texts—on their "essentially contestable" character, as Geertz wrote in 1973—is coupled with a suspicion of any totalizing vision in anthropology, any assumption that cultures confront the anthropologist as undivided and homogeneous wholes. Cultures are fora in which many voices are raised and dissensus rather than consensus prevails. (In his critique of interpretation, Keesing, too, insists on the polyphonic character of cultural reality.) Instead of concentrating on paradigm building (possibly misguided from the outset), anthropologists are encouraged to attend to "problems of epistemology, integration, and discursive forms of representation themselves," to experiment—as Natalie Zemon Davis did in her multimedia project *The Return of Martin Guerre*—with genre. The paradigm interlude occasioned by today's "crisis of representation" is seized on as an opportunity to heighten the reflexive mode in anthropology, which was initially inspired by the interpretive framework.[69]

The new textualism presents itself as a critique of the politics as well as the poetics of the production of anthropological texts.

---

66. Clifford Geertz, *Works and Lives: The Anthropologist as Author* (Stanford, Calif., 1988), p. 9.

67. Marcus and Fischer, *Anthropology as Cultural Critique*, p. 8.

68. Clifford, "Introduction," p. 6.

69. Marcus and Fischer, *Anthropology as Cultural Critique*, p. 9.

Edward Said's *Orientalism* rings a death knell for all authority claimed by the West in representing the rest. The end of empire and the development of a postcolonial situation have inaugurated a new era in which polyphony is located across rather than within cultural borders. As Clifford insists at the outset of his important essay "On Ethnographic Authority," "The West can no longer present itself as the unique purveyor of anthropological knowledge about others": "it has become necessary to imagine a world of generalized ethnography."[70] Clifford pursues this set of themes in his most recent book, *The Predicament of Culture,* which envisions a "changing field of counterdiscourses, syncretisms, and reappropriations originating both outside and inside 'the West'" with respect to which Western forms and discourse are no longer privileged.[71] Debates and contestations surrounding anthropological texts become the occasion for challenging the West's historical monopoly on "orientalizing" the other. In the new textualism, the political and the cultural are once again brought into relation, albeit through examination of the rhetorical properties of texts that arise from and function with respect to determinate historical and political circumstances.

Although the new textualism has a very different agenda from Sahlins's "structural, historical anthropology," a certain recognition of the multidimensionality of reality, and a certain boldness in exploring the theoretical paradoxes that an analysis of that multidimensionality necessarily spawns, unite them. So, too, does their shared acknowledgment of the relevance of extralocal, transcultural, pluralistic, historically constituted, worldly and material entities. *Historical Metaphors* and *Writing Culture* propose alternate routes to the historicization of a field that, until recently, had ignored Maitland's dictum and charted ahistorical, even antihistorical, courses.

70. James Clifford, "On Ethnographic Authority," *Representations* 1 (1983): 119.
71. James Clifford, *The Predicament of Culture* (Cambridge, Mass., 1988), pp. 239–40.

Four

Literature, Criticism, and Historical Imagination: The Literary Challenge of Hayden White and Dominick LaCapra

LLOYD S. KRAMER

Historical writing in the twentieth century has evolved through institutional and intellectual patterns that have produced a perennial historiographical tension. The dominant institutional pattern has been the tendency of historians to define themselves along the increasingly precise lines of academic departments, limited specializations, and disciplinary boundaries. At the same time, however, much of the intellectual innovation among modern historians has resulted from their willingness to draw on other academic disciplines for theoretical and methodological insights, which has led to an expansion and redefinition of the political orientation of traditional historiography. The search for new approaches to the past has led historians to anthropology, economics, psychology, and sociology; now it is leading them to literary criticism. In fact, the one truly distinguishing feature of the new cultural approach to history is the pervasive influence of recent literary criticism, which has taught historians to recognize the active role of language, texts, and narrative structures in the creation and description of historical reality.

This emphasis on the literary dimension of social experience and the literary structure of historical writing provides a new opening for those who seek to expand historical scholarship beyond its limiting traditions, and a new threat for those who seek to defend the discipline within its traditional boundaries as they understand them. The metaphors here suggest a kind of historiographical battle with flank attacks from literary forces and a defensive circling of the disciplinary wagons by "real" historians. Although this battle is waged most often among the anonymous troops of academia (editors and referees of journal articles, departmental search committees, graduate seminars, and so forth), the literary forces have clearly rallied in recent years around the prominent leadership of Hayden White and Dominick LaCapra. These two campaigners have developed the literary assault with impressive intellectual force, though the complexity of their maneuvers has sometimes confused their followers and frequently baffled their opponents. This essay therefore traces the literary maneuvers of the White-LaCapra campaign by simplifying its subtle strategies and by stressing only the main directions of its movements.

The distinctiveness of White and LaCapra within contemporary historiography derives in part from the distinctive qualities of intellectual history, the subdiscipline that has always defied departmental lines by its emphasis on the philosophy, literature, and theoretical writings of past cultures. Intellectual historians often seem excessively abstract and marginal to historians who study elections or battles or diplomacy, and yet the recurring theme of intellectual history is that structures of thought and symbolic meaning are an integral part of everything we know as history. Those who analyze such structures in the texts of past societies find similar structures in the historical writings of the present—which may help to account for the fact that intellectual historians tend to become the theoreticians and critical analysts of the historical discipline as a whole. Both White and LaCapra exemplify this tendency, because they turned to theoretical investigations of modern historiography only after writing intellectual histories of influential authors and cultural developments in the European tradition.[1]

Expanding the Boundaries of History

Despite some important differences in many of their leading themes and interests, my effort to link White and LaCapra in a shared literary critical approach to history will stress their similarities over their differences. These similarities appear most

1. See, for example, White's survey of European intellectual history in Wilson H. Coates, Hayden V. White, and J. Salwyn Schapiro, *The Emergence of Liberal Humanism* (New York, 1966), and in Wilson H. Coates and Hayden V. White, *The Ordeal of Liberal Humanism* (New York, 1970). LaCapra's studies of European intellectuals include *Emile Durkheim: Sociologist and Philosopher* (Ithaca, N.Y., 1972), *A Preface to Sartre* (Ithaca, N.Y., 1978), and *"Madame Bovary" on Trial* (Ithaca, N.Y., 1982). He has also put his methodological theories into practice in a recent book on modern literature, *History, Politics, and the Novel* (Ithaca, N.Y., 1987). Despite the importance of their works on specific figures in European intellectual history, I shall limit my discussion in this essay to the more explicitly theoretical texts that White and LaCapra have written.

I should also note that this essay does not examine the critical responses that these texts have elicited from historians—though anyone who wants to understand the wider historiographical debates should refer to some of the critics as well as to the works of White and LaCapra. See *History and Theory*, Beiheft 19 (1980), for a collection of six critical essays on White's methodology in *Metahistory: The Historical Imagination in Nineteenth-Century Europe* (Baltimore, 1973); earlier substantive discussions of this same work include the review essay by John S. Nelson in *History and Theory* 14 (1975): 74–91, and the review by Michael Ermarth in the *American Historical Review* 80 (1975): 961–63. For analytical essays that deal in various ways with LaCapra's methodological proposals, see John E. Toews, "Intellectual History After the Linguistic Turn: The Autonomy of Meaning and the Irreducibility of Experience," *American Historical Review* 92 (1987): 879–907; Michael Ermarth, "Mindful Matters: The Empire's New Codes and the Plight of Modern European Intellectual History," *Journal of Modern History* 57 (1985): 506–27; and William J. Bouwsma's review essay on the book edited by LaCapra and Steven L. Kaplan, *Modern European Intellectual History: Reappraisals and New Perspectives* (Ithaca, N.Y., 1982), in *History and Theory* 23 (1984): 229–36. See also the criticisms in James T. Kloppenberg, "Deconstructive and Hermeneutic Strategies for Intellectual History: The Recent Work of Dominick LaCapra and David Hollinger," *Intellectual History Newsletter* 9 (1987): 3–22.

For examples of the response to White and LaCapra among literary critics, see Peter De Bolla, "Disfiguring History," *Diacritics* 16, no. 4 (1986): 49–58; and Suzanne Gearhart, "History as Criticism: The Dialogue of History and Literature," *Diacritics* 17, no. 3 (1987): 56–65.

obviously in their shared desire to examine and widen the inherited definitions of history and historical methodology. This project leads both White and LaCapra to question the boundaries that separate history from literature and philosophy, to challenge what they see as the dominant trends in historiography, and to focus on the decisive role of language in our descriptions or conceptions of historical reality. Both believe that greater attention to literary critical perspectives can make historians more innovative and more aware of their own assumptions and repressions. As White and LaCapra point out repeatedly to their sometimes hostile (or uninterested) colleagues, history has tended to remain situated within literary and scientific paradigms that date from the nineteenth century, while both literature and science have moved far beyond those earlier phases of development. The challenge that this White-LaCapra perspective brings to contemporary historians thus concerns the complex problem of opening the essentially nineteenth-century historiographical paradigm of reality and representation to the critical insights that have transformed nineteenth-century attitudes in literature, art, critical theory, and science.

The call for a more varied approach to history carries the influence of a European tradition that evolves from Friedrich Nietzsche into the recent work of Michel Foucault or Jacques Derrida and that examines critically the founding assumptions of knowledge. This tradition, which many historians distrust or dislike, stresses that critical theorists should recover those lost or repressed strands of Western culture that might challenge the reigning epistemological and ontological orthodoxies of our time. Most historians who look for philosophical or political continuities in the Western tradition are not inclined to explore the common assumptions by which they link their own values to the historical worlds they describe in their books. "Since the second half of the nineteenth century," White argues in one of his essays, "history has become increasingly the refuge of all of those 'sane' men who excel at finding the simple in the complex and the familiar in the strange."[2]

---

2. Hayden White, *Tropics of Discourse: Essays in Cultural Criticism* (Baltimore, 1978), p. 50. This book, like other books by White and LaCapra cited

White's account of modern historiography therefore suggests that historians seek more often to close down alternative ways of understanding the world than to open up our vision. "Every discipline . . . is, as Nietzsche saw most clearly, constituted by what it *forbids* its practitioners to do. Every discipline is made up of a set of restrictions on thought and imagination, and none is more hedged about with taboos than professional historiography." Such taboos preclude the use of insights from art and literature because they compel historians to emphasize the distinctions between fiction and fact. Unfortunately, these distinctions ignore the perspectives of modern literary theory and blind historians to the actual processes of their work. "In point of fact, history . . . is made sense of in the same way that the poet or novelist tries to make sense of it, i.e., by endowing what originally appears to be problematical and mysterious with the aspect of a recognizable, because it is a familiar, form."[3] Unlike creative writers, however, historians usually choose not to see the fictive element in their books; on the contrary, they prefer to believe that they have transcended fiction by setting strict guidelines for the discipline of history. "They effect a disciplining of the imagination, in this case the historical imagination, and they set limits on what constitutes a specifically historical event." And yet, in spite of these explicit limits, every attempt to describe historical events necessarily relies on narratives that "display the coherence, integrity, fullness, and closure of an image of life that is and can only be imaginary."[4]

The fictive, imaginary dimension in all accounts of events does not mean that the events did not actually happen, but it does mean that any attempt to *describe* events (even as they are occurring) must rely on various forms of imagination. Furthermore, all accounts of historical realities must inevitably rely on a philosophy of history. In other words, one cannot write history without both philosophy and fictional narratives, and one cannot simply affirm the disciplinary distinction that historians

---

below, consists of essays that were published in various places over a period of several years, but I shall not refer to the specific essay titles in these notes.

3. Ibid., pp. 126, 98.

4. Hayden White, *The Content of the Form: Narrative Discourse and Historical Representation* (Baltimore, 1987), pp. 66, 24.

use to separate themselves from philosophers and literary authors. "The principal difference between history and philosophy of history is that the latter brings the conceptual apparatus
by which the facts are ordered in the discourse to the surface of
the text, while history proper (as it is called) buries it in the interior of the narrative, where it serves as a hidden or implicit
shaping device."[5] White suggests that recognition of the philosophical component in "history proper" and of the fictive element in historical narratives threatens historians only if they
insist on rigidly defining history according to the nineteenth-
century scientific theory that posits a radical distinction between fact and philosophy or between fact and fiction. By challenging that distinction, however, historians can expand the
definition of what they do and thus help to transform the discipline into a more creative, self-conscious, critical enterprise.

The same desire to expand our definitions of history appears in the work of Dominick LaCapra, who, like White, wants
to defamiliarize the texts and contexts of the past. But LaCapra
tends to go beyond White in his emphasis on the contestations
that challenge both the apparent unity of the past and the apparent order of historical narratives that describe it. Where
White's analysis of the fictive and philosophical structures in
historical narratives often suggests their coherent (if unexamined) structural characteristics, LaCapra more often points to
the conflicting tendencies in texts or contexts that defy all historiographical attempts to account for these realities in terms of
full coherence. Thus, from LaCapra's perspective, historical
narratives and the objects of their investigation express internal
tensions that always challenge the deep structures of philosophical and literary order that White discovers in his examination of historical writing.

LaCapra therefore calls for a critical historiography that questions the search for order and coherence that one finds in most
history books. The demand here (as in White) points toward a
wider conception of historical scholarship and historical processes. "One such process," LaCapra explains, "is precisely the

5. White, *Tropics of Discourse*, p. 127. This emphasis on the connection between "proper" history and philosophies of history forms a major theme in
White's detailed study of nineteenth-century historians in *Metahistory*.

interaction between the desire for unity, identity, or purity, and the forces that contest it. The investigation of this process does not imply a simple rejection of conceptions of unity or order in a mindlessly antinomian celebration of chaos and dismemberment. What it calls for is a rethinking of the concept of unity and its analogues in more workable and critical terms."[6] LaCapra thus recognizes that notions of order cannot be discarded in historiography, but he wants historians to see these ideas as an issue for investigation rather than as an unexamined presupposition. Historians who rethink the categories of historical understanding are in fact likely to find a great many submerged voices that contest their historical (and metaphysical) desire for unified, unambiguous meaning.

The historian's task, then, is to develop a "dialogue" in which the autonomous past is allowed to question our recurring attempts to reduce it to order. "It must be actively recognized that the past has its own 'voices' that must be respected," LaCapra writes, "especially when they resist or qualify the interpretations we would like to place on them. A text is a network of resistances, and a dialogue is a two-way affair; a good reader is also an attentive and patient listener."[7] Although this "dialogic" emphasis constitutes LaCapra's model for intellectual history, it becomes relevant for all forms of historical study because the "fields" that historians seek to "master" always exceed the explanatory structures that define them; even the "definitive study" leaves out far more than it says. Every epoch, every important text, and every historical figure encompasses tendencies that defy and contradict the labels on which historiography depends.

LaCapra stresses (like White) that historians inevitably use narrative structures to define historical knowledge and to separate history from other forms of writing, but he also argues (like White) that these categories must not be taken for the thing itself. "Analytic distinctions such as those drawn between his-

6. Dominick LaCapra, *Rethinking Intellectual History: Texts, Contexts, Language* (Ithaca, N.Y., 1983), p. 60. White (*Content of the Form*, p. 21) also discusses the common tendency to seek unified closures in historical narratives, which he attributes to the desire for "moral meaning."

7. LaCapra, *Rethinking Intellectual History*, p. 64.

tory and literature, fact and fiction, concept and metaphor, the serious and the ironic, and so forth, do not define realms of discourse that unproblematically characterize or govern extended uses of language. Instead, what should be taken as a problem for inquiry is the nature of the relationships among various analytically defined distinctions in the actual functioning of language."[8] History can never be entirely separated from literature or philosophy or other disciplinary languages, though it can never be identical to those other discourses either. LaCapra's exploration of the similarities and differences in the various languages that define disciplines and reality thus becomes an attempt to expand the meaning of historical scholarship; rethinking the boundaries of language provides a means for rethinking and expanding the boundaries of history.

The effort to rethink the discipline brings White and LaCapra up against what they take to be the dominant forms of contemporary historical understanding—which White describes as Irony, LaCapra as social history. White argues that modern historians are "locked within an Ironic perspective" that relies on the literary trope of Irony to shape the narrative structure of almost all the works of professional historiography. This perspective develops a skeptical attitude toward the way in which historical actors use language to describe reality by stressing the gap between words and things. When applied to the past, Irony enables historians to take a realistic or superior view of the people and events that they discuss, because people always lack the perspective in their own time to see the disjunction between their words and experience as clearly as historians see it in retrospect. "Irony presupposes the occupation of a 'realistic' perspective on reality [i.e., the historian's], from which a non-figurative representation of the world of experience might be provided."[9] No historical generation can represent its reality to itself in this fully accurate ("nonfigurative") manner, and so Ironic historians become analysts of the gap that separated past descriptions of the world from what was actually happening in the world as historians now understand it.

8. Ibid., p. 57.
9. White, *Metahistory*, p. 38.

The famous nineteenth-century historian Jacob Burckhardt exemplifies for White the development of Ironic tendencies that continue to flourish among historians of our own time. "The voice with which Burckhardt *addressed* his audience was that of the Ironist, the possessor of a higher, sadder wisdom than the audience itself possessed. He *viewed* his object of study, the historical field, Ironically, as a field whose meaning is elusive, unspecifiable, perceivable only to the refined intelligence." Ironic historians like Burckhardt assume that their skeptical view is more realistic than either the limited perspective of persons in the past or the naive perspective of contemporary cultural movements that retain unrealistic, romantic illusions. White himself, however, wants to challenge the view that Irony offers the only realistic view of history. "I maintain that the recognition of this Ironic perspective provides the grounds for a transcendence of it," he argues in the conclusion of *Metahistory*. "If it can be shown that Irony is only one of a *number* of possible perspectives on history, each of which has its own good reasons for existence on a poetic and moral level of awareness, the Ironic attitude will have begun to be deprived of its status as the *necessary* perspective from which to view the historical process."[10] The challenge to Irony should foster alternative forms of historical understanding and narrative, all of which must evolve of course through different modes of language. White's critique of the dominant historiography, as well as his proposal for new kinds of historical writing, therefore gives extensive and almost exclusive attention to the various ways in which historians use language.

Although LaCapra shares White's interest in challenging a dominant historiographical trend, he is more concerned with the prominence of social history than with the trope of Irony. LaCapra readily acknowledges the importance of social history as a method for understanding the past, but he complains that social historians have devalued other historical methods and have often oversimplified the complex reality of historical experience. This tendency toward reductionism has moved from social history into intellectual history in studies of *mentalités* and

10. Ibid., pp. 250, 434.

social histories of ideas that replicate for LaCapra the worst features of social history—the tendency to read both texts and
contexts one-dimensionally. The prestige of social history en-
courages historians to adopt a populist perspective that values
one form of history over others ("history from the bottom up")
and thus ignores other interpretations or levels of historical experience. "The result," argues LaCapra, "is prepossessing and
intimidating when social history claims to be a 'total history' or
at least the cynosure to which all other historical approaches
must be referred."[11]

As LaCapra notes in partial explanation for his own attention
to methodological issues, the ascendancy of social-historical
concerns (for example, popular culture over elite culture) "functions to reinforce hegemonic relations in professional historiography." The priority of social-historical assumptions, in
short, limits our conception of historical reality and of historiography. "If a certain level of culture represents primordial
reality, then it is a very short step to the assumption that those
who study it are the 'real' historians, those who focus on the
most important things."[12] But LaCapra is no more willing to
abandon historiography to the social historians than White is
willing to leave it to the Ironists. A new, critical appreciation for
the close reading of texts and contexts alike would contest the
prominence of social history and "even suggest areas in which
the formulations of social history stand in need of further re-
finement." Most important, perhaps, greater attention to the
way that literary critics and philosophers read great texts would
challenge the social historian's desire to "reduce certain texts to
representative, illustrative, or symptomatic functions."[13]

In contrast to the reductive reading style of social history,
LaCapra urges historians to read historical texts and contexts in
ways that recognize their complexity and that might lead to
new kinds of writing too, since the style one adopts in writing
is connected always with the style one adopts in reading. Reading and writing form two overlapping aspects of the historian's
inescapable relationship with language. LaCapra thus shares

11. Dominick LaCapra, *History and Criticism* (Ithaca, N.Y., 1985), p. 80.
12. Ibid., p. 69.
13. LaCapra, *Rethinking Intellectual History*, pp. 24, 344.

White's assumption that the study of history must always be in some sense the study of language, though this does not mean that one should see the world only as language ("textual imperialism") or language merely as a reflection of the world (reductive "contextualism").[14]

The redefinition of the boundaries and priorities of historiography thus requires above all a new sensitivity to language. And the search for a better understanding of language takes White and LaCapra toward those sources where linguistic issues are explored with greatest insight: literary criticism and the great creative works of the literary tradition. One finds in these sources the most interesting precedents for the possible evolution of historiography. "It would appear," White explains, "that the question confronting contemporary historians is not whether they will utilize a linguistic model to aid them in their work, . . . but what kind of linguistic model they will use."[15] Given the relative indifference to linguistic and literary concerns in traditional historiography, those historians who pursue the linguistic route must soon cross the familiar borders of "real history" into the territory of alien cultures. Literary criticism provides the first important guideposts for a journey that should bring a new understanding of modern historiography and a new interpretative perspective on the texts and contexts of the past. But understanding the unexamined structures of historical thought or writing is only the first step, because the new historians must also undertake the task of expanding and changing the inherited categories of those historiographical structures. The new literary approach to history therefore depends also on insights from fictional or poetic forms of understanding and representation that have been declared out of bounds in historiography. History, of course, cannot simply emulate fiction, because historians must deal with what actually happened in the past. According to White and LaCapra, however, the contemporary representation of that past can and should transgress the methodological borders that our positivistic ancestors have bequeathed to the historical profession.

14. Ibid., pp. 19, 85–86.
15. White, *Content of the Form*, pp. 188–89.

Literary Criticism

The use of literary critical methods in analyzing historical problems and texts raises immediate questions about which forms of literary criticism may be most useful for historians. White and LaCapra see particular relevance in recent French theory, though each takes from this theory a somewhat different emphasis. The themes in White's work relate more often to the perspectives of Michel Foucault, whereas LaCapra prefers the work of Jacques Derrida. But this distinction never becomes an absolute dichotomy because they both draw also on other theorists such as (in White's case) Northrop Frye, Kenneth Burke, and Roman Jakobson, or (in LaCapra's case) Martin Heidegger and Mikhail Bakhtin. Despite their reliance on different theorists, White and LaCapra share the belief that unexamined narrative structures and ontological assumptions prefigure all historical works as well as our understanding of reality outside of books.[16] The great value of literary theory thus derives from its analysis of the codes and rhetorical conventions on which historians unconsciously depend.

Following this literary critical tradition, White, in his study of nineteenth-century historians, *Metahistory,* has attempted to explain the literary codes of classical historiography. He draws especially on Frye and Burke to trace various historiographical forms of emplotment, argument, ideology, and tropes, each of which consists of four distinct categories or possible structures. All works of history, White argues, "contain a deep structural content which is generally poetic, and specifically linguistic in nature, and which serves as the precritically accepted paradigm of what a distinctively 'historical' explanation should be." This level of deep structure becomes the inescapable starting point from which "the historian performs an essentially *poetic* act, in which he *pre*figures the historical field and constitutes it as a domain upon which to bring to bear the specific theories he will use to explain 'what was *really* happening' in it."[17] White's con-

16. See White's account of the theoretical influences on his work in *Metahistory,* pp. 3, 8, 31–33, and LaCapra's references to the role of contemporary theory in his work in *Rethinking Intellectual History,* pp. 21–22, 29, 306–18.

17. White, *Metahistory,* pp. ix–x.

cern with these prefiguring categories leads him to analyze the form of historical works, because the formal structure of a narrative (its metahistorical structure) determines the relevance of any particular fact and the organization of every specific story.

Literary criticism shows White, however, that the historical narrative can only be prefigured in a limited number of structures. To be sure, one could conceivably narrate any historical event with a great many different story lines, but the story achieves its plausibility through its use of familiar "explanatory strategies." The all-important requirement of plausibility means that "the number of strategies available to the historian for endowing events with meaning will be coterminous with the number of generic story types available in the historian's own culture."[18] Most historians, though, do not think critically about these prefigurative limitations when they write their narrative plots of historical events—a point that White reiterates by analyzing works as diverse as those of Michelet, Ranke, Tocqueville, and Burckhardt in the nineteenth century and those of E. P. Thompson and A. J. P. Taylor in the twentieth.[19] Indeed, since these historians (like all others) seek to transform the unfamiliar realities of other places or times into metaphors that make the alien world familiar, their reputations indicate the extent to which their stories make sense within the codes or linguistic expectations of our culture. "Historians, no less than poets, can be said to gain an 'explanatory affect' . . . by building into their narratives patterns of meaning similar to those more explicitly provided by the literary art of the cultures to which they belong."[20] It is White's desire to explain how these "patterns of meaning" operate which takes him far into the terminology of rhetorical theory that most historians neither care about nor understand.

As White explains the field of prefigurative narrative strategies, he identifies four modes of possible emplotment (romantic, tragic, comic, satirical), four modes of possible argument (formist, mechanistic, organicist, contextualist), and four modes

18. Hayden White, "Historical Pluralism," *Critical Inquiry* 12 (1986): 488.
19. White, *Metahistory*, p. 142; and idem, *Tropics of Discourse*, pp. 15–19, 107–14.
20. White, *Tropics of Discourse*, p. 58.

of ideological implication (anarchist, radical, conservative, liberal), all of which depend on the four literary tropes that make the unfamiliar world familiar (Metaphor, Metonymy, Synecdoche, Irony).[21] Empirically oriented historians tend to dismiss White's emphasis on the fundamental, even deterministic, role of literary tropes as a technical jargon that is irrelevant to their research, and theoretically oriented historians (such as LaCapra) often question the rigidity of his tropological categories. It should be noted, however, that White's own view of "tropological figuration" does not establish these patterns as an absolute "law of discourse," because there are "plenty of discourses in which the pattern does not fully appear in the form suggested." He nevertheless continues to argue at all times that narrative discourse cannot escape from the "shadow" of tropes or from the structures of thought that constitute any field of historical research.[22]

In this respect, White's work may be compared to that of Foucault, whose "archaeology of knowledge" provides one model for what White is trying to do for history. Indeed, White's accounts of Foucault tend to carry the commitment of someone who perceives himself in what he is describing.

Foucault suggests [that] the human sciences have remained captive of the *figurative* modes of discourse in which they constituted (rather than simply signified) the objects with which they pretend to deal. And the purpose of Foucault's various studies of the evolution of the human sciences is to disclose the figurative (and ultimately mythic) strategies that sanction the conceptualizing rituals in which these sciences characteristically indulge themselves.

This disclosure of "figurative strategies" in the human sciences inevitably becomes a radical, subversive project, but White seems willing to follow Foucault to the very "'threshold' of historical consciousness itself."[23]

Even an archaeological expedition, though, must have its limits, and White chooses to draw his own line at the entrance to the work of Jacques Derrida. The structuralist concern with

21. These various categories of narrative structure and of tropes receive their fullest explication in White's introduction to *Metahistory*, pp. 7–38.
22. White, *Tropics of Discourse*, pp. 2–3, 12–13.
23. Ibid., pp. 231–32, 239.

language is carried to excess in Derrida (according to White's description in "The Absurdist Moment in Contemporary Literary Theory"), because he "not only thinks the unthinkable but turns it into an idol." Derrida renders being itself absurd by arguing that "there is *only figuration*, [and] hence no privileged position from *within* language by which language can be called into question." White thus argues that Derrida's exploration of language goes too far in asserting that "there is no 'meaning,' only the ghostly ballet of alternative 'meanings' which various modes of figuration provide." Having followed the literary critics this far in the search for figurative meaning, White seems to warn that historians should avoid the "absurdist" influence of Derrida. "We are indentured to an endless series of metaphysical translations from one universe of figuratively provided meaning to another," White complains in reference to Derrida. "And they are all equally figurative."[24] But why does White turn against the literary criticism of Derrida?

This is precisely the question that LaCapra raises in a critical reading of White that shows LaCapra's own inclination to follow the Derridean critics further along the linguistic search for historical meaning. LaCapra suggests that White's attack on Derrida expresses the common tendency in books or in society to scapegoat persons who represent the threatening parts of one's own identity. "For the things Derrida discusses *are* inside White." Although Derrida's emphasis on the figurative role of language and his critical evaluation of the foundations of knowledge also appear in White's analysis of historiography, LaCapra argues that the hostile response to Derrida may be seen "as a turn toward secure 'sanity' and conventional irony in the face of the 'other,' who actually articulates things that are 'inside' White himself—but an 'other' whose articulation is perhaps too disconcerting or at least too alien in formulation to be recognizable."[25] LaCapra thus discusses White from the literary critical perspective that he brings also to his analysis of most other historians and critical theorists; that is, he challenges White's view of Derrida with a poststructuralist critique that resembles Derrida's own critique of Lévi-Strauss or Foucault. In spite of his

24. Ibid., p. 281.
25. LaCapra, *Rethinking Intellectual History*, pp. 79, 78.

efforts to challenge the positivist assumptions of historians, White's theory remains for LaCapra "within the same general frame of reference as the 'scientific' views it turned upside-down. Indeed the informing principle of White's theory of tropes as the foundation of rhetoric and narrative was a generative structuralism that presented one level of discourse (the 'tropical') as determinative in the last instance."[26] LaCapra therefore argues that White shares with other historians the desire for a secure foundation that will explain what we understand as historical reality. Where most historians would locate that reality in the social or political world, White locates it in the tropes that shape historical writing, but in each case the metaphysical desire for full presence, full meaning, and full explanation operates as an unexamined founding assumption.[27] White's tropological categories, in short, displace onto the text the kind of categorical thinking that most historians apply to the context.

LaCapra is attracted to Derridean criticism because it seems to offer a more persuasive account of what actually happens in historical texts and social experience. The categories through which we describe the world are always opposed by other tendencies that are "always already" within the category that they theoretically oppose. In simple terms this means, for example, that it is impossible to conceive of light without darkness or to think of presence without absence; each concept carries or overlaps or supplements the other and therefore precludes the possibility of a complete or pure identity. LaCapra believes that this Derridean insight, which may be called the concept of supplementarity, has great importance for historians who seek constantly to break the world into categorical oppositions and thereby distort the complexity of historical experience and texts. "Supplementarity reveals why analytic distinctions necessarily overlap in 'reality,'" LaCapra writes, "and why it is misleading to take them as dichotomous categories. Analytic or polar opposites always leave a problematic difference or remainder for which they do not fully account."[28]

LaCapra admits (and his critics would insist) that the notion of supplementarity questions the way in which reason orga-

26. Ibid., p. 34.   27. Ibid., p. 76.   28. Ibid., p. 152.

nizes the world, though he also argues that the concept "does not obliterate distinctions, and it cannot be identified with confusion." The necessary distinctions between categories, however, should not be transformed into "transcendental conditions" of knowledge that distort the intricate contestatory process through which the distinctions actually operate. One learns from Derridean critical theory that our attempts to limit the play of supplements inevitably requires the use of fiction. "Analysis provides clear and distinct ideas which define boundaries and confine ambiguity or overlap to marginal, borderline cases. Insofar as analysis defines polar opposites, it constructs ideal types or heuristic fictions."[29]

But these fictions are never entirely successful because the supplements escape constantly across the boundaries established to define analytic categories. Although this process does not mean that historians can or should abandon all categories or all desire for systematic distinctions, it does suggest that they should give far more attention to the ways in which their categories overlap and contest one another. The problem, of course, is to find a method for writing history that would convey the complexity of overlapping categories without abandoning analytic distinctions and therefore passing into complete obscurity or confusion. LaCapra himself is aware of the danger in a "lemming-like fascination for discursive impasses and an obsessive interest in the aberrant and aleatory—tendencies that threaten to identify all controlling limits with totalizing mastery and thus to undermine any conception of critical rationality."[30] Literary criticism need not lead inevitably to this impasse, however, as LaCapra indicates through his extended commentary on the Russian critic Mikhail Bakhtin.

The great value of Bakhtin for LaCapra derives from his emphasis on the interplay between opposing tendencies in literature and in life, an interplay that Bakhtin described most thoroughly in reference to the "dialogic imagination" of Dostoevsky. LaCapra draws on Bakhtin to argue that great novels often portray internal contestations more profoundly than other texts because the literary form sets language free and therefore

29. Ibid.
30. LaCapra, *History and Criticism*, p. 141.

challenges the categories that reign elsewhere in the culture. "Bakhtin's emphasis upon dialogization directed attention to the more ambivalent or undecidable dimensions of texts . . . and highlighted the importance of the border or the threshold where seeming opposites entered into an exchange and possibly coexisted, often in tensely charged relationships."[31] This attention to the dialogic process in great literature becomes relevant to the historical analysis of other texts and contexts in that it stresses the importance of contestatory voices. The texts or social realities of past societies evolve through constant dialogues that must be examined and entered from a variety of perspectives and that cannot be simply reduced to a single, monologic meaning. The dialogic approach to history would therefore open up the discussion between opposing categories on a number of different levels: the dialogue between opposing ideas within specific texts, the dialogue between historians and the past, or the dialogue between texts and contexts. None of these oppositions would form simple dichotomies, however, because the dialogue becomes possible only through those many points at which the oppositions tend "always already" to overlap.

Take, for example, the dialogue between the opposing categories of text and context. According to LaCapra, most historians establish a hierarchical dichotomy between texts and contexts that stresses the abstraction of most texts and the essential reality of social contexts. Texts function in this dichotomy as documents that reveal or reflect a coherent and relatively unified historical place, time, or culture, but the desire to read texts in this way reduces their complexity and also obscures the intricacy of the context itself. Most important, the text/context dichotomy radically deemphasizes the fact that the context does not simply exist as a prelinguistic reality that language faithfully describes. On the contrary, reality is "always already" situated in or shaped by textual processes that historians prefer not to examine. "The context itself is a text of sorts," writes LaCapra; "it calls not for stereotypical, ideological 'descriptions' but for interpretation and informed criticism."[32] The historian should

31. LaCapra, *Rethinking Intellectual History*, p. 313.
32. Ibid., pp. 95–96.

therefore read the context with sensitivity to the literary process of "intertextuality" rather than with the causal notion of reflection. Common beliefs about the opposition between texts and reality simply do not hold up, because "the past arrives in the form of texts and textualized remainders—memoirs, reports, published writings, archives, monuments, and so forth."[33] Yet this textual base of all knowledge about contexts is often "obscured or repressed" among historians who rush headlong toward the stable ground of reality.

The widespread tendency of historians to see the context as the essential and often unified causal force in history suggests to LaCapra the continuing influence of the Western metaphysical tradition in even the most secular and positivistic works of modern historiography. Historians want to describe a reality that exists beyond interpretation or outside texts in ways that recapitulate the ancient metaphysical desire for pure being, and their "contextualism" carries the "Platonism" of a tradition that rests on "an idealized notion of full, essential meaning."[34] To be sure, the prime mover of metaphysics or theology (the Idea or God) gives way to the Context, but the new prime mover works in the same way as the traditional metaphysic by transcending language and providing ultimate meaning. LaCapra therefore seeks to challenge the reigning (metaphysical) dichotomy and to stress the complex similarity between texts and contexts. The "'reading' and interpretation [of the context]," he argues, "pose problems as difficult as those posed by the most intricate written text." Greater appreciation for these problems on the part of historians would no doubt complicate their work, and yet it would transform the hierarchy that presently situates the context at the causal center of history.

A fruitful reversal of perspectives would propose the complex text itself as at times a better model for the reconstruction of the "larger context." The relationship between text and context would then become a question of "intertextual" reading, which cannot be addressed on the basis of reductionist oversimplifications that convert the context into a fully unified or dominant structure saturating the text with a certain meaning.[35]

33. LaCapra, *History and Criticism*, p. 128.
34. LaCapra, *Rethinking Intellectual History*, p. 115.
35. Ibid., p. 117.

Although LaCapra's dialogic model for historical writing by no means denies the existence of contexts outside of books, it clearly redefines those contexts with a linguistic emphasis that challenges any reduction of historical reality to its *essential* (i.e., pretextual) qualities. The belief in a pretextual historical field is nevertheless so pervasive that LaCapra finds it appearing even at times in the work of Hayden White.[36]

White's belief in a pretextual historical reality that is "out there" to be explained by the historian's tropes seems more apparent in his early work, where he explains, for example, that "the historian confronts the historical field in much the same way that the grammarian might confront a new language." Historians use language in this process to "characterize the field and its elements . . . and thus prepare them for . . . explanation and representation."[37] From LaCapra's perspective, this view of the "historical field" retains the dichotomy of texts and contexts, though it situates the essence of historical knowledge in the historian's text rather than in the context. Responding perhaps to this kind of criticism, White's more recent work shares LaCapra's emphasis on the textuality of the "historical field" itself and seeks also to move beyond the classic text/context dichotomy. "The text-context relationship, once an unexamined presupposition of historical investigation, has become a problem," White explains. "And yet this very undecidability of the question of where the text ends and the context begins and the nature of their relationship appears to be a cause for celebration [among intellectual historians]."[38] Many historians may not want to recognize the permanent overlap of those once-distinct textual and contextual categories, but White joins with LaCapra in stressing their complex interaction and in urging the value of literary critical readings of texts and contexts alike. "The historically real, the past real, is that to which I can be referred only by way of an artifact that is textual in nature."[39] There is, in short, no meaningful context without the language (i.e., text) that shapes and defines it.

36. Ibid., pp. 79–80.
37. White, *Metahistory*, p. 30.
38. White, *Content of the Form*, p. 186.
39. Ibid., p. 209.

The emphasis on language, textuality, narrative structures, overlapping categories, and dialogue that White and LaCapra draw from literary criticism serves important functions in helping historians to rethink the nature of both historiography and historical reality. This critical process nevertheless raises the practical question of how one might actually write history that encompasses the linguistic complexities that White and LaCapra describe. In other words, how can one challenge the distinctions or categories or realities of historical discourse and still be a historian? That question leads White and LaCapra from literary criticism to modern literature, which historians might now draw on as freely as they have drawn on science or social science. Literature suggests alternative ways of knowing and describing the world and uses language imaginatively to represent the ambiguous, overlapping categories of life, thought, words, and experience.

Novels and Poetry

One of the most significant tendencies in modern historiography, as White and LaCapra describe it, has been the growing separation between the narrative forms of creative literature and historical writing. Historians adopted a mode of representation in the nineteenth century that resembled contemporary developments in the novel and in science, but they chose not to alter that nineteenth-century mode as creative writers moved on to experiment with multiple-perspective narratives and as scientists began to ask new questions about the nature of science. By limiting its models of representation to the realistic novel and positivist science, history (according to White) "lost sight of its origins in the literary imagination."[40] This repression of origins enabled historians to restrict the range of their metaphors and to deemphasize the similarities between historiography and the imaginative activity of novelists or poets. The desire to separate history from literature can be found in almost all discussions of a "discipline" that has regularly sought to

---

40. White, *Tropics of Discourse*, p. 99; LaCapra discusses the separation of literary and historical narratives in *History and Criticism*, p. 122.

confine the imagination within certain kinds of evidence and certain forms of writing.[41] This disciplining process helped historians to stake out their scientific claims, and yet it gradually relegated history to the margins of a creative, critical intellectual culture that focused increasingly on a wide variety of newer linguistic, theoretical, and experimental issues. Both White and LaCapra suggest that historians might play a greater role in contemporary cultural debates if they opened the discipline to alternative narrative forms; more attention to what the novelists and poets have achieved over the last century would help to overcome what White calls the "contradiction in terms" that appears in most current references to the "historical imagination."[42]

The great value of modern literature for historians lies in its willingness to explore the movement of language and meaning in all aspects of social, political, and personal experience. Creative writers have gone far beyond "the older, stable conceptions of the world which required that they render a literal copy of a presumably static reality," and they realize that all descriptions of the world remain open to challenge.[43] Meanwhile, the historians continue to seek *the* account of the world as it actually existed rather than admit that their partial descriptions always exclude a great many other kinds of important information. The more appropriate starting point for historical narratives should be the recognition "that there is no such thing as a *single* correct view of any object under study but . . . *many* correct views, each requiring its own style of representation." This pluralistic conception offers a number of advantages, including a greater sensitivity to the inescapable perspectivism of historical research. "The historian operating under such a conception," White explains, "could thus be viewed as one who, like the modern artist and scientist, seeks to exploit a certain perspective on the world that does not pretend to exhaust description or analysis."[44]

White's new historian would focus on the mysteries of the past that defy the culture's categories of commonsense under-

41. White, *Content of the Form*, pp. 66–68.
42. White, *Tropics of Discourse*, p. 39.
43. Ibid., p. 50.   44. Ibid., pp. 46–47.

standing. The modern artist has already shown how exploration of the unfamiliar changes the way we understand the world, and in White's view there is no reason (except ideology or fear) for historians to avoid the same realms. "Such a conception of historiography is consistent with the aims of much of contemporary, or at least recent, poetry"—aims that stress the importance of perceiving the "strangeness of ordinary things."[45] True, this attention to the unfamiliar might alienate readers in ways that recall the disconcerting effects of modern art or literature, but White nevertheless urges historians to take this risk in order to break the one-dimensional tendencies of their work and to experiment with new forms of representation.

It would permit historians to conceive of the possibility of using impressionistic, expressionistic, surrealistic, and (perhaps) even actionist modes of representation for dramatizing the significance of data which they have uncovered but which, all too frequently, they are prohibited from seriously contemplating as evidence. If historians of our generation were willing to participate actively in the general intellectual and artistic life of our time, the worth of history would not have to be defended in the timid and ambivalent ways that are now used. The methodological ambiguity of history offers opportunities for creative comment on past and present that no other discipline enjoys.[46]

Greater variety in representation would not eliminate the need for historical evidence; White's poetic historian must, however, redefine the boundaries of evidence and the languages by which that evidence is described, so that history might transform rather than merely confirm our understanding of the world.

The innovations of modern literature also appeal to LaCapra because creative writers have experimented with practically every imaginable narrative form to portray the ambivalent interactions of opposing tendencies in life and thought. LaCapra concedes that "it may not be possible or even desirable" to have historians emulate all of the narrative strategies of the modern novel, but he clearly favors a more varied approach to such narrative conventions as the unified point of view, chronology, and the omniscient narrator.[47] Historians might learn to write

45. Ibid., p. 257.   46. Ibid., pp. 47–48.
47. LaCapra, *History and Criticism*, pp. 122–24.

in new ways if they would follow novelists into those areas of experience and language where critical voices challenge the dominant perspectives of past and present cultures. Although the historical search for fully coherent descriptions of social realities has often resulted in the "elimination or the homogenization of exceptional, contestatory, or even uncanny uses of language in history," LaCapra argues that a close reading of novels could show historians how language functions critically and playfully in the world.[48] Among the various historical uses of language, the most intriguing for LaCapra seems to be that form of imaginative wordplay that appears in carnivalesque social practices and in the carnivalesque style of many great novels.

LaCapra draws again on the work of Bakhtin to argue that premodern popular cultures often reversed the hierarchies of thought and society through comic, carnival farces that brought out the ambiguity of the categories by which official culture ruled the world. As LaCapra explains the phenomenon, however, these carnivalesque practices have been domesticated in the modern world into one-dimensional public or private rituals that lack the laughter and contestation of the popular carnival. The carnivalesque tradition therefore continues into our own society primarily through playful literary inversions of the hierarchies that dominate so much of the social or political world. "In muted but still potent ways," LaCapra explains, "older carnivalesque practices were taken up in (or translated into) high cultural artifacts and at times used to protest newer sociocultural developments."[49] The carnival thus employs farce, comedy, and jokes to portray and contest the world—and to maintain the dialogue that so frequently vanishes in both the social-political order and the historical works that describe it.

The carnivalesque perspective becomes in LaCapra's account a kind of utopian condition toward which society and historians alike might well aspire. "The carnival attitude generates an ambivalent interaction between all basic opposites in language and life," thereby transforming these opposites from "pure binarism" into a situation wherein they are "made to

48. Ibid., pp. 119, 132.
49. Ibid., pp. 76–77.

touch and know one another." Carnivalesque literature and social practice set language free, so that its "reversals effect, or should effect, a generalized displacement of ordinary assumptions."[50] This literary challenge to common social perspectives helps to explain the legal prosecution of certain innovative novels (*Madame Bovary* and *Ulysses*, for example), and it suggests also why LaCapra's dialogic historian might turn to the carnivalesque tradition as a model for linguistic forms that question the rigid dichotomies of Western culture. The carnival "tests and contests all aspects of society and culture through festive laughter: those that are questionable may be readied for change; those that are deemed legitimate may be reinforced."[51] Historians are probably at a disadvantage in depicting this carnivalesque process, because imaginative novelists can juxtapose or reverse categories without reference to what actually happened. Yet LaCapra believes that historians, too, can write about the world with carnivalesque strategies. One finds, for example, precisely this kind of parody and irony running throughout Marx's analytical history of French politics in *The Eighteenth Brumaire of Louis Napoleon*.[52] The narrative perspective of historical farce may not be appropriate for every historical problem, but LaCapra's new carnivalesque historian should at least be willing to attempt similar reversals of conceptual categories and to laugh at history as well as respect it.

The problem, then, might lie in the difficulty of thinking about the world like Rabelais or Cervantes or Heine and also writing about the world like a historian: the "carnivalesque historian" may be another contradiction in terms. But if ambiguous contestations and challenges to hierarchy form an integral part of what has always actually happened in human history, why not choose Rabelais over Ranke as a model for historical representation? Rabelaisian history challenges categories like a good joke, but it is not likely to be taken seriously because it raises so many questions about what historians do and why they do it. History departments will never advertise for "carnivalesque historians" with poetic "historical imaginations"

---

50. LaCapra, *Rethinking Intellectual History*, pp. 298–99.
51. Ibid., p. 306.   52. Ibid., p. 332.

unless they follow White and LaCapra toward (or even beyond) a radical, literary redefinition of both historical writing and historical reality. At the present time, however, most historians resist such redefinitions because they seem to lead straight into relativism and straight out of reality.

Relativism and Reality

The most common criticism of White and LaCapra by professional historians concerns these authors' alleged tendency toward historical relativism. By stressing the decisive role of language and literary codes in all accounts of the world, the literary-critical approach seems to transform historical understanding into a mere projection of researchers who naively take their own categories to be the thing-in-itself. White and LaCapra both deny, however, that they are simply latter-day relativists. White tends to attack the problem of relativism by emphasizing the shared codes of narrative conventions, which nobody can escape to create a completely unique or individual account of the world, whereas LaCapra refutes the accusation of relativism by criticizing the metaphysical assumption (the notion of full presence or pure being), which underlies relativism and links it to positivism.

White's preoccupation with the literary tropes that prefigure historical narratives probably takes him closer than LaCapra to the relativistic conception of the limits of historical knowledge. Insofar as all forms of history are limited by language, White explains, "they are *all equally relativistic,* [and] equally limited by the language chosen in which to delimit what it is possible to say about the subject under study."[53] This linguistic determinism, though, neither dissolves all belief in historical knowledge nor leaves the historian in a hopeless tangle of relativistic projections, because White assumes that we can know many things about the world within these limiting language systems. What we cannot know about the past is the kind of knowledge that appears in the physical sciences. White strongly disagrees with

53. White, *Tropics of Discourse*, p. 117.

those critics who would label him a radical skeptic based on the distinction he makes between scientific knowledge and historical knowledge, the latter coming closer to "the kind of knowledge which literature and art in general give us in recognizable examples." The mistake in White's conception of knowledge for the unreconstructed positivist derives from his assumption that literary and artistic knowledge are as valuable as scientific knowledge in comprehending the world, but White makes no concession to scientists on this point. "Only a willful, tyrannical intelligence," he argues, "could believe that the only kind of knowledge we can aspire to is that represented by the physical sciences."[54]

Linguistic knowledge, for example, may be compared to other forms of knowledge in that it is cumulative and can be translated from one historical era or person to another. In fact, White suggests that his linguistic approach might provide the best method for overcoming the relativistic dilemma that philosophers of history have described in detail.

Because it is a theory of *linguistic* determinism, we can envision a means of translating from one mode of discourse to another, in the same way that we translate from one language to another. This way of conceptualizing the problem of relativism is superior to that which grounds point of view in epoch, place or ideological allegiance, because we can imagine no way of translating between these, while we can imagine ways of translating between different language codes.[55]

White therefore counters the charge of relativism by arguing for a linguistic rather than scientistic conception of knowledge and then suggesting that the knowledge or translation of language codes enables us to go beyond those traditional notions of relativism that sentence historians to the prisonhouse of their own cultural moment.

LaCapra extends the critique of classic relativism somewhat further than White, because he wants to establish the fundamental similarity between positivistic and relativistic conceptions of historical knowledge. The positivism/relativism dichotomy holds up no better for LaCapra than other polar opposites

54. Ibid., p. 23.   55. Ibid., p. 117.

124   *Lloyd S. Kramer*

such as text and context, and he describes the *apparently* opposing views of positivists and relativists as a dispute over details
rather than basic assumptions.

> Extreme documentary objectivism and relativistic subjectivism do not
> constitute genuine alternatives. They are mutually supportive parts
> of the same larger complex. The objectivist historian places the past in
> the "logocentric" position of what Jacques Derrida calls the "tran-
> scendental signified." It is simply there in its sheer reality, and the
> task of the historian is to use sources as documents to reconstruct
> past reality as objectively as he or she can. . . . The relativist simply
> turns objectivist "logocentrism" upside down. The historian places
> himself or herself in the position of "transcendental signifier" that
> "produces" or "makes" the meanings of the past.

Both positivism and relativism therefore ignore the dialogic
conception of historical understanding, which recognizes that
the past (other) is "always already" in the historian and the historian (self) is "always already" inscribed in a linguistic or philosophical past. "Alterity, in other words, is not simply 'out there'
in the past but in 'us' as well," LaCapra explains, "and the comprehensive problem in inquiry is how to understand and to ne-
gotiate varying degrees of proximity and distance in the relation to the 'other' that is both outside and inside ourselves."[56]
LaCapra's dialogic historian thus works within linguistic, philosophical, and historical structures that somehow resemble those
of the past (the similarity that undermines relativism) but that
also change in ways that make even the most familiar historical
realities somehow alien and resistant to our categories (the
difference that undermines positivism). Historical dialogues
evolve constantly along the borders of similarity and difference, which never become as clear or distinct as positivism and
relativism imply.

The intricate connection between the form and the content of
knowledge, which White and LaCapra discuss constantly in
their epistemological arguments, suggests that it is impossible
to transform our methods of historical scholarship without also
transforming our definitions of historical reality. Literature and
literary theory help to expand the search for historical reality

56. LaCapra, *History and Criticism*, pp. 137–38, 140.

into sources and submerged forms of thought that often challenge the hierarchies, social relations, and intellectual categories that control modern societies and modern historiography. This search for lost voices means that White and LaCapra share with the new social history a strong desire to expose those deep structures, assumptions, interests, and relationships that pass unnoticed through the historiography of social elites, politics, and culture, though the emphasis of social historians differs significantly from many of the specific concerns in the literary approach. One might say that the theoretical model for critical social historians derives from Marx, while the theoretical model for a critical, literary method derives from Nietzsche. To be sure, both White and LaCapra give considerable attention to Marx, and they by no means exempt Nietzsche from critical analysis, but the Nietzschean challenge to the reigning assumptions of nineteenth-century historiography provides a forceful, dialogic precedent for the White-LaCapra challenge to twentieth-century historiography.

Although White criticizes Nietzsche more often than La-Capra does, his account of the Nietzschean project in *Metahistory* suggests some striking resemblances to White's own critical analysis of modern historiography. He stresses that Nietzsche attacked the belief "that the historical process has to be explained or emplotted in any particular way" and that he thereby called attention to the multiplicity of possible historical perspectives.[57] Historians were wrong, though, to see only the challenge and negation in Nietzsche's project because, as White explains it, the Nietzschean analysis carried affirmation as well as criticism:

Basically, therefore, Nietzsche divided the ways in which men looked at history into two kinds: a life-denying kind, which pretended to find the single eternally true, or "proper," way of regarding the past; and a life-affirming kind, which encouraged as many different visions of history as there were projects for winning a sense of self in individual human beings. The desire to believe that there was one, eternally true, or "proper," idea of history was, in Nietzsche's opinion, another vestige of the Christian need to believe in the one, true God—or of Chris-

57. White, *Metahistory*, p. 371.

tianity's secular counterpart, Positivist science, with its need to believe in a single, complete, and completely true body of natural laws.[58]

White's description of Nietzsche in this passage might apply
with almost equal relevance to himself or to LaCapra. Indeed,
one's ultimate acceptance or rejection of White and LaCapra is
likely to indicate also one's attitude toward Nietzsche—or toward the value of literary truths. Most historians today would
probably agree that there can be "many different visions of history," and yet they would prefer to exclude the Nietzschean vision or literary vision from real history. This resistance may
stem from a fear that the use of literary perspectives will increasingly separate history from science, but White dismisses
such anxieties by steadfastly reaffirming the legitimacy of non-
scientific forms of knowledge. "The affiliation of narrative historiography with literature and myth should provide no reason for embarrassment," he explains, "because the systems of
meaning-production shared by all three are distillates of the
historical experience of a people, a group, a culture."[59]

LaCapra also wants to connect the historiographical conception of reality with those areas of meaning that literature explores in its greatest works. He, too, looks to Nietzsche and
stresses the influential role of symbolic meaning in all aspects
of the historical process. This emphasis on symbols leads some
critics to charge that LaCapra has taken reality out of history,
though his own view of the problem suggests that he has instead taken history into wider areas of reality. "The objectiv-
ist," LaCapra complains, "falsely sees the attempt to question
precritical and unreflective certainty about the nature of history
as tantamount to denying that people really bleed when they
are cut."[60] LaCapra never denies that people bleed when they
are cut, but he would also stress that every material phenomenon, including blood, war, sex, and dollar bills, carries complex
symbolic meanings that are inextricably bound up with all that
we call reality. "This is the fascinating and the disconcerting
ambivalence of symbols—the fact that nothing entirely escapes

58. Ibid., p. 332.
59. White, *Content of the Form*, pp. 44–45.
60. LaCapra, *History and Criticism*, p. 137.

their signifying power or is simply presented, grasped, or given by them." All attempts to situate reality "out there," beyond interpretation, necessarily depend on symbols for their meaning and significance. "Even the purely transcendental signified [e.g., God] that one tries to protect from the 'contamination' of signification or nomination requires taboos which may be transgressed."[61]

The status of reality therefore becomes for LaCapra so implicated in symbolic ambivalence that most historians may think it disappears in any sense that they can use for research or for narrative accounts. In practical terms, historians must inevitably reduce the play of symbols to some more or less fixed statements about historical realities, though from LaCapra's perspective these statements will almost always be somehow reductive or metaphysical. But the constant movement of symbolic meanings (which can never be finally or fully grasped) does not leave LaCapra's historian without reality; on the contrary, it expands the levels of reality beyond all of our commonsense attempts to describe it in one-dimensional or essentialist language. Reality becomes a bigger problem than we ever imagined.

It is this expanding conception of historical reality and meaning that ultimately makes the literary approach such a potentially rich method for historical research. Although the move from literary theory to practical application can lead to bad history (or difficult, unfamiliar prose) as well as to exhilarating flights of historical imagination, the linguistic emphasis in historiography clearly offers important new strategies for bringing history closer to innovative developments in other areas of modern thought. History cannot and should not become simply another kind of creative literature, in part because historians must continue to develop their own vision and perspectives on reality. Yet there seems to be no reason other than traditional disciplinary considerations to ban the new literary criticism from our efforts to comprehend the nature of historical experience and texts. One finds here another important angle of vision for interpreting the past, though none of its advocates (including

61. LaCapra, *Rethinking Intellectual History*, p. 255.

White and LaCapra) would say that it should be the only approach to history.

Apart from its relevance for the study of historiography, the
literary perspective might help to reanimate critical discussion
among historians and to open those boundaries that tend to
separate historians from the culture of our own time. "One
thing an institution should be," argues LaCapra, "is a setting
for a dialogic encounter in which limiting norms necessary for
life in common are put to tests that may strengthen or transform them. Indeed a humanistic discipline remains vital to the
extent it is possible within it to engage points of view that pose
fundamental questions to one's own."[62] This ideal dialogue
may take us back toward the carnival or it may lead us far outside the circled disciplinary wagons that serve to defend the
territory of real history from the assaults of literature. In any
event, the study of history can surely survive, even flourish,
with more criticism, more imagination, and a lot more laughter.

62. LaCapra, *History and Criticism*, p. 142.

Part Two

New Approaches

Five

The American Parade:
Representations of the
Nineteenth-Century Social Order

MARY RYAN

The *San Francisco Morning Call* began its report on the July Fourth celebration of 1864 with this perfunctory comment: "The chief feature of the day was the great Procession of course." By mid morning, the editor went on, "the streets began to be thronged with platoons, companies and regiments of soldiers, benevolent associations etc., swarming from every point of the compass and marching with music and banners toward the general rendezvous like the gathering hosts of a mighty army." An hour later these contingents of citizens had formed into a linear sequence and proceeded to file through the principal streets of the city "rank after rank, column after column, in seemingly countless numbers."[1] Having traversed much of the city, the marchers quietly disbanded. Not even the editor stayed on to observe the songs and orations that concluded the public commemoration of the nation's birthday.

Accounts like this were commonplace between 1825 and 1880 in the press of the three cities I have investigated: San Francisco, New York, and New Orleans. They indicate that Americans had devised a distinctive and curious mode of public cele-

1. *San Francisco Morning Call*, 6 July 1864.

bration, in which a sizable portion of the urban population organized into "platoons," "companies," "regiments," "ranks and columns," and paraded through the public thoroughfares. This particular type of celebratory performance seems to have been an American invention. In the *Oxford English Dictionary*, the first listing for the modern meaning of the word *parade*, an adaptation of the term for military muster to encompass civic and ceremonial purposes, includes the phrase "especially in the United States."

The parade stands out in the chronicles of American public life as the characteristic genre of nineteenth-century civic ceremony. A grand procession of citizens was "of course" the central event in the cyclical patriotic rite, the Fourth of July celebration, and to a lesser extent of Washington's Birthday. It was also the focal point of local holidays: Evacuation Day in New York, Admission Day in San Francisco, and the anniversary of the Battle of New Orleans. When it came time to celebrate civic improvements—the Erie Canal, the Atlantic cable, the transcontinental railroad—or the erection of any number of new monuments in public squares, a parade was again in order. The parade was called into ceremonial service on somber occasions as well. The procession that accompanied Lincoln's casket through the streets of New York was, in structure and organization if not in mood, like a classic American parade.

The parade presents historians with a kind of cultural performance from which anthropologists have extracted rich meaning. Milton Sanger tells us that these ceremonies "encapsulate a culture." Clifford Geertz finds a more intimate revelation in such public events: they are the "stories a people tell about themselves." And according to John Skorupski, "Ceremony says, 'look this is how things should be, this is the proper, ideal pattern of social life.'"[2]

Translated into the more modest language of historians, the

2. John J. MacAloon, ed., *Rite, Drama, Festival, Spectacle: Rehearsals Toward a Theory of Cultural Performance* (Philadelphia, 1984); and John Skorupski, *Symbol and Theory: A Philosophical Study of Theories of Religion in Social Anthropology* (Cambridge, 1976), p. 84. See Susan G. Davis, *Parades and Power: Street Theatre in Nineteenth-Century Philadelphia* (Philadelphia, 1986), for an excellent account of a variety of processional forms in one city, and an interpretation that differs from my own.

reports of parades are simply very resonant documents. First, the parade offers a well-rounded documentation of past culture; it conjured up an emotional power and aesthetic expressiveness that the simple literary formulation of ideas or values lacked. Second, accounts of parades record the actions as well as the words of the past. In a parade, an organized body, usually of men, marched into the public streets to spell out a common social identity. Third, whatever insights can be drawn from parades offer a very high level of generality. This public performance occurred before a massive audience and engaged a large number of participants—in the extreme case a single parade would find fifty thousand on the line of march and three-quarters of a million more observing on the sidelines. Finally, many parades, including those spotlighted in this analysis, were predicated on some level of public consensus: they were funded and arranged by democratically elected public officials, who designed these pageants to attract and satisfy the city as a whole. By focusing on this variety of celebration, rather than on the holiday festivities that engaged only select groups in the population or processions of a more militant sort, I hope to reconstruct the most general and broadly public picture that American cities presented of themselves.

The appropriate procedures for analyzing such documents might seem comparable to those of literary analysis, for the parade is like a text in its susceptibility to multiple interpretations. But the parade is a peculiar text, intricately entangled with its social and historical context. It has multiple authors: the thousands of marchers who carried their own chosen symbols into one composite ceremony. If there is any overarching meaning, any capsule summary of a culture embedded in this text, it was not the design of an *auteur* but the creation of specific individuals and distinct groups who operated within the social constraints and political possibilities of their time. The parade, then, can tell us something of the historical process whereby cultural meaning is created. The multiple architects of such cultural creations, furthermore, did not simply inscribe meaning onto some preordained literary genre; rather, they devised ceremonial forms specific to their own times, needs, and possibilities.

Thus, before extracting substantive meaning from these doc-

uments, it is necessary to specify some of the characteristics of
the parade as a form of cultural performance. The term *parade*
refers to that ritualized, collective movement through the streets
that took a distinctive form in nineteenth-century American
cities. It had several essential features. First, the parade was
clearly organized into separate marching units, each representing a preestablished social identity. The filing by of these constituent parts of the society, sometimes termed a *desfile*, was the
basic action and structure of the American parade.[3] Second, an
American parade—unlike, for example, an eighteenth-century
French procession, which, according to Robert Darnton, "ended
at a relatively elevated point in the hierarchy of local officials"—
enrolled a large portion of the local population.[4] A New Orleans newspaper editor said of the line of march in 1849, "All
will find a place who wish to join the celebration."[5] Of course,
some exclusionary clauses restricted the invitation to parade,
based chiefly on race and gender. Still, the line of march was
quite open, and rarely was any group who bothered to apply to
the committee of arrangements denied admission. The third
identifying characteristic of the American parade was its seeming aimlessness, or lack of plot, so to speak. The marchers did
not set off single-mindedly for an established civic center, there
to place an offering to a patron saint, profess fealty to a leader,
or enact a civic pageant. This was not a march of governors or
priests who conferred some legitimizing or sanctifying power
on the places they passed. The typical parade simply wove its
serpentine way through all the principal streets of the city,
allowing the participants to present themselves to throngs of
citizens gathered all along the way. Marching units therefore
invested great effort and money adorning their persons with
ribbons, sashes, and bright uniforms. In sum, then, the American parade seemed to be a march for the sake of marching, as
well as for the display of the ordinary citizens who marched.

The parade is, of course, a species of procession, with an-

3. Robert Da Matta, "Carnival in Multiple Planes," in *Rite, Drama, Festival,
Spectacle,* ed. MacAloon, pp. 208–40.
4. Robert Darnton, *The Great Cat Massacre and Other Episodes in French Cultural History* (New York, 1984), pp. 116–24.
5. *New Orleans Picayune,* 4 July 1849.

cient and geographically widespread antecedents. The first notable procession mounted in the United States harked back at least to the Renaissance in its form and imagery. This mobile pageant was conducted in Philadelphia in 1788, to celebrate the ratification of the Constitution. It was draped in classic symbolism and surrounded by public drama and communal festivity. Tradesmen plied their crafts along the route; other marchers impersonated archetypal figures like Christopher Columbus; still others carried sacred icons such as mementos of George Washington; and all proceeded to a definite destination where the participants celebrated their communal bonds by feasting, thousands strong, from a common public larder.[6] In the early Republic, then, the procession had not yet acquired the streamlined characteristics of the parade, nor did it occupy the center of ceremonial time and space. It was not yet a parade.

The civic ceremony that begins my analysis, organized in New York in 1825 to pay proud homage to the completion of the Erie Canal, gave greater definition to the genre of parading. There were many festivities on that day, including a public dinner for three thousand citizens and the ritualized mingling of the waters of Lake Erie and the Atlantic, but the center of public attention and the focal point of civic participation was a procession on land. This long march, a mobile display of a wide spectrum of the corporate groups of the city, supplied the basic form of parading for many years to follow. After 1825, and at an accelerated pace during the 1840s and 1850s, public processions became increasingly commonplace on city streets, and they occupied center stage on such holidays as the Fourth of July, Washington's Birthday, and local anniversaries. Through most of the antebellum period these full-scale, publicly constituted processions shared the streets and the calendar with a panoply of more specialized and spontaneous processions—walks to serenade a nominee for political office, journeys to Sunday school picnics, torchlight drills of the local militia, and public displays of new fire engines.

In the 1850s and through the Civil War, use of the streets grew more restricted as ceremonial energies came to be focused

6. William L. Stone, *History of New York City from Discovery to the Present Day* (New York, 1872), pp. 280–90.

on a few tightly organized parades and circumscribed by elaborate police arrangements. In these decades, the ceremonial form of the parade expanded to incorporate more and more marching units, organized into an ever increasing number and variety of divisions. After mid century, even as the parade form seemed most solid and elaborate, its claim to dominance of public ceremonial life was placed in jeopardy as civic processions began to ravel along cleavages in the urban community. Yet even as late as 1876, a full, hearty, and classic American parade was assembled in all three of my study cities, that is, in the North, South, and West of the United States, to celebrate the centennial of the Declaration of Independence.

The invention of the classic American parade and its installation at the center of public ceremony were, in sum, the product of a distinct, if imprecise, historical period that lasted roughly from 1825 to 1850. Several features of urban history set the context for this cultural creation. First, this was a period of extraordinary demographic growth in each city: New York's population grew sevenfold between 1825 and 1880, when the city harbored 1.2 million residents; the population of New Orleans tripled during the same period; and the wilderness by San Francisco Bay was transformed as an instant city of fifty thousand arose after the Gold Rush and mushroomed to a population of a quarter-million by the closing date of this study. The population of each city diversified as it grew, taking in the foreign-born by the thousands and grudgingly accommodating racial minorities. Each local economy took the critical steps toward industrialization during this same period, as merchants, capitalists, shopkeepers, artisans, industrial workers, and day laborers pursued their conflicting interests in a mixed urban economy. These groups took their clashing interests into the political arena, where fierce contests of popular political parties supplanted the stewardship of older elites. Concurrently, each city was the site of major riots, with scores in New York alone, as well as total breakdowns of political legitimacy—vigilantism in San Francisco, and the military occupation of New Orleans during Reconstruction. A simple cultural functionalism would suggest that the necessity of fostering order in such diverse, turbulent, and contentious populations might lead to the invention of some unifying public rituals.

Yet the antebellum city placed certain constraints on such ceremonial practices, especially physical ones. The dense built environment provided few open spaces large enough for the entire population to enact their communal dramas. A swift march through the public arteries would seem to be the ceremonial path of least resistance, for social as well as spatial reasons. The genius of the parade was that it allowed the many contending constituencies of the city to line up and move through the streets without ever encountering one another face to face, much less stopping to play specified roles in one coordinated pageant. The parade was much like the social world in which it germinated—mobile, voluntaristic, laissez-faire, and open. Like a civic omnibus, the parade offered admission to almost any group with sufficient energy, determination, organizational ability, and internal coherence to board it.

The parade was something more, however, than an automatic, reflexive expression of American pluralism. It was also a positive assertion of democracy. The parade evolved as a civic ceremony at a time when many groups resorted to processions in order to assert their civic rights. Neophyte political parties took to parading when such popular democratic action was still suspect. Tradesmen "turned out" in procession to protest against their bosses. Groups of immigrants, especially the Catholic Irish, marched through the streets to demand the full rights of citizenship in defiance of rampant nativism. These processions—what we might today call demonstrations—were quite properly seen in the 1830s, 1840s and 1850s as insurgent public actions. The multiple architects of the antebellum parade incorporated these gestures of a militant democracy into public ceremony.

The parade can also be seen as a kind of cultural equivalent of what Hanna Pitkin calls "descriptive representation."[7] In the classic parades of the mid nineteenth century, constituent groups in the polity actually presented themselves, rather than abstract symbols, for public view. The parade re-presented the urban population, forming a detailed, descriptive portrait of urban social structure. The thousands who made the effort to

7. Hanna Fenichel Pitkin, *The Concept of Representation* (Berkeley and Los Angeles, 1967).

march in these antebellum parades acted out an implicit political theory, asserting their prerogative to participate actively and in their own right in the creation of urban culture.

Finally, the emergence of the parade was predicated on an open, public political process in which popular forces acted in tandem with constituted authorities. Most civic ceremonies were funded by the city government and organized by a committee of arrangements appointed by elected officials. Private citizens often initiated the original proposal for a celebration, and sometimes called a public meeting to promote it. While the appointed committee arranged certain portions of the day's program—the firing of arms at daybreak, the fireworks in the evening—the organization of the parade was an exercise in popular sovereignty. The first act of the committee of arrangements was to publish an open invitation to a public meeting where any group could apply for a place along the line of march. Despite evidence of contention at some of these meetings and repeated incidents of conflict along the line of the march, antebellum political institutions both tolerated and actively promoted this democratic procedure for creating public culture.[8]

In an ad hoc, experimental way, these institutions gave shape to the parade as the characteristic genre of American celebration. That genre was something like a street railway on which a panoply of different social groups mounted and occupied a string of cars, with each car embodying cultural and historical meaning and giving ceremonial definition to some component of the urban social structure. Filing neatly by in a parade, the parade participants presented a compact documentation of how "society takes cognizance of itself, its major classifications and categories."[9] Because this ceremony permitted countless Americans to write their identities on the streets in full public view, the parade can posit answers to basic questions of concern to social and cultural historians. It reveals, in a particularly powerful, publicly sanctioned way, how contemporaries construed, displayed, and saw the urban social order.

8. *New York Tribune*, 18 March 1850.
9. Barbara Babcock, "Clay Voices: Invoking, Mocking, Celebrating," in *Celebration: Studies in Festivity and Ritual*, ed. Victor Turner (Washington, D.C., 1982), p. 24.

To historians then, the parade constitutes the public, cere-monial language whereby nineteenth-century Americans made order out of an urban universe that teemed with diversity and change. By choosing to join the march in specific contin-gents, paraders acted out a social vocabulary, impressing their group identities on the minds of countless bystanders. Their words were also strung into sentences—the order of the line of march—that adumbrated social ranks and relationships among the contingents. In the composition and order of the parade, historians can read both the vocabulary and the syntax by which social and cultural order was created out of urban multiplicity.

Although the basic cultural performance—the public display of especially salient constituent groups of the community—remained the same between 1825 and 1880, its composition changed in significant ways as the most prevalent contingents were replaced, replenished, and rearranged over time. The fol-lowing account of this metamorphosis highlights three differ-ent principles of parade formation and social classification, based respectively on class, ethnicity, and gender. This pro-gression is roughly chronological as well as topical, reflecting changes in the principles according to which urban culture or-ganized itself on ceremonial occasions.

In the formative years of parading, the ceremonial structure was filled by groups that loosely resembled classes. The march-ing units based their common identity in their occupations and prominently displayed their contributions to the local econ-omy. The Erie Canal procession on 5 November 1825 set the pattern: nearly every marching unit grouped men together according to their occupations, from journeymen tailors to members of the Medical Society. The symbols that these groups carried into the parade identified position within the urban economy as the primary principle of group formation. This was especially true of the artisans, who played such a prominent role in the Erie Canal parade. Some, like the hatters, carried banners honoring the patron of their trade, St. Clement; oth-ers, like the butchers, enacted their workaday role, towing along the parade route animals ready for the slaughter.[10] Although

10. Martha Lamb, *History of the City of New York: Its Origin, Rise, and Prog-ress* (New York, 1880), pp. 696–730; *New York Evening Post*, 3, 5 November 1825.

the artisans were best represented and most ebullient in New York processions, occupation was the basic principle of the line of march in the merchant economy of New Orleans as well. Bodies representing an array of occupations participated in the New Orleans Fourth of July procession of 1837, from the Chamber of Commerce to the Mechanics Society.[11] In New Orleans, be it July Fourth, January Eighth, or Washington's Birthday, the rank order of occupations proceeded from the civic officials and elite occupations on through the tradesmen who took up the rear of the procession. Whereas in New York tradesmen led the procession, some semblance of occupational hierarchy was maintained there as well. The more elite, nonmanual workers—doctors, lawyers, clergymen, and the faculty and students of Columbia University—were all clustered together at the end of the line of march, with the city officials and most honored guests, the Canal commissioners.

In New Orleans this form of parade, which reconstructed society as an inclusive and hierarchical arrangement of corporate groups based primarily on occupation, endured with only minor additions and changes right up to the Civil War. Parades in New York, in contrast, as well as in the stripling town of San Francisco, expressed class in new and more varied ways. First the higher ranks of the social structure dropped out of the line of march. The *New York Herald* noted this striking absence in its description of the parade celebrating the opening of the Croton Aqueduct in 1842. In the division where the bar, the judges, the Chamber of Commerce, and the students and faculty of Columbia were to appear, "none of them were to be seen." Only at a moment of extraordinary national unity, in the funeral procession of President Lincoln, would these more prestigious members of the community parade again. (Even the New York Historical Society marched that year.)[12]

The aristocrats of labor—skilled craftsmen—soon followed the professionals and merchants in withdrawing from the line of march. Although these groups still made a prominent appearance in 1842 in New York, and although a few butchers still carried symbols of their skills in parades of San Francisco even

11. *New Orleans Picayune*, 4 July 1837.
12. *New York Herald*, 15 October 1842; 25 April 1865.

in the 1860s, they never were represented as fully as in the parade of 1825. As artisans exited the parade, however, their positions were taken up by workers of lesser skill. The common laborers of New York, San Francisco, and New Orleans—longshoremen, quarrymen, cartmen, draymen—became regulars in the line of march after mid century. These workers sometimes organized on a new basis, calling themselves either benevolent associations or outright unions. During Lincoln's funeral procession, for example, the largest single contingent was the Workingmen's Union, assembled in twenty-six branches. In San Francisco, trade unions were powerful enough to attempt a wholesale usurpation of public ceremonies. In 1869, much to the chagrin of the local press, the Fourth of July procession was dominated by some twenty-four unions organized into the eight-hour movement.[13] Yet at other times industrial workers put another kind of consciousness on public display. In both New York and San Francisco some workers paraded docilely behind their bosses, carrying the name of an industrial firm rather than an example of their craft into the line of march.

Thus, although signs of economic status had not disappeared from the line of march at mid century, they had certainly become more various and difficult to read. Alongside old craft values and corporate occupational groupings could be found class-conscious industrial workers, compliant employees, and the invisible factor of the more prestigious occupations who disappeared from the line of march entirely. There were even a few attempts, in both New York and San Francisco, to replace the old symbols of production with emblems of a consumer economy. Occasionally after mid century, wagons draped with the manufacturers' names of such commodities as beer, pianos, and sewing machines made brief but colorful appearances in parades. Yet this innovation, a blatant form of advertising, never acquired full legitimacy, and after a brief experiment in San Francisco, advertising cars were barred from the parade.[14] Despite this amorphous conceptualization of class, Americans were not yet ready to place an ethic of consumption in the proud place where craftsmen once carried the icons of skilled production.

13. *San Francisco Chronicle,* 4 July 1869.
14. *Daily Alta California,* 4 July 1868; *New York Tribune,* 31 May 1877.

However defined, emblems suggestive of class lost their privileged ceremonial position around 1850. For the next few decades the line of march was swollen with new contingents whose variety and heterogeneity defied categorization. Throughout this robust yet transitional and anomalous period groups of workers were far outnumbered by contingents composed of the members of voluntary societies. When San Francisco began officially to sponsor Fourth of July processions in the 1850s, it adhered to the new principles of parade composition that had become typical in New York and New Orleans as well. Scattered in the line of march were a few occupational groups: the clergy, the Chamber of Commerce, printers, and stevedores. These contingents were outnumbered, however, by voluntary organizations of four sorts: fraternal orders, militia companies, temperance associations, and ethnic benefit societies.[15] By mid century in each city, the press had devised a shorthand for describing the line of march, dividing these myriad groups into two categories: the military and the civic societies. Such a simple schema could not hide a radical resorting of the cells of the ceremonial community—public group identity was now a matter of voluntary choice between such alternatives as national origins, fraternal associations, and even allegiances to a particular personal code such as temperance. The military contingents were not drafted into service, but made their public appearance as members of volunteer militia companies. Notoriously ill trained in the martial arts, these ubiquitous antebellum associations were devoted above all else to the sport of parading.

To confuse things further, most members of these marching units, whatever the banners they carried into the parade, actually had multiple identities in common. Whatever allegiances they displayed most prominently—martial skills, temperance reform, or fraternal conviviality—most units were bound by ethnic and class ties as well. The military units were generally homogeneous in both class and ethnicity. In New York, for example, the Seventh Regiment was composed of gentlemen, as was the Continental Guard in New Orleans and the Washington Guard in San Francisco. Given the expense involved in out-

15. *Daily Alta California*, 6 July 1853.

fitting oneself for a parade, few militia companies enrolled anyone below the middling economic ranks. The ethnic makeup of
the militia companies was common knowledge—New York's
Seventh Regiment was composed of the native-born; the Sixty-
ninth was Irish; and behind the banner of the Empire Hussars
marched a band of young Jewish men. The story was much the
same in the other cities. In New Orleans, the elite Washington
Artillery acknowledged its ethnicity by officially changing its
name to the Native Americans.[16] Ethnicity and temperance were
also closely, if not predictably, allied. During Lincoln's funeral
procession, for example, the fifth division was identified as a
contingent of temperance societies in one column of the *New
York Herald*, and a collection of Irish societies in another. In fact
the two were probably the same, for Irishmen often marched
behind the banners of temperance. For example, eighteen Roman Catholic Total Abstinence Societies, each associated with a
different parish, marched in New York's centennial parade.[17] In
sum, the individual units that came to dominate parades after
1850 often had dual or even quadruple identities, based in this
instance in temperate habits, ethnic roots, religious practice,
and neighborhood proximity.

The committee of arrangements was hard pressed to create a
logical linear arrangement of all these multifarious marching
units. Aside from the convention of leading off with a contingent of the military, the arrangement of marchers into divisions seemed somewhat arbitrary. The program for Lincoln's
funeral procession was particularly anomalous, reflecting no
doubt the difficulty of the task faced by the committee of arrangements, which had hastily to assemble an unprecedented
number of marching units into a rational order. In this moment
of national sorrow, the organizers of the parade fell back on old
principles of social hierarchy—at least in the front ranks of the
procession, where the elite assembled in groups such as the
Chamber of Commerce and the Union Club, followed immediately by state and local officials. The remainder and bulk of the
procession, however, was grouped into divisions that defied

16. Marcus Cunliffe, *Soldiers and Civilians: The Martial Spirit in America,
1775–1865* (Boston, 1968), pp. 223–30.

17. *New York Herald*, 25 April 1865; 2 July 1876.

comparison and rank ordering: "Fourth: Masonic and Other Orders"; "Fifth: Various Temperance Organizations"; "Sixth: Trades, Societies, Clubs and Associations." Although these categories seemed to encode ethnic differences (with the third and fourth largely native-born, the fifth Irish, and the seventh heavily German), this logic was neither perfect nor explicitly stated.[18] The mid nineteenth century had introduced a whole new ceremonial vocabulary—denoting new voluntary units of the community—but had not devised a new syntax to connect these terms in any logical whole.

When New York City celebrated 4 July 1876, much of this confusion was still visible. Take the seventh division of the centennial parade, for example, which contained old craft workers, including blacksmiths and bricklayers, along with the William Cullen Bryant Club and a contingent of the Cadets of Temperance. Young teetotalers would seem unlikely, and not particularly flattering, companions to the old aristocrats of labor. Within this heterogeneous ceremonial mixture, however, the dominance of one principle of social organization had become more obvious, and that was ethnicity. In New York, two divisions were purely Irish, two were purely German, and another, while primarily Italian, contained explicit subdivisions for Cubans and Swedes. A colored division marched behind the Grand Army of the Republic. Because elite occupations did not join the line of march at all in 1876, and since the first division was given over to a full ethnically mixed assemblage of the military, no stigma of rank applied to any position within the line of march. The parades that celebrated the centennial in both San Francisco and New York were a mosaic of the two cities' ethnic makeup. Of the sixteen divisions in the San Francisco parade, for instance, six were ethnically homogeneous bands: one Scotch, one German, one Italian, and three Irish; Austrians, Scandinavians and Swiss and Portuguese shared two other divisions; and the native sons took up a position near the end of the procession along with the children of the public schools. By this date in New Orleans elite occupations had

18. *New York Herald*, 25 April 1865.

withdrawn, allowing ethnic societies, French and Portuguese as well as Irish and German, to assume dominance.[19]

By 1876, then, the American parade had apparently become an ethnic festival. The *New York Tribune* fumbled for words to characterize the multiethnic pageant that celebrated the centennial, choosing the adjectives "incongruous" and "cosmopolitan" to describe how "German singing bands followed the American militia; German Schutzen corps and Irish temperance societies were in adjacent divisions; trade unions, civic associations and secret societies moved in one body; the Ancient Order of Hibernians and the post of the Army of the Republic were a close company; while Spanish, Swiss, French and Italian associations were combined in the same division."[20] If the *Tribune* were speaking of San Francisco, or to a lesser extent New Orleans, this idyllic picture of ethnic harmony might accurately reflect the ceremonial life of the city as a whole. The actual relationship between ethnicity and public ceremony, however, especially in New York City, is far more complicated and bears further scrutiny.

Well before 1876, ethnicity had begun to erode the public and inclusive character of parading. As the editor of the *Tribune* knew full well, New York parades had fractured along ethnic lines long before and now were reassembled only on special occasions, such as that of 4 July 1876. In 1870 the *Herald* had reported that the closest approximation to an old-fashioned parade was a procession of forty thousand Irish on March 17, a separate holiday that was not accorded official sponsorship.[21] By contrast, the annual Fourth of July parade in New York had degenerated into a short military procession. The festive Irish parade every St. Patrick's Day did not win the approval of the city press, or of their middle-class readers; on the contrary, it brought annual complaints about disruption of business. In 1871, moreover, the Irish proclivity for marching precipitated one of the bloodiest police confrontations in the city's history

19. *New York Herald*, 2 July 1875; *San Francisco Chronicle*, 4 July 1876; *New Orleans Picayune*, 4 July 1876.
20. *New York Tribune*, 4 July 1876.
21. *New York Herald*, 18 March 1869; 18 March 1870.

when the Orange Irish paraded to celebrate the anniversary of the Battle of the Boyne.[22] On St. Patrick's Day two years later, the *New York Times* expressed equal disdain for the Irish and the ritual of the parade. Commenting on the procession of some twenty-five thousand marchers, it opined: "It is difficult in the extreme for the American Mind to understand."[23] Parading, if we are to believe the *Times,* had become an ethnic rather than a civic ritual, and the peculiar avocation of the Irish.

The withdrawal from parades of the ethnic groups that the *Times* called "American" had taken some time to accomplish. Before 1850, parades, whether flush with artisans, freemasons, or temperance reformers, were composed principally of native-born Anglo-Saxons. The native born did not immediately cede this public ceremonial territory to the new arrivals from famine-torn Ireland. On 4 July 1850, the press congratulated the city on the polite reception it gave militia companies representing many different nationalities.[24] At the funeral procession for Zachary Taylor just a few weeks later, however, the *Herald* quietly noted that contingents of Catholic Irish scuffled briefly with a division of the nativist organization, the United Americans.[25] For the next decade the Irish marched defiantly through the most virulent seasons of nativism, and by the late 1850s they seemed to have won out over all ethnic opposition. In 1858 the *New York Herald* commented that parading had become almost synonymous with the ethnic label Irish-American.

On September 1 of that year, however, native-born Protestants took the offensive by converting the celebration of the completion of the Atlantic cable into an undisguised assertion of Anglo-Saxon culture. A bevy of Protestant associations—the St. Nicholas, St. George, St. Andrew, St. David, and Scotch societies—paraded through the streets decorated with anti-Irish taunts. Indeed, the Irish immigrant and virulent opponent of all things English might well take exception to such slogans as "There is no such word as fail for Saxon Blood" or "Severed

22. See extensive accounts of the Orangemen riots in the *Herald, Times,* and *Tribune* for 13 July 1870, and 13 July 1871.
23. *New York Times,* 18 March 1873.
24. *New York Tribune,* 4, 5 July 1850; *New York Herald,* 6 July 1850.
25. *New York Herald,* 23 July 1850.

July 4, 1776, united August 12, 1858."[26] As it turned out, this would be the last time that Anglo-Saxons would play such a prominent role in parades. Furthermore, middle-class associations—the medical society, the bar, mechanics' associations, literary societies—retired from public display at the same time, preferring to spend civic holidays quietly at home or journeying up the Hudson to rural retreats. Class and ethnicity were simultaneously converging and unraveling at this critical juncture in the history of the parade.

The retreat of the native born is an early sign of the decline of parading as a fully public rite, capable of enrolling a wide spectrum of social groups. Ethnicity seemed, furthermore, to provide the umbrella under which the middle and upper classes, including the artisans who flocked into nativist associations, departed from the parade. This process whereby the American parade began to unravel cannot be understood without considering a third social category. The category is gender, and it operated largely to define parading as a male prerogative, offering women only a shadowy position in the line of march.

The parades of the nineteenth century were almost exclusively male affairs. The exceptions to this rule, however, are revealing. Although the evidence is too scanty to sustain a full argument, interesting speculations may be proffered. For example, a few women appeared in the Erie Canal celebration—not in the prosaic parade, but in a procession of boats that sailed to Long Island Sound to ceremonially mingle the waters of the Atlantic and Lake Erie. These choice women were wives of the city elite who traveled in barges with names like the "Lady Clinton" and the "Lady Van Rensselaer." After disembarking, the ladies walked in a body from the Battery to Bowling Green, thus enacting a brief and rare women's parade. This ritual gesture seemed a throwback to a bygone era, best exemplified perhaps by the processions of Renaissance Italy, and still appropriate to aristocratic circles of the early American Republic, in which marital and family alliances were so critical to social standing that female ties were publicly honored.

26. *New York Tribune*, 1 September 1858; *New York Herald*, 1 September 1858.

The common man who marched through the streets in the age of Jackson was unencumbered by such bonds. The classic American parade celebrated Republican manhood, an individual identity exercised through voting, breadwinning, and marching. Nearly every contingent of the parade reflected a male social role, that of the citizen, the public official, the worker, the college student, or the soldier. All participants assumed the masculine posture, stepping high, chest expanded, as they marched into the public ceremony. There were, however, a few references to female contingents in antebellum parades. Two of the many temperance units that marched in New York during the 1840s had suggestive titles: "Happy Wife" and "Lady Franklin." Although these contingents in the parade were probably composed entirely of men, the temperance societies gave at least nominal recognition to the second sex, whom they routinely included in their private, indoor ceremonies. From San Francisco comes another, more definite, notice of women, eight of whom marched as auxiliaries of the Masons. In both these instances, and in other cities as well, those rare women who appeared in marching units were in the company of native-born Protestant males, the contingents most likely to withdraw from parades before the Civil War.[27]

Before they surrendered this public ceremonial space to the foreign born of lowlier economic status, however, these same groups introduced women into their parades in yet another ominous way. A temperance parade on 4 July 1842, composed largely of the native born and middle class, contained this novel contingent: a wagon carrying thirteen young girls representing the thirteen states of the Union—a role that early in the century small boys had played. The middle-class congregation of Whigs who commemorated the erection of a statue of Washington in Union Square in 1847 actually admitted an adult woman to the line of march, where she impersonated the Goddess of Liberty. This classic female symbol appeared once again on a nativist banner in 1850: the Goddess of Liberty was depicted passing the torch of freedom from Washington to the chief official of the

27. *New York Tribune*, 21, 22 October 1847; *San Francisco Chronicle*, 22, 23 February 1872; Davis, *Parades and Power*, p. 42; and Jean Gould Hales, "'Co-Laborers in the Cause': The Women in the Ante-Bellum Nativist Movement," *Civil War History* 25 (1979): 119–38.

United Americans. Women had won at least a symbolic place in the parades of the native born and middle class. Yet by the middle of the century these classes had largely withdrawn from public ceremonial life. In a sense, then, these female symbols portended the ultimate retreat of the middle class and native born into a privatized Victorian culture.

These same symbols continued, however, to be incorporated into the parades of others during and after the Civil War. The Irish, by the 1860s in New York and in San Francisco, had adapted and elaborated the role of women as living symbols. Comely young ladies, sometimes in carriages, sometimes on horseback, were given prominent places in St. Patrick's Day parades, playing the roles of both the Goddess of Liberty and the Maid of Erin. When the Fourth of July was still celebrated with a parade, as in San Francisco in the 1870s, emblems of gender differences headed the line of march. In 1877, the parade began with two divisions of the military, followed by a Goddess of Liberty and thirty-eight young women representing the states of the Union. After the Civil War those military contingents conveyed a new meaning. No longer dashing citizen-soldiers, they were veterans of a bloody war or members of the National Guard, ordered to parade by their commanding general. During the waning days of parading, symbols of sexual dimorphism, of male power and female gentleness, loomed over the city on the Fourth of July. The American eagle and the Goddess of Liberty were favorite images in the fireworks that had become a prominent part of Independence Day celebrations in all three cities. These icons spoke symbolically and vaguely of but two social groups: the male and the female.

The Goddess of Liberty was obviously just an allegorical figure whose presence in the parade did not reflect the actual composition of the procession, which was decidedly male. Throughout the Jacksonian era, indeed, male marchers simply represented themselves, enacting a kind of cultural equivalent of descriptive representation. By contrast, the Goddess of Liberty, the Maid of Erin, and the female embodiment of the thirty-odd states of the Union evoked some abstract concept far removed from the women themselves—an overt expression, perhaps, of their cultural utility. The female symbols were serviceable in a variety of ways. Their status as the quintessential "other" within a male-defined cultural universe made them perfect vehicles for representing the remote notions of national unity and local harmony. Similarly, as nonvoters they could evoke the ideal of a nation or a city freed of partisan divisions. As supposedly domestic creatures, they could stand above the class conflicts generated in the workplace. Defined by their roles as wives and mothers, women provided excellent symbols for ethnic solidarity: through marriage and childbirth they knit the bonds of ethnic communities. Finally, when the Civil War magnified the power of the state, the female allegory of the Goddess of Liberty evoked the soothing, humanizing imagery of maternity and nurturance. These complementary symbols were drawn together explicitly in San Francisco's Fourth of July parade in 1872. The ornamented wagon that carried thirteen fair young women was called the "Ship of State."

The rise of female symbolism represents a mode of civic ritual fundamentally at odds with the parade genre. Instead of displaying the constituent elements of the urban social order, albeit imperfectly and incompletely, these symbols transcended such mundane realities and washed out the actual social differences within the polity. To use Hanna Pitkin's terminology, gender imagery invoked symbolic rather than descriptive representation. The public presentation of civic groups was replaced by signs—goddesses, eagles, and flags—whose imprecise but evocative references manipulated the diffuse feelings of the audience rather than representing the body social and political.

The central but illusive role of gender in this transition can only be alluded to here. At issue is a complex political and cultural history that commenced with those masculinist assumptions of the early Republic which placed women outside the arena of public deliberation and discourse, thereby creating a feminine, depoliticized cultural field for the abstract symbols around which the republic could seek ideological unity. Accordingly, by the early nineteenth century both France and the United States had constructed female allegories to legitimize their fragile new republics.[28] In the Jacksonian era, however,

28. Lynn Hunt, *Politics, Culture, and Class in the French Revolution* (Berkeley and Los Angeles, 1984), pp. 61–66; and Maurice Agulhon, *Marianne into Battle* (Cambridge, 1981).

and in its characteristic ceremony, the parade, these classic female allegories receded from public view, eclipsed by the ceremonial display of the distinct components of the democracy. When, after mid century, that constituency became too contentious, female symbols acquired new currency. By then popular literary culture had invested female symbols with a domestic meaning, proffering a reassuring imagery of purity, passivity, and hence social harmony. At the same time, the association of femininity and privacy lodged a challenge to the cultural authority of public ceremonies in the parade itself. In intricate, still poorly understood ways this serpentine history of gender contributed to the decline of parading as the characteristic genre of American ceremony.

Thus when, as in New York in 1883, it came time again to commemorate an epochal event in the history of civic improvement, the parade was only a small part of the ceremony. The procession that opened the Brooklyn Bridge on May 24 was hardly a parade at all. Only the president of the United States, a long line of municipal officials, and the Seventh Regiment of the National Guard marched across the span of steel and masonry. The rest of the society assembled as a largely undifferentiated mass of spectators. The reporter for the *New York Tribune* found only two sources of relief from the visual monotony of the crowd: the glitter of the soldiers' muskets and the billowing white of the ladies' handkerchiefs. Similarly, the end of Reconstruction in New Orleans was commemorated in a spectacle of gender and power. While the White Leagues, triumphant soldiers who had once ousted the radical Republicans from office, marched through the streets, women in white waved their handkerchiefs in approval. That abstract and dualistic image replaced the complex language of social structure once inscribed in the parade.

Left behind, however, is valuable evidence for historians. The parade offers some answers to the questions about group formation and group identity that have preoccupied historians of nineteenth-century America. The parades of 1825 to 1880 document the development of such concepts as class, ethnicity, and gender, all in forms that were legible to contemporaries. This public ceremonial language was both complex and highly mutable. Any witness to a parade could see that the American city was an intricate mixture of nationalities, occupations, and allegiances. In a lifetime that spanned those fifty years, a spectator along the parade route could see those differences sorted first along lines of occupation, then fragmented into a kaleidoscopic array of voluntary associations, and finally reordered according to ethnicity. In the third quarter of the nineteenth century, the public itself resolved the historian's persistent question about the relative importance of class and ethnic consciousness, in favor of the latter. As symbols of gender became more prominent in these public displays, the syntax as well as the vocabulary of civic celebration began to change. Cultural unity no longer inhered in the representation of the diverse components of the social order but was woven in abstractions that hovered in an imaginary sphere above the line of march.

In its heyday, the parade provided a public lexicon that organized the diverse population of the city into manageable categories. It performed this cultural and social service during times of major social transformation. These buoyant festivals were mounted amid the most inauspicious historical circumstances, as cities grew at an extraordinary rate, took in a diverse array of new immigrants, and incorporated whole new social classes and modes of economic organization. Parading spanned the harrowing transition from urban village to industrial city and survived seasons of rioting, fierce partisan battles, and even a civil war. On parade days, all this confusion was sorted into neat categories and dressed in its Sunday best. The disorder and cacophony that reigned most of the year was ordered into reassuring, visually and audibly pleasing patterns.

The parade was an exercise in self-discipline as well as social discipline. Especially after 1840, its participants, whether organized into actual militia companies or simply mimicking such regimented bodies, all accepted the responsibility to maintain an exacting order in their ranks. Irish benefit societies, for example, exacted a one-dollar fine from any member who smoked, left ranks without permission, or otherwise behaved "improperly" during a parade.[29] Under the pretense of play, thousands of men marched at specified times, in rigid postures, in straight

29. "Articles of Incorporation, Constitution, By-Laws and Rules of Order of the Irish American Benevolent Society" (San Francisco, 1871), p. 29.

ranks, in uniform clothing. Thousands of newcomers to the
city, many of them scarcely rehabilitated peasants, practiced
the etiquette of urban living in public.

The paraders were not only agents of social order, but also
parties to the creation of urban culture. The Irish, in a particularly obstinate way, forced Anglo-Saxon Protestants to acknowledge them as members of American culture as well as citizens.
They actively demonstrated that an ethnic parade, not a melt-
ing pot, would be the most fitting symbol of a multiethnic society. Although this ethnic fragmentation ultimately undermined the parade as a citywide celebration, ethnic affirmation
kept the form alive. The St. Patrick's Day parade was the first of
many examples of independent parading whereby distinctive
social groups imprinted their identity on the public mind.
Blacks would use parading in a similar fashion in Reconstruction New Orleans. Workingmen would write themselves into
ceremonial and social history during the great Labor Day parades of the 1880s. And finally, in the second decade of this
century, suffragists took to the streets in processions and won
for women a representative rather than a symbolic place in public ceremony.

Parades continue to this day, providing a ceremonial method
of forging and asserting the diverse social identities that com-
pose American culture. These groups take to the streets on
Martin Luther King Day, Cinco de Mayo, Gay Pride Day, and
many other occasions. Seldom, however, does a wide array of
different social groups send contingents to a common public
ceremony. The celebration of the centennial of the Statue of
Liberty, for example, gave center stage to the commander in
chief, assorted Hollywood celebrities, corporate executives,
and mass-marketed commodities. The pageantry was choreo-
graphed by public relations experts and advertisers, not ham-
mered out in public meetings. Still, those sporadic isolated parades recall a past, and perhaps inspire a future, in which
diverse social groups could come together both to display themselves and to acknowledge one another.

Six

Texts, Printing, Readings

ROGER CHARTIER

In the prologue to his *Celestina*, published in Saragossa in 1507, Fernando de Rojas asked himself why the work had been understood, appreciated, and used in so many different ways since its first appearance in 1499 at Burgos.[1] The question is simple: how can a text that is the same for everyone who reads it become an "instrument of discord and battle between its readers, creating divergences between them, with each reader having an opinion depending on his own taste?" (instrumento de lid o contienda a sus lectores para ponerlos en diferencias, dando cada una sentencia sobre ella a sabor de su voluntad?) I will use this question, formulated by a classical author about an old text, as my point of departure in delineating basic hypotheses for a history of practices of reading. These practices will be defined to include relationships to printed objects (which are by no means limited to books) and to the texts that readers thus encounter.

For Rojas, the contrasting receptions of the text he presented to the public are due first to the readers themselves, whose

1. Rojas citations are translated from the bilingual Spanish-French edition *La Celestina, Tragicomedia de Calisto y Melibea/La Célestine ou Tragicomédie de Calixte et Mélibée*, attributed to Fernando Rojas (Paris, 1980), pp. 116–19. An English translation of the prologue can be found in Guadalupe Martinez Lacalle, ed., *Celestine or the Tragick-Comedie of Calisto and Melibea*, trans. James Mabbe (London, 1972), pp. 111–14.

contradictory judgments can be traced not only to their diversity of characters and dispositions ("tantas y tan differentes
condiciones") but also to their multiplicity of abilities and expectations. Abilities and expectations are differentiated according to age: *niños, mozos, mancebos, viejos* (little children, school-
boys, young fellows, old men) do not approach writing in the
same way; some do not know how to read, while others have
no desire to or no longer can. Abilities and expectations are also
differentiated according to the highly distinct uses readers make
of the same text.

Rojas notes at least three readings of the *tragicomedia*. The
first focuses not on the story as a whole but rather on certain
detached episodes. It reduces the text to the status of a *cuento de
camino* (travelers' tale), to a story told for passing time, much
like the one that Sancho tells his master in Part One, chapter 20,
of *Don Quixote*. The second reading retains from the tragicomedy nothing more than easily memorized formulas, those *do-
naires y refranes* (pleasantries and proverbs) that provide clichés
and ready-made expressions. These formulas are collected in
the course of a reading that establishes absolutely no intimate
relationship, no individual rapport, between the reader and
what is read. To these practices, which mutilate the work and
miss its true meaning, the author opposes the correct, profit-
able reading. This third reading is the one that grasps the text
in its complex totality without reducing it to mere episodes of a
plot or a collection of impersonal maxims. Those who read the
comedia properly "will understand its essential matter and profit
from it, they will be amused at its wit, and they will store away
in their memories the maxims and sayings of the philosophers,
in order, when the proper time comes, to use them to advantage" (coligen la suma para su provecho, ríen lo donoso, las
sentencias y dichos de filósofos guardan en su memoria para
trasponer en lugares convenibles a sus actos y propósitos).
They thus put into operation a plural reading that distinguishes
the comic from the serious, and that extracts the moral that best
illuminates each person's life, whose "first person" is appli-
cable to everyone.

In its way, Rojas's prologue clearly indicates the central tension of every history of reading—and this is why he is worthy

of our consideration. Should we place at the center of such a history the text given to be read or the reader who takes it up? The reader is, in effect, always thought by the author (or the commentator) to be necessarily subjugated to a single meaning, to a correct interpretation, to an authorized reading. To understand reading, in this view, would be above all to identify the discursive arrangements that constrain it and that impose on it a signification that is intrinsic and independent of any deciphering. But in thus postulating the absolute efficacy of the text tyrannically to dictate the meaning of the work to the reader, do we not in fact deny all autonomy in the act of reading? The latter is virtually absorbed and annihilated in both the explicit protocols and the implicit devices that are intended to regulate or control it. In this manner, reading is thought of as inscribed in the text, an effect automatically produced by the very strategy of writing peculiar to the work or its genre.

Nevertheless, experience shows that reading is not simply submission to textual machinery. Whatever it may be, reading is a creative practice, which invents singular meanings and significations that are not reducible to the intentions of authors of texts or producers of books. Reading is a response, a labor, or, as Michel de Certeau puts it, an act of "poaching" (*braconnage*).[2] But how do we make sense of this living, personal, striking experience? If each reading by each reader is actually a secret, singular creation, is it still possible to organize this indistinguishable plurality of individual acts according to shared regularities? Is it even possible to envision knowing anything certain about it? How can we consider at one and the same time the irreducible freedom of readers and the constraints meant to curb this freedom?

This fundamental tension runs through literary criticism, which is torn between two fundamentally different approaches. On the one hand there are the approaches that deduce the reading or the reader from the text's own internal structures; on the other there are approaches—such as the phenomenology of the act of reading or "reception aesthetics"—that attempt to

2. Michel de Certeau, "Lire: un braconnage," in *L'Invention du quotidien, L'Arts de Faire* (Paris, 1980), pp. 279–96; English translation *The Practice of Everyday Life*, trans. Steven Rendall (Berkeley and Los Angeles, 1984).

locate individual or shared determinations which govern modes of interpretation from outside of the text.[3] The tension is also central in philosophical endeavors that, like the work of Ricoeur, consider how the narrative configurations that form stories (of fiction or history) remodel the private consciousness and the temporal experience of subjects. In such a perspective, the act of reading is strategically situated at the point of "application" (*Anwendung*, in the hermeneutic lexicon) where the world of the text meets that of the reader, where the interpretation of the work ends in the interpretation of the self. Reading is to be understood as an "appropriation" of the text, both because it actualizes the text's semantic potential and because it creates a mediation for knowledge of the self through comprehension of the text.[4]

In what way can a historical perspective help to resolve the contradictions in literary theory or the difficulties of phenomenological philosophy, which while defining reading as a concrete act does not consider pertinent the multiple variations that at different times and places organize its contrasting forms? History offers two approaches that are necessarily linked: reconstructing the diversity of older readings from their sparse and multiple traces, and recognizing the strategies by which authors and publishers tried to impose an orthodoxy or a prescribed reading on the text. Among these strategies, some are explicit and rely on discourse (in prefaces, prologues, commentaries, notes), and others implicit, making of the text a machinery that by necessity must impose a comprehension held to be legitimate. Guided or trapped, the reader invariably finds himself inscribed in the text, but in turn the text is itself inscribed variously in its different readers. Thus it is necessary to bring together two perspectives that are often disjointed: on the one hand, the study of the way in which texts and the printed works that convey them organize the prescribed read-

3. Wolfgang Iser, *Der Akt des Lesens, Theorie ästhetischer Wirkung* (Munich, 1976); English translation *The Act of Reading: A Theory of Aesthetic Response* (Baltimore, 1978). Hans Robert Jauss, *Literaturgeschichte als Provokation* (Frankfurt-am-Main, 1974).

4. Paul Ricoeur, *Temps et récit*, 3 vols. (Paris, 1983–85), vol. 3, esp. pp. 228–63. Volumes 1 and 2 published in English as *Time and Narrative*, trans. Cathleen McLaughlin and David Pellauer (Chicago, 1984).

ing; and on the other, the collection of actual readings tracked down in individual confessions or reconstructed on the level of communities of readers—those "interpretive communities" whose members share the same reading styles and the same strategies of interpretation.[5]

Let us return to our Spanish master. For Rojas, the diverse opinions on the *Celestina* are to be linked first to the many differences in abilities, expectations, and predispositions of its readers. But the opinions also depend on how the readers "read" the text. It is clear that Rojas addresses a reader who reads the prologue to himself, in silence, in private. Yet not all readings of the tragicomedy are of this nature: "So then, when ten persons congregate to hear this play there will naturally be a variety of reactions among them. Who will deny that there will arise dissension about something which may be understood in so many different ways?" (Así que cuando diez personas se juntaren a oír esta comedia, en quien quepa esta diferencia de condiciones, come suele acaecer, ¿quién negará que haya contienda en cosa que de tantas maneras se entienda?). Ten listeners gathered around a text read out loud: here "reading" is actually listening to speech that is read. The practice was common, for in the edition of 1500 the "corrector de la impresión" tells how the text should be read aloud. One of the stanzas that he adds to the work is entitled "On the way to read this tragicomedy" (Dice el modo que se ha de tener leyendo esta tragicomedia). The "lector" he envisions must know how to vary the tone, play the parts of all the characters, convey asides by speaking through his teeth—in short, mobilize "a thousand arts and methods" (mil artes y modos) of reading in order to capture the attention of "los oyentes," the listeners. Along with the *Celestina*, other texts such as pastorals or chivalric romances are the favored texts of these readings, where, for a few people, the spoken word offers a written text even to those who could read it themselves.

Rojas's notation opens several paths of inquiry. The first concerns the sociability of reading, a fundamental counterpoint to the privatization of the act of reading, to its retreat into the inti-

5. Stanley Fish, *Is There a Text in This Class? The Authority of Interpretive Communities* (Cambridge, Mass., 1980), pp. 167–73.

macy of solitude. From the sixteenth to the eighteenth century, reading out loud survived in the tavern and the coach, the salon and the café, in high society and in the household. This history remains to be written.[6] A second path leads to the analysis of the relationship between textuality and orality. To be sure, between the culture of the tale and of storytelling on the one hand and that of writing on the other the differences are great, and aptly characterized by Cervantes in the passage from *Don Quixote* cited above.[7] To pass the time while standing guard one night, Sancho undertakes to tell stories to his master. But his method—interrupting the account with commentaries and digressions that result in repetition upon repetition and that project the narrator into the story and relate the story back to the present situation—makes his listener wildly impatient: "If thou tellest thy tale in this manner, cried Don Quixote, repeating every circumstance twice over, it will not be finished these two days; proceed therefore, connectedly, and rehearse it, like a man of understanding: otherwise, thou hadst better hold thy tongue" (Si desa manera cuentas tu cuento, Sancho —dijo don Quijote—, repitiendo dos veces lo que vas diciendo, no acabarás en dos días; dilo seguidamente, y cuéntalo como hombre de entendimiento, y si no, no digas nada.) A man of books par excellence, even to crazy excess, Don Quixote becomes irritated by a story that lacks the form of those he ordinarily reads; Quixote really wants Sancho's recitation to conform to the rules of linear, objective, hierarchical writing. The distance between these expectations of a reader and the oral practice as Sancho learned it is insurmountable: "In my country, answered Sancho, all the old stories are told in this manner, neither can I tell it in any other; nor is it civil in your worship, to desire I should change the custom" (De la misma manera que yo lo cuento —respondió Sancho— se cuentan en mi tierra todas las conse-

6. Cf. Roger Chartier, "Les Pratiques de l'écrit," in *Histoire de la vie privée*, ed. Philippe Ariès and Georges Duby, vol. 3: *De la Renaissance aux Lumières*, ed. Roger Chartier (Paris, 1986), pp. 113–61; and idem, "Leisure and Sociability: Reading Aloud in Modern Europe," in *Urban Life in the Renaissance*, ed. Susan Zimerman and Ronald Weissman (London, 1988).

7. Miguel de Cervantes, *El ingenioso hidalgo Don Quijote de la Mancha*, ed. John Jay Allen (Madrid, 1984), 1:237–39; English translation from *The Adventures of Don Quixote de la Mancha*, trans. Tobias Smollett, intro. Carlos Fuentes (New York, 1986).

jas, y yo no sé contarlo de otra, ni es bien que vuestra merced me pide que haga usos nuevos). Resigned, Don Quixote reluctantly agrees to listen to this text that is so different from those contained in his precious books: "Take thy own way, said the Knight, and since it is the will of fate, that I should hear thee, pray go on" (Di como quisieres —respondió don Quijote—; que pues la suerte quiere que no pueda dejar de escucharte, prosigue).

The discrepancy, then, between the spoken recitation and the printed script is great. We must bear in mind, however, that the links between the two are numerous. For one thing, formulas of oral culture are often inscribed in texts destined for a large public. *Occasionnels* (ephemera, yet having perhaps a longer life than the English term implies) that use in written form the storytellers' methods of recitation or the variations introduced in the popular editions of fairy tales by borrowing from folkloric traditions are good examples of these joinings of the spoken with the printed word.[8] Moreover, this continuing dependence assures the return of multiple texts into oral forms, where they are destined to be read aloud: for example, in monastic exercises or preaching, in reading for pleasure or family teaching.

But for Rojas there is another reason that could confound the understanding of the text he offered to his readers: the unfortunate intervention of the printers themselves. He in effect deplores the additions they felt they could make, against his will and against the recommendations of the ancients: "The very printers have wounded the text: they have put unnecessary headings and summaries at the beginning of the acts, which was a custom not followed by ancient authors" (Que aun los impresores han dado sus pinturas, poniendo rúbricas o sumarios al principio de cada acto, narrando en breve lo que dentro contenía: una cosa bien escusada, según lo que los antiguos escritores usaron).

8. See, for example, Roger Chartier, "La Pendue miraculeusement sauvée. Etude d'un occasionnel," and Catherine Velay-Vallantin, "Le Miroir des contes. Perrault dans les Bibliothèques bleues," in *Les Usages de l'imprimé (XVe–XIXe siècle)*, ed. Roger Chartier (Paris, 1987), pp. 83–127 and 129–55; English translation *The Culture of Print*, trans. Lydia G. Cochrane (Cambridge, 1989).

This observation can establish a fundamental distinction between the text and print, between the work of writing and that of making the book. As an American bibliographer justly observed, "Whatever they may do, authors do *not* write books. Books are not written at all. They are manufactured by scribes and other artisans, by mechanics and other engineers, and by printing presses and other machines."[9] In contrast to the representation of the ideal, abstract text—which is stable because it is detached from all materiality, a representation elaborated by literature itself—it is essential to remember that no text exists outside of the support that enables it to be read; any comprehension of a writing, no matter what kind it is, depends on the forms in which it reaches its reader. Thus a sorting out of two types of apparatus becomes necessary, between those entailed by the putting into text, the strategies of writing, the intentions of the "author," and those resulting from the manufacture of the book or publication, produced by editorial decision or through workshop procedures, which are aimed at readers or readings that may not be at all like those the author intended. This gap, which is the space in which meaning is constructed, has too often been overlooked, not only by the classical approaches, which consider the work itself as a pure text whose typographical forms do not matter, but also by reception theory (*Rezeptionstheorie*), which postulates a direct, immediate relationship between the "text" and the reader, between the "textual signals" used by the author and the "horizon of expectation" of those he addresses.

Here, it seems to me, we find an illegitimate simplification of the process by which works take on meaning. Restoration of its true complexity requires consideration of the close-knit relationship among three poles: the text itself, the object that conveys the text, and the act that grasps it. Variations in this triangular relationship produce in effect changes in meaning, which can be organized in a few models. First, there is the case of a stable text presented for reading in printed forms that themselves change. In studying the variations in the printing of

9. Roger E. Stoddard, "Morphology and the Book from an American Perspective," *Printing History* 17 (1987): 2–14.

William Congreve's plays in the seventeenth and eighteenth centuries, D. F. MacKenzie was able to show how apparently small and limited typographical transformations (the shift from a format of quarto to octavo, the use of an ornament to separate scenes, the numbering of episodes with roman numerals, the list of characters' names at the beginning of each scene, the mention of who enters and who exits, the indication of the speaker's name) had major effects on the status given to the work, on how it was read, even on the way the author himself considered it. A new readability was created by the format, which made the book easier to carry, and by the layout, which restored something of the dramatic sense of movement and of time in print. A new readability, but also a new horizon of reception, for the forms used in the 1710 octavo edition had seemingly "classicized" the text—which might be what led Congreve to purify the writing here and there, in order to make it conform to the text's new legitimacy.[10]

In the same way, it seems to me that the editorial history of Molière's comedies has a significant impact on the reconstruction of contemporary understandings of them. With *George Dandin*, for example, four changes must be taken into account. First, there was a shift from separate editions of the play in the form of small books that were closely linked with performances, to its publication as part of edited series, individually or in continuous pagination, whereby the play was inscribed in a corpus and its meaning contaminated by its proximity to other comedies. Second, as print became theatricalized, beginning with the 1682 edition the number of stage directions, particularly the cues, progressively multiplied, thus allowing Molière's sense of the scene to be preserved in readings detached from the immediacy of the performance. Third, the introduction of illustrations, also in 1682, required a series of choices to be made (which scene to illustrate, how to represent characters and interpret stage directions) and constituted a protocol of reading

10. Donald F. MacKenzie, "Topography and Meaning: The Case of William Congreve," in *Buch und Buchhandel in Europa im achtzehnten Jahrhundert*, ed. Giles Barber and Bernhard Fabian (Hamburg, 1981), pp. 81–126; see also idem, "The Book as an Expressive Form," *Bibliography and the Sociology of Texts*, The Panizzi Lectures, 1985 (London, 1986), pp. 1–21.

for the text that it accompanied. And fourth, after 1734 a single edition appeared, containing the comedy itself, the text of the pastoral in which the comedy had been inserted, and the account of the 1668 festival at Versailles where both had been included during the first performance—as if at the beginning of the eighteenth century the play, now situated at a historical distance, was supposed to be restored to the context of its creation. Thus the text, unchanged since the first editions in 1669, now changes because the apparatus in which it is to be read has changed.[11]

The second model concerns the way in which changes in the printed form of a text govern the transformations in its meaning. This is the case, for example, with the titles in the corpus of French chapbooks (the "Bibliothèque bleue"), an editorial formula aimed at winning over the most numerous (and most popular) readership between 1700 and the mid 1800s. The common characteristics of these editions are above all material and commercial. The material side of publication involved paperbound books, covered generally with blue paper (but also red or marbled), printed with type that was old and mismatched, illustrated with second-hand woodcuts, and with a picture frequently taking the place of the publisher's insignia on the title page. Commercially, even if the length of the works varied, their prices always remained low, much lower than those books that were produced for a more refined and thus more expensive market. Thus, the Bibliothèque bleue required that costs be calculated quite precisely so that a book could be sold at the lowest possible price.

The texts of the Bibliothèque bleue were not written for such editorial ends. The politics of the inventors of the formula (the printers of Troyes, later copied in Rouen, Caen, Limoges, and Avignon) consisted of picking out from a repertoire of already published texts those works that seemed to them to meet the expectations and abilities of the vast public they hoped to attract. From this formula, two essential corollaries followed: the texts published as chapbooks were not "popular" in and of

11. I am in the process of doing a study of this comedy under the provisional title *Le Social en représentation. Lectures de George Dandin* (Paris, forthcoming).

themselves but came from all genres, from all eras, and from all kinds of literature, and all had already enjoyed a relatively long editorial life in classic published form before becoming a part of the Bibliothèque bleue. Thus devotional literature and religious exercises, fairy tales and novels, and handbooks all were included. Between publication of the original text and manufacture of the chapbook edition, the gap could be great and was always marked by a series of editions with nothing "popular" about them.

The cultural specificity of the materials published in the Bibliothèque bleue, then, stemmed not from the erudite and diverse texts themselves but from editorial intervention intended to make them conform to the reading ability of the buyers whom the publishers wanted to attract. This work of adaptation modified the text as it was given in the previous edition, which in turn served as copy for the printers of "popular" books. The adaptation was informed by the image the printers had of the competence and cultural expectations of readers who were unfamiliar with books. The printers undertook three kinds of transformations of the text: they shortened the texts, removed chapters, episodes, or digressions deemed superfluous, and simplified the wording by stripping sentences of their relative and incidental clauses; they broke up the text by creating new chapters and adding paragraphs, titles, and summaries; and they censored allusions deemed to be blasphemous or sacrilegious, descriptions considered licentious, and scatological or indecent expressions. The logic behind this adaptive work was thus twofold: it aimed to control the texts by submitting them to the demands of Counter-Reform religion and morals, while at the same time intending to make them more accessible to inexperienced readers.

The implicit reading that such a work sought to create can be characterized as a reading that required visible landmarks (hence anticipatory titles and summary recapitulations, or even woodcuts functioning as protocols of reading or mnemonic devices). This kind of reading was comfortable only with brief, self-contained, often disjointed sequences and apparently was satisfied with minimal global coherence. This manner of reading was not at all that of the literate elites, who were familiar with books and adept at deciphering and mastering texts in their entirety. Unlike the scholar, the rudimentary reader could tolerate the dross left in the text by hasty and cheap manufacturing processes (for example, the countless misprints, cuts in the wrong places, confusions of names and words, multiple errors). Chapbook readers (or at least the majority of them, for notables too bought the books for pleasure, curiosity, or collecting) read in what seems to have been a discontinuous, fragmented way that accommodated gaps and incoherences.

The rudimentary reader was also comfortable with books that included texts he already knew, at least partially or approximately. Often read out loud—but not only (or perhaps not at all) during those evenings devoted to public readings called *veillées*—the chapbooks could be memorized by listeners who, when actually faced with the books, recognized them more than they discovered them. And more generally, even outside of this direct listening, most people read books with a previously gained knowledge that was easily evoked in the act of reading. This knowledge was gained from the recurrence of coded forms, from the repetition of themes, and from the books' images (even if these originally had no relation to the text they illustrated). This "preknowledge," as it were, was mobilized to produce comprehension of what was read—a comprehension not necessarily in conformity with that desired by the producer of the text or the maker of the book, or with that which a sharp and well-informed reading could construct. "Popular" reading can thus be traced to these particularities, both formal and typographic (taking the latter in the largest sense of the term, as found, for example, in MacKenzie), of the publication of the chapbooks and to the modifications they imposed on the texts on which they were based. In this context, then, popular reading is understood as a relation to the text unlike that of literate culture.

A third model of this relationship among text, book, and understanding appears when a text that is stable in content and fixed in form becomes the object of contrasting readings. "A book is changed by the fact that it does not change even when the world changes," declared Pierre Bourdieu.[12] To make the proposition compatible with the smaller scale of this essay, let us add: "even when its mode of reading changes." We need to develop indicators of the major divisions that can organize a history of reading practices (of the use of texts, even the uses of the *same* text)—for example between reading out loud, for one-self or for others, and reading in silence; between reading in-wardly and privately and reading publicly; between religious reading and lay reading; and between "intensive" reading and "extensive" reading (to borrow the terminology of R. Engel-sing).[13] Beyond these macroscopic cleavages, the historian must seek to determine the dominant paradigms of reading in a com-munity of readers in a given time and place. These include, for example, the Puritan readings of the seventeenth and eigh-teenth centuries or the "Rousseauist" reading of the Enlighten-ment or, yet again, the "magical" reading of traditional peasant societies. Each of these "manners of reading" has its own spe-cific gestures, its proper uses of the book, and its particular ref-erential text (the Bible, the *Nouvelle Héloïse*, the Grand and Petit Albert). The mode of reading, which is dictated by the book it-self or by its interpreters, provides the archetype of all reading, whatever kind it may be.[14] Characterization of these modes of reading is therefore indispensable to any approach that aims to reconstruct how texts could be apprehended, understood, and handled.

The final remarks of Rojas in the prologue of the *Celestina* concern the very genre of the text: "Others have made quite a to-do about the name of the play, saying it was not a comedy

12. Pierre Bourdieu and Roger Chartier, "La Lecture: une pratique cul-turelle," in *Pratiques de la lecture,* ed. Roger Chartier (Marseille, 1985), pp. 217–39.

13. Rolf Engelsing, "Die Perioden der Lesergeschichte in der Neuzeit. Das statistische Ausmass und die soziokulturelle Bedeutung der Lektüre," *Archiv für Geschichte des Buchwesens* 10 (1969): 946–1002.

14. David Hall, "Introduction: The Uses of Literacy in New England, 1500–1850," in *Printing and Society in Early Modern America,* ed. William L. Joyce et al. (Worcester, Mass., 1983), pp. 1–47; Robert Darnton, "Readers Re-spond to Rousseau: The Fabrication of Romantic Sensitivity," in *The Great Cat Massacre and Other Episodes in French Cultural History* (New York, 1984), pp. 214–56; Daniel Fabre, "Le Livre et sa magie," in *Pratiques de la lecture,* ed. Chartier, pp. 182–206.

but a tragedy, since it ended so sadly. The first author wished to give it a description that would reflect what happens in the beginning, and so he called it a comedy. I have found myself in a dilemma, and I have cut the Gordian knot by calling the play a tragicomedy" (Otros han litigado sobre el nombre, diciendo que no se había de llamar comedia, pues acababa en tristeza, sino que se llamase tragedia. El primer auctor quiso dar denominación del principio, que fué placer, y llamóla comedia. Yo, viendo estas discordias, entre estos estremos partí agora por medio la porfía, y llaméla tragicomedia). The notation leads to two series of reflections. First and foremost, it reminds us that the explicit indicators by which texts are designated and classified create expectations of the reading and anticipations of understanding. That is the case as well for the indication of the genre, which links the text to be read to other texts that have already been read and which signals to the reader the appropriate "preknowledge" in which to locate the text.

A similar process takes place with purely formal or material indicators—the format and the image, for example. From the folio to smaller formats, a hierarchy exists that links the format of the book, the genre of the text, and the moment and mode of reading. In the eighteenth century Lord Chesterfield bore witness to this fact: "Solid folios are the people of business with whom I converse in the morning. Quartos are the easier mixed company with whom I sit after dinner; and I pass my evenings in the light, and often frivolous chitchat of small octavos and duodecimos."[15] Such a hierarchy is, moreover, directly inherited from the days when books were copied by hand. This hierarchy distinguished the book that had to be laid flat in order to be read; the humanist book, which was more manageable in its medium format and suitable for both classic and newer texts; and the portable book, the *libellus*, a pocketbook and bedside book with multiple uses and more numerous readers.[16] The im-

---

15. Cited in Stoddard, "Morphology and the Book."
16. Alphonse Petrucci, "Alle origine del libro moderno: libri de banco, libri da bisaccia, libretti da mano," in *Libri, scrittura e pubblico nel Rinascimento: Guida storica e critica*, ed. Alphonse Petrucci (Rome, 1979), pp. 137–56; and idem, "Il libro manoscritto," in *Letteratura italiana*, vol. 2: *Produzione e consumo* (Turin, 1983), pp. 499–524.

age on the frontispiece or title page, along the border of the text, or on the last page also classified the text and suggested a reading. It provided the protocol of the reading, the identifying index.

Rojas also leads us to think that the history of genres, both textual and typographical, could provide the underpinnings for the history of discourse as formulated by Foucault.[17] Understanding the series of discourses in their discontinuity, stripping principles of their regularity, and identifying their particular rationalities all presuppose, I believe, that the constraints and demands of the very forms in which they are to be read be taken into account. Hence we must pay attention to the laws of production and to the obligatory devices governing every class or series of texts that have become books—the lives of saints as well as the books of hours, the *occasionnels* and Bibliothèque bleue, the *folhetos de cordel* and chapbooks, the emblem books and programs of civic processions, and so on. Hence, moreover, we must trace the shifts from one genre to another, when a given form becomes invested with issues that are normally foreign to it or with themes that are generally expressed elsewhere and in other ways. In the seventeenth century, for example, at the time of the acute crisis known as the Fronde, the "general politicization of printing" placed all textual and typographic genres of large circulation and public reading (from the letter to the gazette, from the song to the narrative account) at the disposal of the conflicting parties.[18] The critical and genealogical study of discourses in series can thus find support in a project that takes each text or collection of texts and considers the intersections between the history of the variations in their content and the history of the transformations they undergo when being put into print.

These working hypotheses are backed by several critical reevaluations that call into question the certainties and habits of French cultural history. The first concerns the classic uses of the

17. Michel Foucault, *L'Ordre du discours* (Paris, 1970); English translation "The Discourse on Language," trans. A. M. Sheridan Smith, in *The Archaeology of Knowledge* (New York, 1972).

18. Christian Jouhaud, *Mazarinades, la Fronde des mots* (Paris, 1985); and the critical note of Michel de Certeau, "L'Expérimentation d'une méthode: les mazarinades de Christian Jouhaud," *Annales, E.S.C.* 41 (1986): 507–12.

notion of popular culture. This notion no longer appears to hold up against three fundamental doubts. First and foremost, it no longer seems tenable to try to establish strict correspondences between cultural cleavages and social hierarchies, creating simplistic relationships between particular cultural objects or forms and specific social groups. On the contrary, it is necessary to recognize the fluid circulation and shared practices that cross social boundaries. Numerous examples exist of the "popular" uses of objects, ideas, and codes that were not considered as such (think of the readings of Menocchio, the Friulian miller);[19] conversely, the rejection by the dominant culture of forms rooted in the common culture came late. Second, it does not seem possible to identify the absolute difference and the radical specificity of popular culture on the basis of its own texts, beliefs, or codes. The materials that convey the practices and thoughts of ordinary people are always mixed, blending forms and themes, invention and tradition, literate culture and folklore.

Finally, the macroscopic opposition between "popular" and "high" culture has lost its pertinence. An inventory of the multiple divisions that fragment the social body is preferable to this massive partition, which often defines the common people by default as the collection of those outside elite society. Their ordering follows several principles that make manifest the divergences or oppositions between men and women, townspeople and rural folk, Protestants and Catholics, but also between generations, occupations, and neighborhoods. For far too long, French sociocultural history has accepted a reductive definition of the social, identified only with the hierarchy of wealth and its conditions. This approach has lost sight of the fact that other differences, based on gender as well as on territorial or religious affiliations, were also clearly social. Such differences could make sense of the plurality of cultural practices, proving at least as and perhaps more effective than the opposition of dominant/dominated or the socioprofessional hierarchy.

19. Carlo Ginzburg, *Il formaggio e i vermi. Il cosmo di un mugnaio del' 1500* (Turin, 1976); English translation *The Cheese and the Worms: The Cosmos of a Sixteenth-Century Miller*, trans. John Tedeschi and Anne Tedeschi (New York, 1982).

Thus, because it ignores borrowings and exchanges, because it masks the multiplicity of differences, because it presupposes a priori the validity of a set of divisions that remains to be established, the concept of popular culture—which provided the foundation for the first pioneering studies about chapbooks—must now be called into question.

We must likewise question the long-recognized contrast between the completely oral and gestural forms of so-called traditional cultures on the one hand and the circulation of writing, first in manuscript and then in printed form, on the other, a contrast that delimits a separate, minority culture. The division has encouraged the partitioning of the approaches to these two modes of cultural acquisition and transmission; it has rigidly separated historical anthropology (which, even if it works with texts, is attached to systems of gestures, to the use of words, and to ritual apparatuses) from a more classic cultural history dedicated to studying the production and circulation of writing. Thus formulated, the opposition of oral and written fails to account for the situation that existed from the sixteenth to the eighteenth century when media and multiple practices still overlapped.

Some of these overlaps associate the spoken word and writing: either a spoken word fixes itself in writing or, conversely, a text returns in oral form through the mediation of reading out loud. Other overlaps connect writings and gestures. Numerous texts overtly aim to negate their own status as discourse in order to produce, at the practical level, behavior or practices held to be legitimate or useful. Manuals on how to prepare for death, books on religious exercises, guides to good manners, and handbooks are among many examples of genres that attempt to internalize necessary or appropriate gestures. Furthermore, writing is installed at the very heart of the most central forms of traditional culture; festivals or entries, for instance, are surrounded by written notices of all kinds and commented on in programs that explain their meaning, and ecclesiastical rituals often require written objects to be placed at the center of the ceremony. The history of cultural practices must consider these interpenetrations and restore some of the complex trajectories that run from the spoken word to the written text, from writing that is read to gestures that are performed, from the printed book to reading aloud.

One concept seems useful here, that of appropriation: because, understood more sociologically than phenomenologically, the notion of appropriation makes it possible to appreciate the differences in cultural apportionment, in the creative invention that lies at the very heart of the reception process. A retrospective sociology that has long made the unequal distribution of objects the primary criterion of the cultural hierarchy must be replaced by a different approach that focuses attention on differentiated and contrasting uses of the same goods, the same texts, and the same ideas. Such a perspective does not preclude identifying differences (including socially rooted differences), but it displaces the very arena of their identification because it no longer involves social qualification of the works as a whole (for example, designation of Bibliothèque bleue texts as "popular literature"). Instead, it characterizes the practices that differentially appropriate the materials circulating in a given society.

The statistical approach that once seemed to dominate French cultural history and that sought to weigh the unequal social distribution of serializable objects, discourses, and acts therefore no longer suffices. By presuming overly simplistic correspondences between social levels and cultural boundaries and seizing upon the most repetitive and reductionist expressions of ideas and behaviors, such a course misses the essential, that is, the contrasting manner in which groups or individuals utilize shared themes or forms. Without abandoning the measures and the series, the history of texts and of books must be above all a reconstitution of variations in practices—in other words, a history of reading.

Thought of in this way, the emphasis on cultural appropriations also enables us to see that texts or words intended to mold thoughts and actions are never wholly effective and radically acculturating. The practices of appropriation always create uses or representations that are hardly reducible to the wills or intentions of those who produce discourse and norms. During the Catholic reform, for instance, the imposition of new devotions was accompanied by recastings and reinterpretations that profoundly transformed them. The devotion to the Blessed Sacrament, which was central in post-Tridentine pastoral work and iconography, was strongly contaminated by the ancient cult of relics and subverted by a demand for exteriorization that insisted on public and spectacular practices (the exposition of the sacrament, the benediction, and the procession) no longer easily accepted by ecclesiastical authority. And the devotion to the Rosary often reasserted the gestures and meanings traditionally attached to the cult of the Virgin of Mercy.[20] Between the institution and the community, between the normative model and the collective experience, the game was always two way. So-called popular religion was at once acculturated and acculturating: neither totally controlled nor absolutely free, it affirmed the specific modes of belief at the very core of the acceptance of new models of spirituality.

By the same token, the act of reading cannot be effaced in the text itself, nor can significations be annihilated in imposed meanings. The acceptance of messages and models always operates through adjustments, arrangements, or resistances. That is the lesson of Richard Hoggart's book *The Uses of Literacy*.[21] In 1950s England, the culture of the popular classes, far from being reduced to that embodied in the productions of mass culture, was characterized by a relationship of defiance and defensiveness vis-à-vis the messages it received and consumed. Large-circulation newspapers, tabloids, advertisements, horoscopes, and songs are always the object of an oblique or distracted attention that reads or understands them with pleasure and suspicion, at once fascinated and distanced. Belief and disbelief go together, and the acceptance of the truth in what one reads or hears does not diminish the fundamental doubts retained about this presumed authenticity. Does Hoggart in fact provide a key for understanding the particularity of the relationship between the least literate public and the texts that aim to govern and distract them, from the Bibliothèque bleue to the

---

20. Alphonse Dupront, "De la religion populaire," in *Du Sacré, croisades et pèlerinages, images et langages* (Paris, 1987), pp. 419–66; and the preface in Marie-Hélène Froeschlé-Chopard, *La Religion populaire en Provence orientale au XVIIIe siècle* (Paris, 1980), pp. 5–31.

21. Richard Hoggart, *The Uses of Literacy* (London, 1971).

soap opera? Or is it better to place this characterization within the *longue durée* of differential modes of belief that can ascertain similar ambivalences at completely other social levels in other historical situations?[22] At any rate, Hoggart's work reminds us of the reader's creative autonomy in the face of the machineries that try to control him.

Here, the idea of appropriation is not taken in the sense defined by Foucault in *Discourse on Language*. Foucault considered the "social appropriation of discourses" as a procedure that controls them and an apparatus that limits their distribution—in other words, as one of the grand systems of the subjugation of discourse.[23] My perspective is different without being contradictory, because it focuses attention not on exclusions by confiscation but on the differences within shared usage, such as those indicated by Pierre Bourdieu: "The taste, propensity and aptitude for appropriation (material and/or symbolic) of a specific class of objects or of classified or classifying practices, is the generating formula behind style of life. It is a unitary ensemble of distinctive preferences which express the same intention in the specific logic of each one of the symbolic subspaces."[24] Which is to say that contrasting practices must be understood as competitions, that their differences are organized by strategies of distinction or imitation, and that the diverse uses of the same cultural goods are rooted in the stable predispositions proper to each group.

Consequently, we have a choice between two models for making sense of texts, books, and their readers. The first contrasts discipline and invention, presenting these categories not as antagonistic but as an interrelated pair. Every textual or typographic arrangement that aims to create control and constraint always secretes tactics that tame or subvert it; conversely, there is no production or cultural practice that does not rely on materials imposed by tradition, authority, or the market and

22. Paul Veyne, *Les Grecs ont-ils cru à leurs mythes? Essai sur l'imagination constituante* (Paris, 1983); English translation *Did the Greeks Believe in Their Myths? An Essay on the Constitutive Imagination*, trans. Paula Wissing (Chicago, 1988).

23. Foucault, *L'Ordre du discours*, pp. 45–47.

24. As quoted in Pierre Bourdieu, *La Distinction. Critique sociale du jugement* (Paris, 1979), p. 193; English translation *Distinction: A Social Critique of the Judgement of Taste*, trans. Richard Nice (Cambridge, Mass., 1984).

that is not subjected to surveillance and censures from those who have power over words or gestures. Thus, a presumed "popular" spontaneity cannot be simply opposed to the coercions imposed by the authorities; what must be recognized is how liberties that are always restrained (by conventions, codes, constraints) and disciplines that are always upset articulate with each other.

Discipline and invention must be considered, but so must distinction and divulgation. This second pair of interdependent ideas enables us to posit an understanding of the circulation of objects and cultural models that is not reductive to a simple process of diffusion, one generally thought to descend along the social ladder. The processes of imitation or vulgarization are more complex and more dynamic and must be considered, above all, as struggles of competition. In these struggles every divulgation, conceded or won, produces simultaneously the search for a new distinction. Thus, once the book became a more common object and less distinctive by its being merely possessed, the manners of reading took over the task of showing variations, of making manifest differences in the social hierarchy. Simplistic, rigid representations of social domination or cultural diffusion must thus be replaced. Following Elias and Bourdieu, we can develop a means of understanding that recognizes the reproduction of distances at the very interior of the mechanisms of imitation, competition in the midst of sharing, and the constitution of new distinctions in the very processes of disclosure.[25]

These hypotheses and ideas enable us to attempt the study of print practices in former societies. These practices are a good entry point into European culture of the fifteenth to nineteenth centuries for two reasons. First, they fix or convey speech, which means that they cement sociabilities and prescribe behavior, cross into both private and public space, and give rise to belief, imagination, and action. They overturn the whole culture, coming to terms with traditional forms of communication

---

25. Norbert Elias, *Über den Prozess der Zivilisation. Soziogenetische und psychogenetische Untersuchungen*, 2 vols. (Frankfurt-am-Main, 1979; first published Basel, 1939), 2:312–454; English translation *The Civilizing Process*, 2 vols., trans. Edmund Jephcott (New York, 1982).

and establishing new distinctions. Second, they permit the circulation of writing on an unprecedented scale. Printing lowers the cost of the book's manufacture because the cost is distributed among all the copies of an edition rather than being supported by a single copy. In addition, printing shortens the time of production, which was very long for books in manuscript. After Gutenberg, the entire culture of the West could be considered a culture of print, because the products of presses and typographical composition, rather than being reserved for administrative and ecclesiastical uses as in China or Korea, themselves influenced all relations and practices.

We are left with a twofold ambition and a twofold task. On a small scale, we must understand the multiple, differentiated, contradictory uses of print, because competing authorities had faith in its powers and readers handled it according to their abilities or their expectations.[26] From a larger perspective, we must reinscribe the emergence of the printing press in the long-term history of the forms of the book or the supports of texts (from the *volumen* to the *codex*, from the book to the screen) and in the history of reading practices. Here, cultural history might find a new niche at the crossroads of textual criticism, the history of the book, and cultural sociology.

26. See the studies collected in Roger Chartier, *The Cultural Uses of Print in Early Modern France* (Princeton, N.J., 1987), and in *Les Usages de l'imprimé*.

Seven

Bodies, Details, and the Humanitarian Narrative

THOMAS W. LAQUEUR

Compassion itself eludes logic. There is no proportion
between the pity we feel and the extent of the pain by
which pity is aroused. . . . Perhaps it is necessary that it
can be so. If we had to and were able to suffer the
sufferings of everyone, we could not live. Perhaps the
dreadful gift of pity for many is granted only to
saints . . . and to all of us there remains in the best of
cases only the sporadic pity addressed to the single
individual, the Mitmensch, *the co-man: the human being*
of flesh and blood standing before us, within the reach of
our providentially myopic senses.
Primo Levi, *The Drowned and the Saved*

This essay asks how details about the suffering bodies of others engender compassion and how that compassion comes to be understood as a moral imperative to undertake ameliorative action. It is about the origins of eighteenth- and early-nineteenth-century humanitarianism.

Beginning in the eighteenth century, a new cluster of nar-

I delivered an early version of this paper as the Farnham Lecture at Princeton University in the Spring of 1987 and am immensely grateful for criticisms offered there by Peter Brown, Laura Engelstein, Isabel Hull, Peter Mandler, Joan Scott, and Lawrence Stone. I also want to thank Robert Abzug, Francis Ferguson, Catherine Gallagher, Stephen Greenblatt, Samuel Haber, Thomas Haskell, Lisbeth Hasse, Wendy Lesser, Randy McGowan, Gail Saliterman, Randolph Starn, Reginald Zelnik, and members of the History of Medicine and Culture Seminar at Berkeley, especially Ian Burney and Caroline Welberry, for their thoughtful and demanding criticisms of subsequent drafts.

ratives came to speak in extraordinarily detailed fashion about the pains and deaths of ordinary people in such a way as to make apparent the causal chains that might connect the actions of its readers with the suffering of its subjects. This aesthetic enterprise, various forms of which I will consider under the rubric "the humanitarian narrative," is characterized in the first place by its reliance on detail as the sign of truth. The realistic novel, the autopsy, the clinical report, and the social inquiry are all children of the empiricist revolution of the seventeenth century.[1] Unprecedented quantities of fact, of minute observations, about people who had before been beneath notice become the building blocks of the "reality effect," of the literary technique through which the experiences of others are represented as real in the humanitarian narrative.

In the second place, the humanitarian narrative relies on the personal body, not only as the locus of pain but also as the common bond between those who suffer and those who would help and as the object of the scientific discourse through which the causal links between an evil, a victim, and a benefactor are forged. The body is, of course, also the object of Christian mercy, of *misericordia*. But there is a difference. Christ's command to clothe, feed, and shelter the needy is construed in the Gospel as doing likewise to His body: "Verily I say unto you, inasmuch as ye have done it to one of the least of these my brethren, ye have done it unto me" (Matthew 25:40). The universal body of the risen God who ascended into heaven mediates here between sufferer and those performing acts of mercy. In the humanitarian narratives of the eighteenth and nineteenth centuries, in contrast, the individual body, alive or dead, came to have a power of its own. Indeed, the corpse, more so even than the vivified flesh, enabled the imagination to penetrate the life of another. A life that had ended could be retrospectively and definitively represented, while one still in

---

1. This point regarding the novel is of course one of the central theses of Ian Watt's *The Rise of the Novel: Studies in Defoe, Richardson, and Fielding* (Berkeley and Los Angeles, 1964). More generally on the new power of empirical evidence, see Barbara Shapiro, *Probability and Certainty in Seventeenth-Century England: A Study of the Relationships Between Natural Science, Religion, History, Law, and Literature* (Princeton, N.J., 1983).

progress remained elusive. "What draws the reader of a novel," Walter Benjamin observed, "is the hope of warming his shivering life with a death he reads about."[2]

Finally, and most importantly for the actual politics of reform, humanitarian narrative exposes the lineaments of causality and of human agency: ameliorative action is represented as possible, effective, and therefore morally imperative. Someone or something did something that caused pain, suffering, or death and that could, under certain circumstances, have been avoided or mitigated. In sharp contrast to tragedy, in which we feel for the suffering of the protagonist precisely because it is universal and beyond help—there is no invitation, or possibility, to do anything to prevent Macbeth's misdeeds and their consequences— the humanitarian narrative describes particular suffering and offers a model for precise social action.

The genre subsists in the matrix of detailed cause and effect, specific wrong and specific action. Coal miners die because of faulty ventilation fans, and seamstresses because of bad air and overwork; children lose their hands because drive belts are exposed, and Little Dick in *Oliver Twist* dies in direct consequence of the neglect he suffers at the hands of the overseers of the poor. Particular chemicals and industrial practices lead with epidemiological precision to particular diseases in groups of workers. In all these instances an analytic of suffering exposes the means for its relief. Great causes seem to spring from the power of *a* lacerated back, *a* diseased countenance, *a* premature death, to goad the moral imagination. For example, Granville Sharpe, one of the major figures in early British abolitionism, reports that he became involved with the plight of slaves when he discovered a black man, Jonathan Strong, waiting at the door of his brother William Sharpe to be treated for wounds inflicted on his back by his West Indian owner.[3] The wounds of one man, not the abstract wrongs of slavery, cried out, pierced his heart, and propelled him into the abolitionist cause.

For John Howard, the prison reformer, details likewise plead their own case, both for truth and for virtuous action: "My de-

2. Walter Benjamin, *Illuminations* (New York, 1971), pp. 100–101.
3. See Roger Anstey, *The Atlantic Slave Trade and British Abolition 1760– 1810* (London, 1975), p. 244.

scription will to some readers appear too minute; I chose rather to relate circumstances, than to characterize in general terms. By these, the legislature will be better acquainted with the real state of gaols." The bodies of prisoners assaulted his sensibilities: "their sallow meager countenances declare, without words, that they are very miserable." He saw much distress, he says, "but my attention was principally fixed by the gaol-fever and the smallpox." Again, the flesh speaks. From the minutiae of prison conditions and corporeal decay, which he so meticulously recorded, from these "scenes of calamity" sprang his personal crusade—"I grew daily more anxious to alleviate [them]." Details speak both to Howard's private consciousness and, through his narratives, to the outside world.[4]

I do not want to claim that narratives of the sort I have just described are the only means of arousing compassion or action. In Harriet Beecher Stowe's *Uncle Tom's Cabin,* for example, the breakup of the slave family, far more than the slave's lacerated back, is the imaginative vehicle for abolitionist sentiment. Rousseau argues that the displacement of concern from oneself to others, to the love of the whole, is accomplished through the abolition of property, that selfishness is a product of ownership. The narratives with which I am concerned worked in precisely the opposite way.[5] They created a sense of property in the objects of compassion, they appropriated them to the consciousness of would-be benefactors. My claim, therefore, is more modest: that a particular cluster of humanitarian narratives created "sympathetic passions"—bridged the gulf between facts, compassion, and action—in a wide variety of places and circumstances, but by no means exclusively or universally.

David Hume suggests how these narratives might work. A beautiful fish, a wild animal, a spectacular landscape, or indeed "anything that neither belongs, nor is related to us," he says, inspires in us no pride or vanity. The fault, however, lies not in the objects themselves but in their relationship to us. They are too detached and distant to arouse passion. Only when these "external objects acquire any particular relation to ourselves,

4. John Howard, *The State of Prisons* (London, 1929), sec. 7, p. 158; sec. 1, p. 1; introduction, p. xix.
5. I owe these points to my colleague Samuel Haber.

and are associated or connected with us," do they engage the emotions.[6] Ownership is for Hume the most obvious way for this to happen, and "humanitarians" do implicitly claim a proprietary interest in those whom they aid. They speak more authoritatively for the sufferings of the wronged than those who suffer can speak themselves. But, more generally, Hume is suggesting that moral concern and action are engendered not by the logic of the relationship between human beings but by the pain of a stranger crying out—*as if the pain were one's own or that of someone near.*

I begin my discussion of humanitarian narratives with the novel because it is the most obvious and most famous of the new genres of the eighteenth century and the one in which the relationship between the facts in the world, fictions about them, and the response of readers have been most discussed. Indeed, the novel, as Michael McKeon has argued, was created to mediate between the divided worlds of truth and of virtue: "The origins of the novel's mediatory project mark the discovery not of the relation between these realms but of an increasing division between them that is too great to ignore."[7] The novel is in a sense a genre born out of the problem Hume so neatly dissected when he said that it is not "contrary to reason to prefer the destruction of the whole world to the scratching of my finger."[8]

Although the novel is neither the earliest nor the prototypical form of humanitarian narrative, its creators are uniquely self-conscious of the power of their literary strategies. By "denying their own mode of production as mere fictions," as one critic puts it; by employing a variety of mimetic techniques (the

---

6. David Hume, *A Treatise of Human Nature*, ed. L. A. Selby-Bigge (Oxford, 1965), 2(9):303.

7. Michael McKeon, *The Origins of the English Novel, 1600–1740* (Baltimore, 1987), pp. 419–20.

8. Hume, *Treatise of Human Nature*, 3(iii):416. This fact of human nature had to be acknowledged as a given of moral discourse and yet also as a barrier to be more or less overcome. "If he were to lose his little finger to-morrow," said Adam Smith, "he would not sleep to-night. But, provided he never saw them, he will snore with the most profound security over the ruin of a hundred millions of his brethren, and the destruction of that immense multitude

narrator's claim that he or she is simply reporting on what happened in the outside world, the use of an immediate past tense, the accumulation of circumstantial detail, etc.), the novel creates a "lived" experience that gains authority by seeming to be a report of "actual experience."[9] Early in the history of the novel, when the conventions of realistic fiction had not yet taken root, writers had to labor hard to create the "realism effect." Defoe, for example, protests that his fictions are true: *Moll Flanders* is a slightly edited version of the protagonist's own account; Alexander Selkirk swears in proper legal form that his life is the basis of *Robinson Crusoe*. The epistolary novel relies on the intimacy of the letter to make its readers feel that they have instant access, despite print, to the thoughts and feelings of the correspondents in question.

The capacity of these sorts of narratives to elicit compassion is obvious. Anyone who has read about the black death in *Journal of a Plague Year*, the mine explosion in Zola's *Germinal*, or the prolonged death of Clarissa and of frail Paul Dombey is affected by these reports of the death of others. A common body, a shared organic nature, bonds reader and character. Here are the denouements of lives/stories that we believe and that touch us. And, although the rhetorical purpose of each of these episodes is different, all share a narrational technique that enforces commitment to the reality of human suffering and to its claim for sympathy.

But the novel is only the most self-conscious of the new "humanitarian narratives." The case history and autopsy develop at the same time and share both the techniques of the novel and its assumptions about agency. They constitute step-by-step ac-

---

seems plainly an object less interesting to him, than this paltry misfortune of his own" (Smith, *Theory of Moral Sentiments*, ed. A. L. Macfie and D. D. Raphael [Oxford, 1976], 3[3.4]:136–37). Jane Austen makes the same point, though with self-critical irony and with the hint that tending one's own moral garden is preferable to necessarily ill-conceived efforts to meddle in the affairs of strangers (see below). I am grateful to Wendy Lesser and Lisbeth Hasse, who suggested that I read Hume in connection with this paper, and to David Keightley, Barry Stroud, and Richard Teichgraeber for helping me to find and understand the relevant passages in both Hume and Smith.

9. Lennard J. Davis, *Factual Fictions: The Origins of the English Novel* (New York, 1983), pp. 155, 212–13, and passim.

counts of the history of the body in relation to itself and to social conditions, and provide therefore a model for the intelligibility of misfortune. Whether their rhetoric is intended to
lead to action or not, the medical writings I will consider present in purest form the amassing and ordering of vast quantities of detail so as to make real the pain of others and to offer a
logic of specific intervention. They expose, more explicitly than
the novel, the possibilities of action and mastery.

Case histories and autopsies thus constitute humanitarian
narratives not only because of their policy implications or because doctors were leading figures in a wide range of reform
movements both in Great Britain and on the Continent, but
also because they make bodies the common ground of humanitarian sensibility and explicate the history of their suffering.
Humanitarianism, while devoted to saving human lives, focuses its attention most powerfully on the dead and becomes a
guide to the mastery of death.

Like early novels, early versions of the medical narrative
with which I am concerned take the time to justify themselves—
to vindicate their subject matter and to stake out their claims as
a literary form. The great early-eighteenth-century Dutch phy-
sician Hermann Boerhaave defends his rummaging around in
the still sacred body in search of the organic foundation of a
patient's pain and suffering by claiming that through his enterprise other physicians will be better able to recognize the disease's "secret and dubious characteristics." He devotes considerable space to circumstantial detail, to "the singularity of the
disease," to making his readers believe that his stories are true
and beyond reproach. Because the conventions whereby the
veracity of medical narrative could be taken for granted are not
yet in place, he must distinguish himself explicitly from "de-
praved, insincere, and tenacious men who derive pleasure
from uncertain and suspicious tales spread among the popu-
lace." While novelists were creating a new fiction out of the
elements of news reports of dubious veracity, doctors like
Boerhaave labored to develop a new kind of factual medical re-
portage with claims to truth that would not be compromised by
association with a popular medical tall-tales tradition and sto-

ries of monstrous births, miraculous recoveries, or extraordinary physical endurance.[10]

Moreover, in both novels and medical reports, the reader is asked to sympathize with, to feel vicariously through, the body of the patient/protagonist. Boerhaave reads his patient's thoughts and speaks his words for him. "He then tried to tell me of the malady he was suffering, but could not; when he intended to talk, the pain prevented him." "Would that he could tell of this," the narrator laments: "'Think Boerhaave, what sufferings have tried my patience; you know what pains I suffered! Think what this is whose immensity forces groans from me that I cannot suppress.'"[11] The level of circumstantial detail is Balzacian. Boerhaave's readers know, for example, precisely what the man with the ruptured esophagus ate during his fatal illness, yet the narrator invites trust by admitting tiny gaps in his knowledge: he is unsure whether the sweetbreads were lightly roasted or fried, whether the duck that the patient swallowed but could not digest had been the breast or the thigh, whether the wine was from the Moselle or not. Who would not believe so scrupulously honest a guide?

When the patient dies and readers are allowed to discover what caused so much pain—that is, when the post mortem dissection is recounted—the precariousness and novelty of the genre become most evident. The self-confident rhetorical moves, the explicit procedures of nineteenth-century protocols, for example, are missing. Boerhaave instead labors to convey the sufferings of others in a new clinical way. He draws his readers in, bit by minute, detailed bit, so that they might discover the truths of the bodies in question. He opens the chest in one of his cases only slightly, he inserts his finger and explores. Only then does he confess, as though startled by a revelation: "I realized that there could be no more trustworthy way

10. Hermann Boerhaave, "Description of Another Dreadful and Unusual Disease," trans. Maria Wilkins Smith, *Journal of the History of Medicine* 23 (1968): 334; idem, "Atrocis, nec descripti prius, morbi historia" (History of a grievous disease not previously described), trans. Vincent J. Derbes, M.D., and Robert E. Mitchell, *Bulletin of the Medical Library Association* 43 (1955): 220.

11. Boerhaave, "History of a Grievous Disease," p. 222.

of observing the interior than by laying open the whole chest."
When he finally locates the tumor that had suffocated his patient, Boerhaave exclaims: "Imagine for yourself, my reader,
how horrified we were to see this huge and shapeless monstrosity in that spot, instead of the normal landmark of noble
viscera, and how we all touched and contemplated it."[12] Gothic
horror is brought home. There, in the body, is the organic pathology, in all its particularity, the very sight of which elicits
horror and compassion.

As for the man who suffered so mightily that he could not
speak, Boerhaave reports breathlessly on coming upon a rupture of the pleura: "But this was a monstrous and horrible thing
which was swollen! When I gently turned the tip of my finger
in the wound, it came upon a hiatus; it reached upon a rupture
of the esophagus. . . . I hardly believed what I found, and in
my amazement I called the others, showed them this strange
and odd thing." The autopsy stops here—as it would not have
a century later—because "religion, reverence, and piety prevented further scrutiny and laceration of the corpse." Pages
and pages have gone by, and finally Boerhaave reveals the
cause of so much pain and the fate of the painstakingly described meal. In summation, Boerhaave disarms his readers: "I
am sure my narration must have bored you."[13]

The humanitarian claims of these case histories are twofold.
In the first place, they construe suffering so as to elicit sympathy and display secular mastery of the body. But they also make
more rhetorically specific arguments for humane concern. Doctors in the eighteenth century subscribed explicitly to the "party
of humanity" as an element of their professional self-definition.
By the middle of the nineteenth century they no longer need to
proclaim this affiliation in their scientific writings; humane concerns are taken for granted. In autopsy protocols, as in the
naturalistic novel, humanitarian sensibilities are so much assumed that they go unspoken.

The connection between humanitarian as well as other political claims, on the one hand, and narratives of the body on the
other are still explicit in late-eighteenth-century medical writ-

12. Boerhaave, "Description of Another Disease," pp. 345, 347.
13. Boerhaave, "History of a Grievous Disease," p. 235.

ings. William Hunter, the leading British surgeon of the period, for example, published an extraordinarily compassionate defense of women accused of murdering their infant children.[14] It is framed as the expansion of a letter he had written earlier to a country magistrate who had asked him for advice in defending a particular girl accused of infanticide. This magistrate believed the girl to be innocent, though she had been found guilty, and he solicited the professional expertise of his friend the surgeon to support his case.

Hunter writes in a narrational voice familiar to readers of *Pamela* or *Clarissa*. First he claims, as would the novelist— explicitly in early-eighteenth-century works, less so later—that he has special knowledge of his subject, special knowledge of the "female character": "I have been in on their secrets, their counsellor and advisor in the moments of their greatest distress in body and mind."[15] The doctor, like the novelist and the humanitarian generally, has the authority to expose for scrutiny the subjective consciousness of others and to do so more effectively than they could themselves.

Hunter next invites readers to enter into the minds and bodies of supposed murderers and thereby feel for—or perhaps more precisely, through—them. "Women who are pregnant without daring to avow their condition are commonly objects of the greatest compassion. . . . Think seriously about what [under such circumstances] a fellow creature must feel." Women who kill their children, perhaps in an effort to take their own lives, might well be in a state of frenzy, fever, or lunacy. If they "raise our horror," they should "raise our pity too." But the real criminals are men, Hunter continues. While the would-be mother is "weak, credulous and deluded," the father, "having gained satisfaction, forgets his promises of marriage."[16] (The community and the justices of the peace, Hunter might have added, were increasingly unable or unwilling to enforce a promise of marriage; this situation led to a greatly increased bastardy rate and to greater temptation to commit infanticide.) A woman

14. William Hunter, "On the Uncertainty of the Signs of Death," *Medical Observations and Inquiries* (London, 1784), 6:269–90.

15. Ibid., p. 269.

16. Ibid., pp. 270–71.

with no shame would not try to hide a birth. Deception in Hunter's version of the story becomes itself a sign of virtue and an invitation to sympathize with the deceiver.

Implicitly, the authority for these commonplaces is Hunter's vast and famous clinical practice.[17] Much of the tract is taken up with social and anatomical details that solicit and justify his readers' compassion for women accused of murdering their babies. He tells of a newborn infant who was found dead in the room of its mother, a servant girl. Its lungs floated, so the child was presumed to have been born alive. Yet the mother did not murder it, as we, and contemporary authorities, might heartlessly have supposed. The servant had indeed hidden her pregnancy, but not with the intention of committing infanticide. She had made secret plans to have the child at a nearby house. When labor began, pain and terror overcame her and she fainted. When she awoke, the dead child lay in her wet clothes. She then put it in a box, where it was found. The landlady from whom she had planned to rent a room corroborated this story, and the girl was acquitted.[18]

But most of Hunter's testimony is more clinical. He stakes his credibility on experience with great numbers of bodies: live newborn children, stillborn children, as well as babies in various states of decay.[19] A scientific sensationalism demands the attention and sympathy of his audience. Hunter warns against always believing the floating-lung test, in which a dead infant's lungs are placed in water and if they float the child is presumed to have drawn a breath.[20] Lungs may float because of putrefac-

17. As Roy Porter argues, Hunter was the great medical entrepreneur of his time. His writing and anatomical teaching were widely known and were, far more than would be the case today, part of the cultural life of his times. See Roy Porter, "William Hunter: A Surgeon and Gentleman," in *William Hunter and the Eighteenth-Century Medical World*, ed. W. F. Bynum and Roy Porter (Cambridge, 1985), pp. 7–34.

18. Hunter, "On the Uncertainty," pp. 275–77. This set of extenuating circumstances is a commonplace in reports of infanticide, a stock defense.

19. Ibid., pp. 281–82.

20. Ibid., pp. 284–85. This test was based on the seventeenth-century Dutch naturalist Jan Swammerdam's observations and entered the forensic literature in 1690 when Johann Schreyer used it in defense of a woman accused of infanticide (*Erörterung und Erläuterung der Frage: Ob es ein gewiss Zeichen, ween eine todtend Kindes Lunge im Wasser untersinckt, dass solches in Mutter-Leibe gestorben sey?* [Zeitz, 1690]).

tion or because a mother breathed into her stillborn infant's mouth. He tells of a jury that had wanted, mistakenly, to convict a woman of murder because it believed that marks on her dead child could only have been made while the child was still alive and that only the accused had been in a position to inflict them. But Hunter offers to soften up the body in warm water, compress it, cool it again, and thereby produce identical marks on a decidedly dead body. The jury mercifully takes the point without the experiment having to be conducted. And on and on. "All of these facts," Hunter hopes, "may be the means of saving some unhappy and innocent women."[21]

The social narratives that Hunter interweaves with forensic medicine are absolutely standard eighteenth-century fare. Indeed, they gain power precisely because they are repeated in so many different contexts and become, through repetition and through association with the authority of medicine and law, the means for comprehending the actions of others. A coroner's inquest tells of a maid to Lady Tyrconnell who had kept her pregnancy secret from her fellow servants and who then delivered a premature but, according to the surgeon's evidence, live baby girl. In this version, the maid was saved by the detailed evidence of a housekeeper who testified that the accused had prepared baby clothes and had thus probably not intended, by murder, to hide her pregnancy forever. In printed reports of Old Bailey trials, in execution broadsheets of cases in which the defense failed, in ballads, and in forensic medicine texts, the tale is retold with slight modifications. The narrative form for "humanitarian" sympathy and action is thus widely disseminated.[22]

I do not want to imply that Hunter's interest in saving innocent women is purely altruistic or that the criminal law's greater or lesser zeal to prosecute infanticide is determined by transcendent principles of justice.[23] Clearly Hunter is staking out professional turf against the laity in general, against ignorant

21. Ibid., p. 290.
22. MS Westminster Coroner's Inquests, Westminster Abbey, 14 Jan. 1764.
23. See Thomas L. Haskell, "Capitalism and the Origins of the Humanitarian Sensibility," Part 1, *American Historical Review* 90 (1985): 339–61, esp. pp. 343–45, for a brilliant discussion of the relationship between class and other interests on the one hand and the intention to do good on the other.

magistrates, and against the legal profession. The great virtue of the modern age, as a later expert in medical jurisprudence put it, is that "the innermost recesses of human science are laid open"; knowledge once absent or exclusive is "rendered obvious, or at least accessible to the public at large."[24] And doctors, of course, are the ones who make all this possible.

Hunter and his colleagues are declaring epistemological sovereignty over the bodies and minds of others. Indeed, the medical man may know more about their actions and motivations than they know themselves. One of the leading forensic-medicine texts of the early nineteenth century cites the case of a distraught "poor woman of the name of Grimshaw" who confessed in minute detail to the murder of her child. But evidence from the doctor who examined the body belied her admission of guilt. When confronted with this exonerating testimony she "seemed much distressed in mind, and said in a low voice, 'I thought I had murdered the child, but I will leave it to the doctors to tell whether I did it.'"[25]

The central role of the body in exposing evil and creating a common ground of sensibility is clear. Its connection with humanitarian narrative is more apparent—and more explicitly intertwined with other cultural agendas—in the writings of another famous late-eighteenth-century doctor, John Ferriar of Manchester. He was the leader of a group of physicians active in factory reform, public health, and other good works and wrote extensively on a wide range of medical topics, including the

24. Michael J. Ryan, *A Manual of Medical Jurisprudence* (Philadelphia, 1832), p. 1.

25. William A. Guy, *Principles of Forensic Medicine* (New York, 1845; first published London, 1844), p. 14. Because gender and professional politics are inextricably linked, general claims are difficult to make. It is tempting to argue that Hunter, Guy, and their exclusively male colleagues are asserting a domination over the bodies and persons of their female clients. Yet the case cited just before the one I discuss involves six sailors who swore in great detail to having murdered the captain of a frigate. Medical examination of their states of mind proved that they had neither committed the crime nor so much as seen the officer in question. The professional imperative, which Guy wants to instill in his students, is to make careful inquiry into the states of mind of confessing parties and to collate carefully all the evidence. Regina Marantz, in *Sympathy and Science: Women Physicians in American Medicine* (New York, 1985), gives a nuanced and complex assessment of the relationship between gender and professional commitment.

physiology of dying.[26] Medical interest in death was institutionally bound up in England with humanitarianism. In the 1780s,
for example, the "Humane Society" was founded to resur-
rect those who seemed dead—victims of drowning, lightning,
trauma—but who could be saved if doctors and the public
learned to distinguish real from apparent death and applied the
appropriate first aid measures to victims in whom the spark of
life still smoldered. The Society sponsored research and writing both on the signs of death and on resuscitation techniques.

Ferriar's emphasis is somewhat different in that he is less interested in apparent death or the danger of premature burial
than in the right to die decently. The body is once again the
locus of discourse; an understanding of disease processes provides the narrative frame for attentive and considerate nursing.
Struggle in the last moments, Ferriar argues, would be eased if
those who tended the dying understood the physiology of
fleeting life. Biology dictates that it is merciful simply to let the
chronically ill go. "The approach of actual death produces a
sensation similar to falling asleep. The disturbance of respira-
tion is the only apparent source of uneasiness to the dying"
and should elicit no countermeasures. "Alternate tossing of the
arms" as death approaches may be an effort to assist the muscles
of the chest and aid breathing. In many cases, there is a considerable interval "between insensibility and the absolute cessa-
tion of existence"; the superstitious, cruel, and unnatural custom of moving a dying person from a bed to a hard mattress to
make it easier to "quit life" ought therefore to be stopped in the
interest of humanity. Ferriar condemns premature laying out,

26. Ferriar's work constitutes one of the most cogent and well-documented
early arguments for the centrality of the body in understanding and mastering industrial society. It is also a sustained call on the rich to regard disease as
a social concern for self-interested if not humanitarian reasons. "All infec-
tious poisons [Ferriar was an ardent miasmatist] originate in the human
body." These poisons begin with the poor, who in the new towns live exposed to all manner of pestilence, dirt, and decay. "By secret avenues it
reaches the most opulent, and severely revenges their neglect, or insensibility
to the wretchedness surrounding them" (John Ferriar, *Medical Histories and
Reflections* [London, 1792], 1:241). "Thus it appears," he says a few pages later,
"that the safety of the rich is ultimately connected with the welfare of the
poor and that a minute and constant attention to their wants, is not less an act
of self-preservation than of virtue" (1:246).

forcing liquids into a mouth that cannot swallow, "ignorant practitioners [who] torment [the] patient with unavailing attempts to stimulate the dissolving system," and unnecessary noise and bustle. Science is here explicitly in the service of "humanity."[27]

Ferriar's paper was reprinted by the Society for Bettering the Condition of the Poor as part of its program to improve the sensibilities of the poor, whose "brutality," it was thought, arose from ignorance. "Sound sense and medical knowledge," the Society hoped, would "find their way into the cottage, and assist the child, the wife, and the neighbor, in their last offices to their dying friend."[28] This wish is clearly not transcendently selfless. Medical imperialism is at work; the journal in which the article appears is dedicated to the preservation of paternal relations between rich and poor. Nevertheless, through this discourse of the body a common ground of feeling is established and the cognitive pathways for intervention laid in place.[29]

On a far more massive and pervasive scale, the parliamentary inquiry performs the same function.[30] Beginning in the early nineteenth century, variously constituted committees and commissions produced an extraordinary number of hitherto untold stories of human suffering. These in turn had an immense public life in their original "blue book" form and in the novels, tracts, and newspapers that in turn borrowed from the "blue books." Like novels and medical case histories, the parliamentary inquiry is characterized by rich layers of detail and by a more or less explicit commitment to expose the naturalistic origins of suffering. The body is again central. There was no more powerful symbol of degradation, no greater prod to the

27. John Ferriar, "Extract from Dr. Ferriar's Directions as to the Treatment of the Dying," *Reports of the Society for Bettering the Condition of the Poor* 2, 7 (1799): 286–92.

28. Ibid., p. 286.

29. Ferriar's case is particularly interesting because, while he clearly regarded medicine as the great engine of moral reform and thought nothing of direct, uninvited intervention in the lives of the poor, he thought it unethical for doctors to attend the dying on the grounds that where they could offer no help they should offer no services and collect no fees. His account of deathbed practice is thus less self-serving than it might appear.

30. I speak here specifically of England, but the accumulation of detail for purposes of reform is a European phenomenon. See, for example, William Coleman, *Death Is a Social Disease: Public Health and Political Economy in Early Industrial France* (Madison, Wis., 1982).

dormant moral conscience, than the image of the half-naked young girl pulling a coal wagon up a dark, low tunnel in the famous 1842 report on women and children in mines and manufacturing. Inquiry is explicitly tied to sympathy for the plight of strangers. The "interests of humanity demand consideration," said the first parliamentary select committee to investigate mine disasters in its technically sophisticated 1835 report. No "object of pecuniary interest or personal gain, or even the assumed advantages of public competition," can justify the owners of mines exposing men and boys to situations in which they are far from adequately protected.[31]

Before there were public inquiries, little was known about the dangers of mining, or of any other occupation for that matter. Such dangers figured in almost no stories except for the occasional broadsheet announcing the occurrence of a disaster and the number of men and boys killed. In 1813 a private committee was established in Newcastle to look into the dismally frequent accidents that took the lives and broke the bodies of miners. This committee observed that "townships and parishes were extremely negligent in calling upon coroners in cases of accidents"—that is, in calling on an officer of the crown to generate narratives about the deaths of miners.[32]

The 1835 parliamentary committee, and subsequent ones as well, made mining deaths a public issue, and in doing so created a new politics of narrative: what story, whose story, with what details should the story be told, by whom, and with whose account of agency? Many accidents, the 1835 committee learned, were simply never investigated. In Staffordshire, for example, if a rope broke, sending men careening back into a pit, a coroner's jury was called to pronounce on the mishap. But if the mine caved in, no inquiry was held. Why? "I know of no reason," says one witness, "only that it has not been customary." It was, in short, "customary" to regard inadequate support structures as God's work and outside the bounds of human agency, whereas frayed ropes were by convention the fault of someone.[33]

31. *Report of the Select Committee of the House of Commons on Accidents in Mines, Together with the Minutes of Evidence* 1835 (603) XX, p. v.
32. Ibid., pp. v, 22.
33. Ibid., Qs 3070, 3076–77, p. 22.

If an investigation did take place, the political question arose
of how far into the facts and into the victim's body it ought to
proceed. An extensive inquiry into a particularly catastrophic
explosion that killed over one hundred men in a pit near Walls-
end ended with the verdict that the explosion was due to some
"cause or causes . . . to the jury unknown" and that John Giles,
the representative corpse over whose burnt, bruised, and suffocated body the inquest was held, had died "accidentally, ca-
sually and by misfortune."[34]

This sort of verdict depended, as critics pointed out, on at
least two social facts that influenced its production. First, the
story was one about working miners told to, and ultimately by, a
jury whose members had an economic interest in a no-fault verdict and from which miners were systematically excluded.[35] But
more importantly, the verdict depended on a theory of causality—itself, of course, socially determined—that dictated what
facts were gathered and how they were interpreted. Many bodies, for example, as one medical witness pointed out, emerged
from explosions with nary a scratch on them. Why? Because
the main cause of death in explosions was from suffocation.
And why did the public not know this fact? Because the coroner did not inquire, "Why are so many killed? True you have
had an explosion, but why have so many perished?" as he
should have. And had he asked these questions, the public
would have learned that the danger in mines was not just from
gas but from improper ventilation doors that allowed an explosion to suck all the air from working areas, thereby leaving
miners, who would otherwise have survived a blast, dead from
lack of fresh air.[36] The greed of mine owners would, in short, be
shown to have killed those who on another account were dead
from an unavoidable explosion.

A government inspector of mines made the same sort of case

34. Ibid., p. 188. A copy of the inquisition submitted as part of the prepared testimony of a witness, Mr. John Buddle, is here reprinted.
35. See on these points the testimony of Martin Jude, a collier for thirty-
four years and subsequently an innkeeper and union official, in *First Report of
the Select Committee on Accidents in Coal Mines with Minutes of Evidence 1852–53*
(254) XX, Qs 1836, 1838; *Second Report . . . 1853* (740) XX, Q 2415.
36. *Report of the Select Committee of the House of Lords to Inquire into the Best
Means of Preventing the Occurrence of Dangerous Accidents in Coal Mines, with
Minutes of Evidence 1849* (613) VII, Q 1424. Since, as one broadsheet account of

to an 1852 committee convened, as were the others I have quoted from, "in the interests of humanity." What could be done, the committee asked, about reducing the death toll, which then stood at about one thousand a year? Coroners, he replied, "preclude all evidence excepting what bears immediately upon the accident; they will not allow evidence as to the general management and ventilation of the mine." Therefore explosions which might have justified criminal prosecutions of overseers or mine management were "passed over and *made* accidental death." An expert on jurisprudential medicine testified that coroners insisted on searching only for the immediate cause of death and that their scrutiny of mining catastrophes had "not been conducted exactly with the care and discrimination it ought to have been." The committee seems to have agreed, recommending that "more diligent inquiry should be made than has hitherto been customary into the remote as well as the proximate causes of explosion and loss of life."[37] The "high objects of humanity," said A. H. Wylie to parliamentary commissioners in 1864, as well as the "security of life among a hard-working and deserving portion of her Majesty's subjects," demanded more thorough inquiry.[38]

Marx was acutely aware of the rhetorical payoffs and dangers

---

a mine accident puts it, the men who could throw "any light on the catastrophe" were dead in the pit, autopsy and other forms of inquiry had to tell their story. The account is couched in terms of what caused "her" (mines are always referred to in the feminine) to take the lives she took. In this case it was not the explosion itself but, according to a surgeon, breathing the after-damp that killed the body being "sat upon" (Crime Box 3, John Johnson Collection, Bodleian Library, Oxford University).

37. *Report from the SCHC on Coal Mines, Together with the Proceedings of the Committee, Minutes of Evidence* 1852 (509) V, p. viii, Qs 841, 962, 1712.

38. *Appendix B to the Report of the Commissioners to Inquire into the Condition of All Mines in Great Britain* 1864 (3389) XXIV, pt. 2, pp. 459, 450, and 450–63 passim. This comment summarizes criticism of an inquiry into the deaths of a group of men whose box went careening into the sides of a mine shaft when the chain supporting the box broke. Verdict: "accidental death." "The question of the quality of the chain, and its breaking strain, were not gone into." A second inquiry into the deaths by scalding of two men when a boiler blew up was also defined as accidental death, despite the fact that the boiler was already old and corroded when it was installed nine years previously and that it had been jury-rigged to work "just a little bit longer" only two months prior to the fatal accident.

of such inquiries into the bodies of abused workers. He cites them frequently in the only part of *Capital* concerned with the daily lives and feelings of laborers, and he is clearly somewhat embarrassed by their novelistic, sentimental appeal. One week, to cite one of his many, many examples, all the London papers reported the oft-told story of "Death from Simple Overwork." Mary Anne Walkley, Marx recounts, worked as a needlewoman in one of London's "best millinery establishments" with sixty other girls, thirty in a room, for 26 1/2 hours uninterruptedly. They had available to them only one-third the cubic feet of air necessary for good health. (A long footnote reports that three hundred cubic feet are required for sleeping, five hundred for waking activities.) Mary Anne Walkley slept in a crowded bedroom divided from the other girls by boards. On Friday she was taken ill; on Sunday she was dead. Mr. Keys, the surgeon who was summoned too late to her deathbed, testified that "Mary Anne Walkley had died from long hours of work in an overcrowded workroom, and a too small and badly ventilated bedroom." "In order to give the doctor a lesson in good manners," Marx continues sardonically, "the coroner's jury thereupon brought in a verdict that 'the deceased had died of apoplexy, but there was reason to fear that her death had been accelerated by overwork in a crowded workroom.'" He concludes ambiguously with a quote from the free trade *Morning Star*, a paper whose politics he deplored but whose sentimental sensationalism he was willing to employ: "Our white slaves, who are worked into the grave, for the most part silently pine and die."[39]

These discussions of suffering and death are but tiny fragments of a vast literature, rich and unsettling in detail, that subsumes misfortune in a new moral and social discourse. Engineers point out how this or that sort of ventilation system will make mines safer. Doctors publish autopsies and epidemiological works that with novelistic precision tie the broken bodies of miners to their milieu, and particularly to whatever in that milieu might have been altered to produce a better outcome. Mountains of facts create the effect of reality in tales of suffer-

39. Karl Marx, *Capital*, trans. Ben Fowles (New York, 1977), 1(10.3): 364–65. I am grateful to Cathy Gallagher for calling these paragraphs to my attention.

ing and invite remedial action. An account of fever in one village notes that the local butcher killed his animals in the midst
of habitations, that the cottages were of rough stone and roofed
with heavy, locally quarried slabs, that green slime covered
pools of refuse, and so on. Along with the family history, personal history, and results of physical examination of some sixty-
three Cornish miners, a gigantic table reveals that one miner
had a cup of tea and bread and butter for breakfast; another
had the same plus a little meat made in the form of a pasty,
"with dough not 1/2 pound when cooked; he also takes milk,
eggs and vegetables." Another miner, although generally temperate, did have a pint or two now and then.[40] The statistical
body becomes here the lived body, which eats particular foods
and lives in a particular sort of house.

Like industrial novels, inquests use such detail in stories that
locate the lives and sufferings of others in a social context,
making them intelligible to readers of other places and periods.
Both genres are the product, and in some measure the creator,
of a mass public that feels itself implicated in the particular evils
that befall others and able to control these evils by incorporating them into narrative and action.

The autopsy in its maturity, like the nineteenth-century novel
and the inquest, can assume that its readers recognize its genre.
It is about what really happened. The body, almost by convention, is recognizable as a shared locus of sympathy binding
reader to text, and both to social context. But even more dra-
matically than either inquest or novel, the autopsy, a century
after Boerhaave, assumes a clear understanding of cause and
effect. Doctors might not have been able to prevent the death of
a particular patient, but the epistemological stage is set for the
mastery of death and consequently of lesser misfortunes. Further knowledge and technology, not a commitment to inter-
vene, are all that lack for an assault on physiological or moral
pathology. Thus, the systematic investigation of a particular patient's demise is paradigmatic of the sorts of narrative structures that make "humanitarianism" possible, even though—or

40. *Report of the Commissioners to Inquire into the Condition of All Mines in
Great Britain* 1864 (3389) XXIV, pt. 2, pp. 11, 31, and passim.

perhaps because—these narratives are written in the icy language of science.

Rudolph Virchow—one of the founders of social medicine with his study of typhus among Silesian weavers, a major liberal politician in the 1848 Frankfurt Parliament, and the author of the canonical pathology textbook of the late nineteenth century—brought the genre of the autopsy to fruition. What Haydn was to the symphony, Virchow was to the post mortem examination.[41]

Virchow begins his classic *Description and Explanation of the Method of Performing Post-Mortem Examinations* with a plea for a "regular method for pathologico-anatomical investigation" and with dire warnings of the disasters that would follow from sloppy, unsystematic observation. There would be no difficulty in collecting "a great number of examples in which the faulty performance of the autopsy had rendered obscure cases which, in themselves, [were] clear and simple, and had made unintelligible those which were at all ambiguous."[42] He sets out in exquisite detail how and why one ought to proceed through a body from outside in. In forensic practice one must open the abdomen before the thorax but not dissect it: note the position of the diaphragm and then go on to the chest cavity. By leaving the organs of the abdomen in place, one can more accurately observe the state of the blood in the ventricles of the heart. For pages he explicates the meaning of each procedure, denouncing hasty conclusions, insisting on order and method.

Finally, Virchow offers four examples of the master at work. Each case gives the impression of a great bulldozer of knowledge piling up facts, not in indiscriminate heaps, but in neatly ordered piles so that they might be intelligible to the trained observer. A calm intellectual power and confidence pervades each account. Case 1: "A man unknown. Dead when brought in. Face covered with blood. Left side of face, particularly about the ear, of a bluish-red color."[43]

41. For the history of the autopsy generally, see Lester S. King and Marjorie C. Meehan, "A History of the Autopsy," *American Journal of Pathology* 73 (1973): 514–45.

42. Rudolph Virchow, *A Description and Explanation of the Method of Performing Post-Mortem Examinations in the Dead-House of the Berlin Charity Hospital*, trans. T. P. Smith (London, 1880), p. 6.

43. Ibid., pp. 44–54.

Systematically, carefully, in full control, the pathologist un-
masks the secrets of the body. He brings to light what was not
(or even could not have been) known about a person before
death. Height, 1.75 meters; strongly built . . . adipose tissue
slight . . . hair on head abundant . . . front teeth perfect, molar
teeth more or less carious and defective . . . hands large . . .
nails long, the projecting edges filled with thick black dirt . . .
nothing particular about the body externally except that the
prepuce is unusually short, and covers no more than the edge
of the glans . . . no lesions evident on the penis. (We are still
only on the first page.) Gradually we work our way in and
through the body and conclude that this man died of ulcerative
consumption of the lung—that is, tuberculosis. He suffocated
from a slow pulmonary hemorrhage and edema; he did not
succumb simply to loss of blood or to occlusion of the airways
from extravasated fluid. Whether the morbid process began in
bronchiectasis or caseous, or necrotizing, pneumonia one cannot tell, but the latter finally supervened. Thus, not only the
cause of death but also its history and its essence—the specific
lung lesion of pulmonary tuberculosis—have been discovered
and made known.

All the stories I have produced so far have a specific rhetorical
purpose more or less related to the production of humanitarian
sentiment and reform. Even Virchow's account is a model of
what medicine, through the formal investigative procedure of
the autopsy, can offer to the world generally, to the police, to
public health, to literature (it is the model of Flaubert's and
Zola's naturalism)—to the human comprehension of death. But
I want to suggest that certain sorts of stories, whatever their
purpose, have the capacity to engender the kind of moral concern that arose in the late eighteenth century.

I thus conclude with a tale pieced together in 1764; I hesitate
to say "written," because no one would claim to be its author. In
many ways this story belies what I take to be its effect, because
it is about poor people who seem emotionally indifferent to the
fact that they find a dead child on a dungheap. No one in the
story seems the slightest bit moved by the unsavory denoue-
ment. So in an important sense I—and you—will read it against
the grain.

At the same time, however, my final narrative is evidence of a cultural propensity to produce extraordinarily full stories about the misfortunes of the poor even when the rhetorical purpose of such production remains hidden to us and ambiguous to its producers. A circumstantial web of sympathy is woven almost of its own accord. The genre is the coroner's inquest, itself a medieval institution. But the density of fact—of detail—about the precipitate deaths of ordinary people is rare before the eighteenth century. Before then, coroner's inquests, for example, generally reported simply that a body was found and that it came to be in that state because of "misadventure" or "causes unknown," "accident" or "suicide." One presumes that some discussion was held before the coroner's jury rendered this verdict, but if so it is rarely recorded. Nor were professional finders of fact about bodies—that is, doctors—consulted in any but a very small number of cases.[44]

My story is from an "Information taken the sixth day of February, 1764, at the Parish of St. Ann's within the Liberty of Westminster in the County of Middlesex, on an inquisition taken on View of the Body of a Newborn Female Child lying dead in the said Parish Liberty and County."[45] It could have been from hundreds of other inquisitions, Old Bailey reports, or broadsheets. My inquest begins with William Hawkins, who worked for one Henry Sawkin. A gardener, Hawkins had on the previous Saturday morning been employed hauling dung. Between eleven and twelve he was filling his master's cart out of a hole covered with broken boards in a yard off Oxford Street. According to Hawkins, for some time while he was pitching dung two young men stood around watching him. After a while one of them, Hawkins reports, said that he, Hawkins, ought to be careful with his fork because there was a cloth under-

44. We actually do not know whether detailed depositions were kept before the 1750s, when new procedures for paying coroners may have encouraged them to keep more of the records they produced. We do know, however, that almost no depositions as extensive as the quite routine one I discuss below exist prior to the mid eighteenth century, except for a few isolated instances. I am indebted to Michael MacDonald of the University of Wisconsin, who has made the most extensive recent study of inquests, for this information.

45. Among the MS Westminster Coroner's Inquests, Westminster Abbey Muniments Room.

neath the dung. Hawkins looked but saw nothing. After he had pitched a bit more dung, however, he did indeed come upon a linen cloth in which a baby girl was "wrapt up very tight and tied with a string, [with] one of the deceased's feet being out of the said cloth."

He opened the cloth and saw the rest of the baby, which, he thought, must have been dead for some time. No one, he says, could have seen the cloth in which the baby was wrapped simply by passing along Oxford Road. A woman working for the Overseers of the Poor soon came and took the body.

The jurors hearing this case are next told by George Wilkinson—who lodges with one Mr. Williams, a butcher, and who, with his friend John Turner of Newport Alley, had been to Covent Garden to buy some greens on that particular Saturday morning—that he, Wilkinson, "having occasion to ease himself, and on going into a Dung hole in Oxford Road for that purpose," saw a cloth with something wrapped in it. He said to his friend, John Turner, "I believe I have found a prize." But of course when he opened it he found instead the corpse of a child. The two men reported their discovery to a Mr. Porter at the King's Arms and then returned with a group of people to the dung hole where the encounter that Hawkins described had taken place. When the carter took up the child and opened the cloth neither Wilkinson nor anyone else saw any marks of violence. All agreed the child had been dead for some time.

Turner—the friend—is questioned and corroborates all of this. He points out, however, that he did not touch the body and cannot say whether it was alive or dead. Moreover, while he and Wilkinson were talking, a man and a woman came up. The man "advised [them] to leave the Child there, for they otherwise would be obliged to Bury it." It is not clear whether "they" refers to the couple, who might have abandoned the child on the dungheap to avoid funeral expenses, or to the men who found the body. Turner confirms that they did put the child back in the dung and that they have no idea who left it there initially, nor when it was left.

Finally, a surgeon/apothecary is called who testifies that the bone on the forepart of the baby's head is pressed down and separated (more than is normal, one presumes) from the other bones of the head. He thinks that pressure to the head killed the baby, whose tied umbilical cord is evidence that she was born alive.

The document says no more; no verdict is attached. It lay undisturbed until I opened it; the grains of sand that had been used to dry the ink fell out onto my notebook. Its purpose remains unclear, since nothing but the surgeon's views seem relevant to determining the cause of the baby girl's death. The mysterious man and woman who might have killed the child are passed over in less than a sentence. The piece is immensely revealing of all sorts of things: the lack of concern about where one relieved oneself in the midst of a big city; the fact that the smell of all this excrement is so taken for granted that it does not warrant comment; the concern of the putative parents that if the child were recognized as theirs it would have to be properly buried at their expense.

But the case's very graininess, its texture of bodies and things, takes over even without any of these observations or immediate rhetorical purpose. Some people have begun thinking and feeling in new ways. Almost in spite of themselves, new sorts of stories are being told and new understandings are becoming possible. A narrative habit has begun to form in the eighteenth century that will eventually make dead babies in dungheaps a thing to inspire compassion, even if that compassion—as the history of cruelty in our times makes abundantly clear—is so easily shut off.

By making formal aspects of narrative itself a central actor in the history of humanitarianism I do not, however, claim that stories exercise power independently of an audience whose responses are determined by material and ideological conditions outside the realm of language. Narrative as an actor in games of power and the heart is no more, but also no less, independent of its social context or of its intellectual milieu than are new religious ideas, new class interests, or new gender relations. Far from escaping the questions of social history, I want to embrace them on new ground. For example, everyone acknowledges the importance of evangelicalism in the moral reform movements of the eighteenth century. But it has long been clear that evangelicalism did not itself subscribe to new moral precepts that would for the first time have extended compassion to slaves, fallen women, or child workers. Nor was the theology of evangelical conversion new. Why, then, did old notions of good and redemption lead to new actions?

It was once enough to point to the fortuitous rise of a generation of transcendently good men and women. This will no longer do. Nor is the reduction of religious interests to a more or less self-conscious expression of class interests satisfactory.[46] But a common historical ground appears if we juxtapose humanitarian narratives of the sort I have been discussing with a science of the heart, as John Wesley called it. The production of the personal conversion account on the one hand and Howard's prison inquiries on the other, of a medical case history and a narrative of slave suffering, become part of a single cultural propensity to use detailed description of the body as a common locus of understanding and sensibility. Pointing out family resemblances over a wide discursive field does not, of course, solve the problem of their ultimate origin, if indeed a stable first cause exists. But it does suggest that one might investigate the social conditions for the rise, not just of evangelicalism or some other movement or intellectual tendency, but of realistic narratives of the lived body generally.

Finally, my concentration on narrative does not constitute a denial of the connection between humanitarianism and capitalism. Rather, I follow Thomas Haskell in suggesting that class interest is not the only mediator between culture and the marketplace. There is an "isomorphism between modes of thought common to economic life and to judgments of moral responsibility" that binds the world of the market to that of conscience. Haskell turns Weber on his head: the market shapes character as much or more than character shapes the market. The market for Haskell need not have been, but did happen to be, the force that induced caring for a wide variety of unfortunates. Contract is the nub of this connection. Through contract, two conditions of humanitarian concern—a sense of obligation and a faith in

46. There is no better critique of this view than in Haskell, "Capitalism and the Humanitarian Sensibility," Part 1, pp. 341–53.

the remote consequences of actions—are made evident and valorized.[47]

I want to argue similarly regarding the narrative forms through which humanitarianism is thought. A civilized world as imagined by Adam Smith or his Scottish enlightenment colleagues—a world of common sensibility and shared sympathy, of common desires and drives, of scientific rational predictability—is the world of the humanitarian narrative. And conversely in their view, both economic desires and moral sensibility are perverted by the same social pathologies, the same backwardness in cultural evolution.

By concentrating on texts I hope to have gone beyond them to suggest that the social history of humanitarianism must include a history and sociology of narrative forms. A new question is posed: under what conditions can we speak of other individuals so as to care for them?

Sadly, narrative forms like the novel, inquiry, and autopsy, however much they might be at the service of a "party of humanity," do not of themselves engender a particular moral response. Quite to the contrary, some would say. The Marxist critic Georg Lukács, for example, condemns the naturalist novel of Flaubert and Zola, which is based explicitly on medicine as the model descriptive science, for its moral neutrality—in contrast to the morally ordered universe of Dickens. Berthold Brecht goes further to argue that, far from inciting to action, the sorts of enthralling narratives I have discussed merely milk sentiment and defer revolutionary action. Moral indignation is spent on fictional suffering, while real suffering is left in peace.[48] In modern medicine, technology and the languages of science obscure rather than illuminate the realities of death.

Furthermore, humanitarian narrative—indeed, the claim for the possibility of powerful concern for humanity generally (that

47. Thomas L. Haskell, "Capitalism and the Origins of the Humanitarian Sensibility," Part 2, *American Historical Review* 90 (1985): 547 and passim.

48. The attraction of narrative over reality is of course not Brecht's discovery. Augustine berates himself for weeping over the story of Dido's ill-fated love of Aeneas "while amid such things, dying to you [God], . . . I most wretchedly bore myself about with dry eyes"—even his own state is less powerfully present to him than the one conveyed by fiction (*The Confessions of St. Augustine*, trans. John K. Ryan [Garden City, N.Y., 1960], 1(13.20): 56.

is, not just for oneself or those naturally near)—created dialectically its antithesis. "How horrible it is to have so many killed!" Jane Austen wrote to her sister Mary after two British victories in the Peninsular Wars. "And what a mercy one cares for none of them!"[49] With self-undermining irony she acknowledges both the horror of mass death and the relief that her naval brothers were safely elsewhere, both an awareness of the correct moral ordering of deaths and gratitude for not feeling it as acutely as its enormity demands. It is as it should and must be, she says, that she could bear with a distancing detachment the news of military slaughter and at the same time be concerned for Mary lest the departure of a clergyman from the parish diminish her social life, be comforted at there "being two Curates now lodging in Brookham, besides their own Mr. Warneford from Dorking, so that I think she must fall in love with one or the other," and be genuinely distressed that "poor F. Cage has suffered a good deal from her accident."[50] Austen understood Hume's point that it is not irrational to care more for one's own finger than for the deaths of millions of Chinese.

Fifty years later, in an age when both humanitarianism and its opposition were shriller, Dickens makes the same point, but more hysterically. The word *humanitarian* had by then come into use and was almost exclusively a term of contempt describing the moral perversion of caring more for those at a distance than for those near. Mrs. Jellyby in *Bleak House* is Dickens's most famous parody of the type. She is furiously busy with helping the natives of distant Borrioboola-Gha by introducing the cultivation of coffee beans, while her own house is "not only very untidy, but very dirty," her younger children miserable, and her eldest daughter furious that her mother seems to

49. R. W. Chapman, ed., *Jane Austen's Letters*, 2d ed. (London, 1952), p. 286 (no. 73, Friday, 31 May 1811). I presume these remarks are in response to news of the British victories in the battles of Fuentes de Onoro and Albuera, 5 and 16 May 1811. Neither of Jane Austen's naval brothers were present at those conflicts: Charles John had just returned from North America, and Francis William, the future admiral, was engaged in blockading the French coast (G. H. Tucker, *A Goodly Heritage: A History of Jane Austen's Family* [Manchester, 1983], pp. 176, 185).

50. *Jane Austen's Letters*, pp. 319–20, 324 (no. 82, to Cassandra Austen, 15 September 1813).

place her duty to the Africans above her duty to her family: "Oh don't talk of duty as a child, Miss Summerson; where's Ma's duty as a parent?"[51] Decades later others undermine Dickens's own creation of sympathy for the ultimately distanced person, the fictional creature. "Nell, in the *Old Curiosity Shop*, was killed for the market, as a butcher kills a lamb," John Ruskin complained; one would have to have a heart of stone not to laugh at her death, as Oscar Wilde put it in a famous epigram.[52]

Any history of humanitarianism and humanitarian narrative, these criticisms remind me, will require a careful analysis of both its production and its reception.[53] It will require an inquiry into both explicit moral messages and the central question of why the moral franchise is extended at any given time to one group but not another.

Here, however, I maintain only that the extension of compassion to others and the moral imperative to act on their behalf depend on habits of feeling and theories of causation that are also the foundation of the new sorts of narrative I have described. Moreover, these narratives did—the Mrs. Jellybys of the world not to the contrary—allow some people to bridge the gap between themselves and strangers, between fact and action. Narrative functioned, I suggest, to arouse the "sympathetic passions" and make "is" seem, at least for a moment, to imply "ought."

51. Charles Dickens, *Bleak House* (New York, 1983), chap. 4, p. 35; chap. 5, p. 44.

52. Quoted in Regenia Gagnier, *Idylls of the Marketplace: Oscar Wilde and the Victorian Public* (Stanford, Calif., 1986), pp. 22–23.

53. David Miller has produced a brilliant and sustained analysis of the power of narrative forms. I am thinking particularly of his "Discipline in Different Voices: Bureaucracy, Police, Family, and *Bleak House*," *Representations* 1 (1983): 59–91; and "The Novel and the Police," *Glyph* 8 (1981): 127–47.

Eight

Seeing Culture in a Room for a Renaissance Prince

RANDOLPH STARN

Over the past few years I have been looking with an art historian at pictures in the surviving council halls and audience rooms of medieval and Renaissance Italy. These rooms of state and their decorations are sites where art—especially painting—and politics were programmatically conjoined in three different centuries under three different regimes: civic republics in the fourteenth century, princely courts in the fifteenth, and "triumphalist" states in the sixteenth. In looking at the pictures, I am especially interested in seeing how regimes of power correspond to regimes of symbolic practice or, more precisely, how different artistic styles and modes of picturing encode distinct political messages and ideologies.[1]

This paper grows out of work for a book on rooms of state in medieval and Renaissance Italy that I have been writing in collaboration with my Berkeley colleague Loren Partridge. An earlier version was presented at the Harvard Center for Italian Renaissance Studies at Villa I Tatti in Florence, and I want to thank the I Tatti community, in particular my hosts there, Louise and William Clubb, for a cordial reception. Further thanks to Thomas Laqueur and to members of my graduate seminar, especially Susan Grayzel, for their helpful comments.

1. I analyze such correspondences in a republican setting in "The Republican Regime of the 'Room of Peace' in Siena, 1338–40," *Representations* 18 (1987): 1–34; on "triumphalism," see Loren Partridge and Randolph Starn, "Triumphalism and the Sala Regia in the Vatican," *Papers in Art History from the Pennsylvania State University* (forthcoming).

There is, of course, nothing new about working on the frontier between history and art, especially not in Renaissance studies, where interdisciplinary trespassing was common from the start. If anything, the double vision of the art-and-context studies of recent years actually reinstates an old academic division of labor by introducing history as a provider of background, meaning, or message for art to reflect, express, or communicate. If, however, the "linguistic turn" and cultural anthropology are the royal roads of a "new" cultural history, then I shall leave most of the traffic to the other contributors to this volume. Since the iconographers are already committed to "reading" images as texts, and the social historians of art to treating them as cultural artifacts, the really innovative task is to look at these images critically. In the scattered and uneven returns of recent work in cultural history, what I identify with most readily is the more or less explicit premise that cultural historians must be concerned as much with form as with content and, further, that the formal properties of cultural performances or productions *have* content as representations of structures of authority. This line of inquiry draws much of its energy from a "poststructuralist" moment or mood that has its own cultural history. In short, it has come to seem newly possible and pressing to see art as a form of power while at the same time charting the traces of power represented in the forms of art.

The frescoes painted by Andrea Mantegna (1431–1506) in the castle of the Gonzaga lords at Mantua are a good case study, not only because they are famous icons of Renaissance culture, but also because they constitute a dazzling display of the cultural and political claims of pictorial forms.[2] The pictures occupy two adjacent walls and the ceiling of the room known since the late sixteenth century as the Camera degli Sposi, or "Bridal Chamber." In the interpretive tradition of which the

2. The authority on the Camera is Rodolfo Signorini, whose years of research and writing have culminated in a sumptuous monograph, *Hoc Opus Tenue: la Camera dipinta di Andrea Mantegna; lettura storica, iconografica e iconologica* (Parma, 1985); like all scholars interested in Renaissance Mantua, I am indebted to Professor Signorini for sharing his unstinting enthusiasm and learning with me. I should also like to thank Professor Antonio Paolucci and Dr. Ugo Bazzotti of the Soprintendenza per i Beni Artistici e Storici in Mantua for facilitating a visit to Mantegna's Camera in the summer of 1986.

1. Andrea Mantegna, Camera degli Sposi, Palazzo Ducale, Mantua, 1465–74. The Court of Ludovico and Barbara Gonzaga (detail). Photograph courtesy of the Gabinetto Fotografico Nazionale, Rome.

frescoes are themselves a part, the scenes of the court of Ludovico and Barbara Gonzaga (fig. 1) and of the so-called Meeting, on the north and west walls respectively, are usually regarded as model illustrations of the picture-as-window prescribed by Renaissance art theory and elaborated in Renaissance painting; in effect, they invite the viewer to look through a framed opening into another "world" coextensive with but other than one's own. Such pictures guide us through the picture surface to a world that is seemingly registered and recorded; their paradoxical achievement as art is to deflect attention from their artistry into the archives, texts, and circumstances that they appear to be about. The painted ceiling (figs. 2–3) engineers even more elaborate effects. We see complex architecture centered on the oculus that opens to a fictive morning sky—all on a simple vault. Enigmatic figures in virtuoso poses appear around the central opening, and the painted decorations of the vault simulate garlands and ribbons, sculptural relief, medallions of ancient emperors, and scenes in mosaic from classical mythology. Although the documentation is thin, we know that Mantegna worked on the room between 1465 and 1474, that it was used as a multipurpose audience room and bedchamber, and that it was noticed and admired by contemporaries. Vividly restored just a few years ago, the spectacle still impresses even the distracted crowds that are herded through the showplaces of the Gonzaga lords of Mantua.

In what follows I will limit discussion to the painted ceiling. Although this part of the room calls for a more extended treatment than I can give it here, it does bring together in one place a full Renaissance repertory of pictorial effects that seem, at first sight, to be the most idealized and least political in the ensemble. The physical act of looking upward brings with it a contrast between one "world" and another, between the courtly settings of the palace and a realm that in all respects rises over and above the space beneath. While the lower area defines a zone of public, purposeful, and mostly male activity, the vault is set apart as a higher region of leisure, inspiration, and learning, of the feminine, the angelic, the exotic, and the antique. We see distinctions here, so it seems, between "high culture" and a more mundane, if hardly informal, one; but since the contrasts come together in the same room, we can also interpret them as complementary sides of a Renaissance commonplace. The *vita activa* of the walls, we might say, sustains the *vita contemplativa* of the ceiling, which in turn supposedly inspires, legitimates, and perfects the activity represented below. These are perfectly plausible interpretations. They have the authority of Renaissance traditions and of traditional views of the Renaissance behind them; the court of Mantua itself would surely have appreciated the flattering claim that it recognized and ultimately resolved the tensions of Renaissance culture. But the virtues of

2. Camera degli Sposi, ceiling. Photograph courtesy of the Gabinetto Fotografico Nazionale, Rome.

such accounts are not without liabilities. These interpretations take brilliantly assertive and demanding pictures as passive illustrations of prescribed themes, and they put us in the position of rehearsing a self-serving ideology as our own interpretation.

So, rather than setting sights on what the painted ceiling allegedly represents, I want to consider some implications of *how* it represents. This means starting from the responses that the

3. Camera degli Sposi, oculus. Photograph courtesy of the Gabinetto Fotografico Nazionale, Rome.

pictures solicit from the viewer, from the three modes of visual attention which I call the glance, the measured view, and the scan. Since the evidence is mostly visual (which is consistent with the etymology of the word *evidence,* I might point out), we do not need much of the culling of supporting texts that usually passes for cultural history or, for that matter, art history. Even so, this is not merely a formal exercise. As we shall see, the ways in which we are invited to look are not only embedded in the culture and politics of the Renaissance court; they are also constituent forms of its political culture.

The Glance

Looking up, the viewer's eyes are soon drawn to the "eyes" of the ceiling: the oculus and the look of what appear to be three girls peering over the rim. Thus, practically from first sight, the ceiling is an invitation to visual play and punning whereby permanent and calculated effects appear as casual and transitory details. Some figures positively dare us to doubt. The hand poised on the pole holding the barrel out in space can just as well be imagined as pushing that all too slender support away as securing it; the fruit held by the plump putto across the way, too large for the pudgy hand, may be about to drop at any moment. These little dramas occur in an architecture that never existed, under a painted sky illuminated by a fictitious morning light.

There is no way of knowing just how to take the three "girls," whose eyes seem to prompt these impressions—whether they are taunting, flirtatious, amused, or something else again (fig. 4). They appear a little to one side, in the opening that is itself set apart as a playful yet somehow celestial realm. Off center, seemingly intent but without clear motivation, directed but indeterminate, their look comes to us as a glance. In his treatise on painting from the 1430s, Leon Battista Alberti advises painters to make their pictures more animated and convincing by including at least one figure that seems to address the viewer, calling attention to the scene and offering a knowing commentary.[3] We could leave it at that, with Mantegna's trio as an illustration. But I want to follow their glances along a familiar trajectory of Renaissance courtly culture, which leads art to aestheticize epistemology and both art and epistemology to practice politics. What Alberti does not say, among other things, is that the beckoning function *requires* the response it pretends only to solicit, for by positing a contingent response, the painting acknowledges the need for a beholder. Unlike the trees in Bishop Berkeley's forest that, until noticed, cannot be said to exist, the three figures watch for the answering gaze that confirms their existence. In this sense their look, far from being desultory, is a sign of necessary dependency, and the apparent playfulness is a serious bid for recognition.

Through this appeal to a visual exchange where considerations of seeing and knowing are practically inseparable we enter into a courtly calculus of status and power.[4] In the first

3. Leon Battista Alberti, *On Painting*, rev. ed., trans. John R. Spencer (New Haven, Conn., 1966), p. 78.

4. On this large issue I have profited especially from Stephen J. Greenblatt, *Renaissance Self-Fashioning* (Chicago, 1980), and Frank Whigham, Jr., *Ambition and Privilege: The Social Tropes of Elizabethan Courtesy Theory* (Berkeley and Los Angeles, 1984).

4. Camera degli Sposi, oculus (detail).

place, there is what we may think of—and surely see at work on Mantegna's ceiling—as the fundamental rule of visual exchange at court: "We are seen, therefore we are." As Castiglione puts it in *The Book of the Courtier,* the courtier shows himself "remembering the place where he is, and in the presence of whom, with proper devices, apt poses, and witty inventions that may draw on him the eyes of the lookers on as the magnet attracts iron."[5] In the exclusive little theaters of court life, to adopt one of its own metaphors, the world, or what we know of it, exists in the beholder's eye. Audiences spring up everywhere, including an internalized one that expects an external show appropriate to the occasion, or, in Renaissance terms, governed by decorum. Anything like a private self is only the impresario that directs the production or the residual consciousness that remains after it is done. Since the audience is itself suspect as a sum of calculating poses, there is nothing that can

5. Baldassare Castiglione, *Book of the Courtier,* trans. Charles Singleton (Garden City, N.Y., 1957), p. 72.

be relied on, no secure referent, to bring the performance to an end. In this shifting state of affairs, heaven might truly lie in the look of Mantegna's painted maidens.

Yet the fixed look is designed to seem spontaneous and the contrivance casual. The impression of being "followed" by a painting is a familiar one, especially in cases where we can fix on some riveting detail—a pointing gesture, a radically fore-shortened object, a human eye.[6] But rules of effortlessness and interdeterminacy at court—the *sprezzatura* or "nonchalance" of Castiglione's model courtier, or the *grazia* of the perfect courtly artifact—are also at work here, as successive aesthetic and so-cial escalations of the fundamental rule of visual exchange at court. The more standardized the gesture, the more super-fluous it is likely to seem; the more ritualized the performance, the more it discounts by its predictability the need that it be seen at all. Gestures that anybody can learn will not close the charmed circle of the court to interlopers and so preserve the fiction that its privileges are inborn and natural signs of good breeding. Hence the appeal at court of the game, the puzzle, or the joke, activities in which the move is up to the player, and in that sense spontaneous, while the norms of play are closely regulated, and in that sense arbitrary and conventional. Even though someone must lose in these sublimated versions of the courtly scramble for place, all the initiated have insiders' pre-rogatives that effectively disenfranchise everyone else; win or lose, they know how the game is played. If we knew for certain that the painted glances in Mantegna's work were playing such games, then they would not be playing to perfection. Clear meanings remain beneath the threshold of easy recognition. The absence of transparent intelligibility that incites our desire to be let in on the secret also tests our credentials to share in-side knowledge.

That such effects are projected through the looks (in various

6. Michael Kubovy explains this phenomenon well: "If you are looking down the barrel of a gun, you need to take only a very small step sideways in order not to be looking down the barrel of a gun. We say here that objects are represented in a visually unstable situation. . . . It is quite natural, therefore, that we perform the unconscious inference: the object is shown in a visually unstable orientation; I am moving enough to destabilize the view; the view is not destabilized; therefore, the object must be turning to follow me" (Kubovy, *The Psychology of Perspective and Renaissance Art* [Cambridge, 1986], pp. 85–86).

senses) of female figures points to rules of gender in the courtly
arts of seeing and being seen. Although the women on the ceiling seem, however mysteriously, to be actively motivated and
engaged, their only very conspicuous function is to look or to
be seen. Even the figure whose gesture with the comb seems
straightforward will cease to act—or so we imagine—when the
primping is done. But how do we really know that these figures
are meant to represent women? I have taken this identification
for granted so far, but the evidence is hardly certain. We see
only heads, at most a glimpse of neck and shoulder; the "girl"
with the comb could easily be a "boy," whereas the "Moorish
maidservant" with the checkered headdress might just as well
be, say, a "Berber prince." My point is not that the figures represent males, but rather that there is nothing incontrovertibly
female about them—in other words, they are gendered by the
"feminine" role they perform. According to conventional Renaissance (male) lore, "it is the eyes of a woman that do more to
attract and allure a man to love . . . than any other beautiful
and remarkable part." The equally standard response calls for
the feminine glance to be returned and mastered: "Fix your
glance lasciviously on her eyes because your thoughts . . . will
descend to the woman's heart, penetrating through the entry-
way of her eyes . . . to the most secret parts, almost as if they
were poison, corrupting the blood, imprinting your name and
your desire firmly in her heart."[7] If Mantegna's figures are feminine, they are surely not innocent girls. As objects of the look
that they themselves seem coyly to invite, they authorize the
desire of the male viewer and submit to its mastery. These are
conventions of femininity that hardly had to be invented in recent theorizing about gender; they are, after all, commonplaces
of the "analysis" of women in courtly literature—the same conventions, it has been argued, that are reinscribed in the rules of
courtly behavior and that, in effect, feminize the persona of the

7. Federico Luigini da Udine, *Il libro della bella donna* (Venice, 1553), in
Trattati del Cinquecento sulla donna, ed. Giuseppe Zonta (Bari, 1913), p. 235;
and Francesco Sansovino, *Ragionamenti d'amore* (Venice, 1545), in *Trattati
d'amore del Cinquecento*, ed. Giuseppe Zonta (Bari, 1912), p. 167. I quote from
A. Christine Junkerman, "*Bellissima Donna*: An Interdisciplinary Study of Ve-
netian Sensuous Half-Length Images" (Ph.D. diss., University of California,
Berkeley, 1988).

courtier.[8] In any case, we do not need to look further than the Camera degli Sposi to see the combination of seductive appeal and compliant submission that signals the roles of the Eternal Feminine and the Perfect Courtier.

The fact that these effects have provoked stereotypically "masculine" reactions says something for their gendered character. In the face of ambiguity and indeterminacy, art historians have usually attempted to impose an unequivocal meaning, or master text, on this imagery. One such reading sees the women in the oculus as a kind of celestial transfiguration of Barbara Gonzaga and the women at court; another looks on the scene as a Renaissance version of a medieval-chivalric court of love, set in a *locus amoenus* where women, beauty, art, and eros offer relief from the rigid decorum and proprieties of court life.[9] The most specific readings point to classical texts, most convincingly to Lucian's *The Hall*, which Rodolfo Signorini has argued is the key to the "program" of the whole ensemble and of the ceiling in particular.[10] Lucian sets his rhetorical showpiece in a painted room that the text proceeds to describe in a mock debate over the relative powers of speech and vision. The apparent correlation between the text and the women in the oculus clinches Signorini's case. Referring to the gilded vault of a perfect room, Lucian's orator contrasts its harmonious beauty with false extravagance and likens the difference to that between the beauty of the woman with modest adornments, including "a ribbon that confines the luxuriance of her hair," and the false glamor of the courtesan who layers on "extraneous charms."

8. Cf. the tentative remarks in Joan Kelly's 1977 essay "Did Women Have a Renaissance?" reprinted in *Women, History, and Theory* (Chicago, 1986), pp. 19–50; and the papers in Margaret W. Ferguson, Maureen Quilligan, and Nancy J. Vickers, eds., *Rewriting the Renaissance: The Discourse of Sexual Difference in Early Modern Europe* (Chicago, 1986), many of which take the connection of gender and courtly politics as a set theme.

9. Ronald Lightbown, *Mantegna* (Berkeley and Los Angeles, 1986), p. 103; Cristelle Baskins, "The Locus Amoenus and the Princely Court: Mantegna's Camera degli Sposi" (unpublished paper read at the Berkeley-Stanford graduate colloquium in art history, 1983).

10. Signorini, *Hoc Opus Tenue*, pp. 228–48; the proposal of Germano Mulazzani ("La fonte letteraria della 'Camera degli Sposi' di Mantegna," *Arte Lombarda*, n.s., 50 [1978]: 33–46) that Mantegna's "source" was Pliny the Younger's Panegyric to Trajan is unconvincing.

The text declares that the beautiful hall "has nothing to do with barbarian eyes, Persian flattery, or Sultanic vainglory"; such a place "wants a cultured man for a spectator . . . who applies thought to what he sees."[11] Taking these cues from Lucian, the viewer would step into the place of that "cultured man," contrast the true beauties with the false charms of the woman with her exotic "oriental" attendant, and so compel the obedience of these feminine apparitions to the dictates of the text.

But this explanation is only partly convincing at best. In the first place, details appear in the text that do not show up in the pictures, and vice versa. Then too, the debate over definitions of beauty and some of the examples are hardly unique to Lucian in classical literature, and the pictures, suggesting various references and stimulating different associations, cannot be held to illustrate a single meaning.[12] Indeed, if Mantegna's painting were to illustrate Lucian, it would need to challenge the mastery of the text over the image, because this is how the debate ends. "Is not then a hall so beautiful and admirable a dangerous adversary to a speaker?" demands the defender of sight after asserting the power of what can be seen in the painted room over anything that can be said about it. The foregone conclusion is that "word-painting is but a paltry thing."[13]

Thus the most compelling textual reading turns us back to the image. Not the least of the ironies here is that the search for a secure iconographical meaning misses how much the glances of the figures actually give away. Their look is an epistemological prerequisite or inauguration of viewing; it also brings an "end"—both a purpose and a point of completion—into sight. By looking from the oculus into the room, the three figures direct the viewer to a central position, offering him at a glance the

11. Lucian, *The Hall*, Loeb Classical Library Lucian, ed. and trans. A. M. Harmon, vol. 1 (Cambridge, Mass., 1953), pp. 185, 183.

12. To take only one example of discrepancies, according to the text (ibid., p. 185), the modest beauty (only one is mentioned) also wears, besides a ribbon, a gold chain, a ring, and earrings; the courtesan is dressed all in purple. For similar tropes of beauty, see Eduardo Saccone, "Grazia, Sprezzatura, Affettazione in the Courtier," in *Castiglione: The Real and the Ideal in Renaissance Culture*, ed. Robert W. Hanning and David Rosand (New Haven, Conn., 1983), pp. 45–48, 55–56.

13. Lucian, *The Hall*, p. 199.

place of honor and the tribute of desire. In responding, the viewer becomes in turn patron, impresario, producer, *and* production of a command performance. Originally the preeminent viewer would have been the prince, and in this sense the play in paint, acknowledging and confirming the necessity of his presence, would have been political all along.

The Measured View

Although we are drawn toward the middle of the vault by the glancing look, a different visual logic takes effect once we focus on the oculus. A circle, a center, a hub of painted architecture opening through the vault, an illusionary disk of sky—the oculus consolidates both the surface pattern and the perspectival scheme of the ceiling. The conspiratorial eyes and the artful poses seem by contrast relatively incidental, distracting, and dispensable. We are released by this contrast from the charms of the glance, but only to be enmeshed in another, more demanding way of seeing.[14]

In two-dimensional outline, the oculus of the Camera degli Sposi is a set of concentric circles inscribed in the square of the false architectural ribbing that frames them. This arrangement brings together the centeredness and symmetry of two practically universal symbols of perfection. Encompassing space but having no beginning or end, the circle stands in many cultures for the cosmic, the celestial, and the eternal, whereas the square, "earth" to the circle's "heaven," represents stability, solidity, and measure.[15] A famous Renaissance icon of perfection, Leonardo's drawing after the classical text of Vitruvius, actually inscribes a male nude within a square and a circle. Real anat-

14. This distinction owes much to Norman Bryson, *Vision and Painting: The Logic of the Gaze* (New Haven, Conn., 1983), esp. chap. 5, "The Gaze and the Glance"; I use the weak term *measured view* both to avoid confusion with the technical meaning of "gaze" in Lacanian theory and to indicate a rather more limited range of effects that Lacan himself confines, in the seminars on "The Look as the *objet petit a*," to the "geometral dimension—a partial dimension in the field of the gaze, a dimension that has nothing to do with vision itself" (Jacques Lacan, *The Four Fundamental Concepts of Psychoanalysis*, trans. Alan Sheridan [New York, 1977], p. 88).

15. See, for example, Maryvonne Perrot, *Le Symbolisme de la roue* (Paris, 1980).

omy is not equal to Leonardo's fantastic geometry, of course, but according to the Gestalt psychologist Rudolf Arnheim, human perceptions of the world do combine the two spatial systems represented by the circle and the square. One gives the essential orientation of a centric point and a horizon, the other the "dimensions of up and down and of left and right, indispensable for any description of human experience under the dominion of gravity."[16] Mantegna's square-and-circle design foists a double order on the viewer, once in its centering geometry, and once again as an archetype of perfect proportion.

But the oculus is also one of the great incunabula of perspective painting, and in its illusionistic third dimension it functions as a hub or tube conducting the eye through the imaginary architecture. Perspective theory remains complex and controversial despite the familiarity of perspective technique.[17] Part of the difficulty lies in the tendency of the theory to conflate optics and geometry, on the supposition that how we actually see is practically identical with geometrical procedures for representing a three-dimensional world in two dimensions; at stake here is the large issue of whether perspective is in some sense "natural." Another problem is that theoretical consistency is not necessarily reflected in the pragmatic operations of the workshop. For our purposes, a few basic principles will suffice. In the Renaissance theory of perspective invented (or codified) by Alberti, one line, a "principal ray," runs from the eye of a hypothetical beholder to a central vanishing point. Fanning out from the base of this line a "visual cone," designating the viewer's field of vision, extends up to the picture plane. Starting in reverse from the vanishing point, the pictorial space is treated as another cone or pyramid extending out to the picture plane, and here the characteristic geometrical grid is laid out plotting recession in space in converging lines and reductions of scale. Thus, while the vanishing point, a focal stop or "plug" to infinite recession, corresponds to the retina of the viewer, the cone or pyramid "outside" the picture corresponds in this

16. Rudolf Arnheim, *The Power of the Center: A Study of Composition in the Visual Arts* (Berkeley and Los Angeles, 1982), p. x.

17. I rely here on the recent critical survey of the literature in Kubovy, *Psychology of Perception*, esp. chaps. 1, 4, and 10.

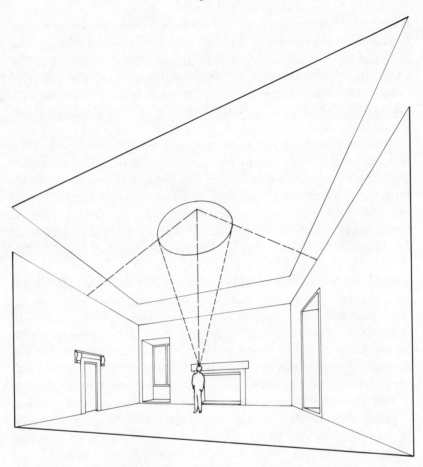

5. Diagram of the "measured view." Drawn by Carolyn Van Lang.

subliminal or supplementary effect of perspectival construction to the one "inside" it.[18]

Without too much exaggeration, the oculus in the Camera degli Sposi can be diagrammed *as* a diagram of a Renaissance analysis of pictorial space. Seen in this way (fig. 5), the perimeter of the opening becomes the outer boundary of a visual field at the point where its base intersects the picture plane. The parapet is represented as slightly but uniformly tilted in, so that if we imagine it projected upward it forms a cone with the van-

18. Cf. Bryson, *Vision and Painting*, pp. 103–10, and the diagrams in Lacan, *Four Fundamental Concepts*, pp. 91, 106.

ishing point at the apex. A line projected from the viewer's eye to the focal point inside the opening defines accordingly the limits of the distance the eye is supposed to see. And since the vanishing point anchors a pyramidal or conical inversion of "our" side of the picture, it is as though we are ourselves on line with an alien gaze meeting and then passing our own at the circle of the opening.

This schema imposes a strict visual discipline in return for the image of a finite world mastered by the beholder and proportioned to the beholder's eye. On the one hand, it draws attention to a centric point and a circular model of the visual field; in one-point perspective, a "correct" point of view is fixed, monocular, and focused from an arbitrary distance (just how rigidly remains open to discussion). On the other hand, these visual power plays are also empowering. The position assumed by the beholder scales the figures and objects represented inside the picture both to one another and to their imagined distance from the picture plane. Through the series of correspondences on either "side" of the picture plane—the vanishing point and the point of projection from the eye, for example—the spectator becomes the destination and source, creature and creator, sight and site, in this little kingdom of the eye.

The interplay between such abstract relations and what is actually represented at the center of the vault enhances the feeling that we are privy to the operations of an omniscient authority.[19] The oculus looks unnervingly like the iris and pupil of a gigantic eye. The cherubs shown standing inside the opening appear as if seen from directly beneath; since they are tortuously foreshortened—practically dismembered—at these extremes of perspective, their antic gestures are understandable. Above the parapet, however, the figures are not drastically foreshortened but represented at sharp angles to the central viewpoint; they appear to lean into space, as if to defy the steep geometry of central projection—a typical strategy, it turns out, for exempting human figures from the distortions of a theoreti-

---

19. I do not mean to argue that this was necessarily Mantegna's conscious intention, but it is worth noting that Kubovy (*Psychology of Perspective*, pp. 1–16) devotes a whole chapter to the explicit visual punning in Mantegna's work.

cally rigid perspectival construction.[20] Even the apparently innocent detail of the large cloud hovers in an air of visual magic. It is off center, ragged and gray, with traces of sublunary light— all this in contrast to an underlying symmetry and geometrical order that seem to transcend the accidents of ordinary space and time. Moreover, the cloud intrudes on and masks the central area where the vanishing point belongs. In what amounts to a philosophical joke, the vanishing point cannot be seen, as if to confirm that vanishing is invisible and that points are geometrical notions, not real places; and yet the mask of the cloud gives the appearance of an object or a site from which light seems to be refracted, in a sense acknowledging that perspective technique does make virtual fetishes of notional points.[21] These visual teasers, broadly hinting that the ceiling is subject to a superior power and a controlling intelligence, summon up the kind of metaphysical shiver that comes with being initiated into a secret order of knowledge.

Much more could be said about the formal operations of composition and perspective, but where power, control, and order are so clearly on display, politics cannot be far behind, least of all in a Renaissance room of state. Let us bring the patron of the picture and chief resident of the room back into the position that was his by right. Looking up, the prince finds his attention fixed by the measured view of the picture. He is master of all he surveys there, in part of course because the room is small and because he has commissioned everything in it. But the view of the oculus is made to order in the further sense that it is proportioned to his perspective and subject to his gaze. The geometric patterns suggest that this order is beyond contingency and change, while the perspective construction makes an otherwise utopian vision plausible and brings it under visual control. From the central vanishing point a steady gaze, a subliminal god's eye manufactured by the machinery of perspective construction, seems to be fixed on the prince. Al-

---

20. Arnheim, *Power of the Center*, pp. 16–18; see also Kubovy, *Psychology of Perspective*, pp. 116–21.

21. See Hubert Damisch, *Théorie du nuage: pour une histoire de peinture* (Paris, 1972).

though analogies between geometric perfection and the perfect order supposedly conferred by princely rule were commonplace in Renaissance political discourse, the humanist orator would have needed many words to say what the painting shows.

The Scan

The power of the effects we have been considering—the enticements of the glance, the controlling composition and perspective—is such that the rest of the ceiling comes as a visual anticlimax. A tour de force in design and execution, the painted vaulting looks by comparison functional, decorative, and didactic. Playing a supporting role to more spectacular performances, it supplies an ingenious architecture to cover the room, a symmetrical and richly textured backdrop, an iconographic script of classical references accompanied by a classicizing repertory of formal details. Where the oculus captures and concentrates attention, the ceiling diffuses it in the philistine pleasures of marveling at the *trompe l'oeil* or in the scholarly equivalent of inventorying iconographic details. There are, in short, profound differences in the way we respond to the oculus and to the false vaulting painted around it. In what follows I shall suggest that the vaulting elicits from the viewer yet another way of looking, a kind of visual scansion. As I see it, this scanning operation has aesthetic and functional charges as distinctive as anything we have seen at the center of the room, among them the classicizing aura essential to the "Renaissance" look of Mantegna's art.

I use the word *scan* to characterize the sweeping way of seeing that picks up a pattern, distinguishes, and then pieces together the shape of a design (fig. 6). To take visual bearings on the vault, the viewer's eyes follow patterns across the surface, along the painted ribs, and around the visual runways the ribbing defines. They may trace the long curve from one corbel embedded in the wall to another diagonally across; at junctions where one band of painted ribbing crosses another there are turns to take the eyes along alternative routes and so into the constituent parts of the overarching pattern. When the ceiling comes into focus as a whole, it is as an assemblage of modules: circles,

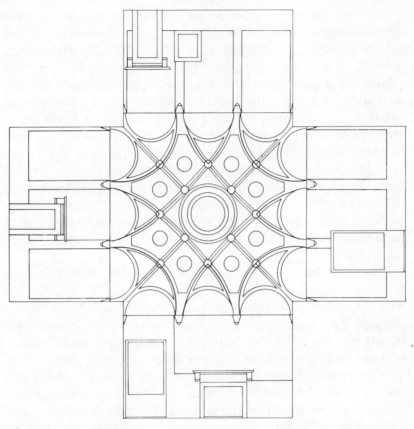

6. Diagram of walls and vault of the Camera degli Sposi. Drawn by Carolyn Van Lang.

squares, triangles. The concentric circles of the oculus ripple out to the circle of medallions that seem to revolve around the central opening; the square of painted ribs framing the center seems itself to be set in another square, turned a few degrees, which can be traced around the tops of the lunettes. Eight diamond or lozenge shapes are grouped around the perimeter of the inner square, the triangular corners of which connect as halves of a visual hourglass with the vaulting over the central of the three lunettes on each wall. Once the viewer is caught in the labyrinth or mandala of this visual circuitry, it takes an act of will, a kind of counterattention, to break the spell.

All the more so because the patterning that draws attention across the surfaces of the vaulting above also directs the viewer around the room on the pavement below. The ceiling cannot be seen all at once as the oculus can. To take everything in, the viewer must go around or across the room, following the design above or picking up double directions in the patterning of the floor, which mimics that of the ceiling. There is no privileged point of view, only a succession of possible viewpoints. Even before studying the inscriptions and examining the *trompe l'oeil* details, the viewer can map out the design visually and on foot. The most conspicuous of the sets and series of elements in the design invite attention each in its own right, but the connections between them suggest that whatever is to be learned from the effort will fall into fixed patterns and comprehensive formulas.

This schematic ordering—regular, repetitive, literally superficial—is essential to the classicizing or "antique" effect. It is true, of course, that the format and the subject matter of the vaulting are classical in type. The model for the dome with oculus was probably the Pantheon, even though the version in Mantua looks quite different from the prototype in Rome. The details are eclectic but generically antique, from the sham medallions, swags, mosaics, and sculpted reliefs to the Roman emperors and episodes from the myths of Hercules, Orpheus, and Arion. Nevertheless, Mantegna was not copying an ancient original wholesale. The critics, for all the professional obsession with classical precedents in Renaissance studies, have been forced to conclude that Mantegna's sources were various and scattered and, in any case, that he adapted them freely to his purposes.[22] This conclusion would be surprising only if classicism were a matter of making perfect copies. Renaissance writers themselves distinguished between literary imitation, where real ancient texts were available, and imitation in the visual arts, where the models were mostly fragmentary or altogether lost. In Alberti's famous preface to his treatise on

22. See, for example, Signorini, *Hoc Opus Tenue*, pp. 101–10, 152–70, 214–28; Lightbown, *Mantegna*, pp. 100–101; and, in another context, Andrew Martindale, *The Triumphs of Caesar by Andrea Mantegna* (London, 1979), pp. 56–74.

painting, the accomplishments of the "new ancients" of early-fifteenth-century Florence were all the greater because they had so little to go on. But even in literature, imitation is obviously not strictly imitative. The Borges story comes to mind, in which the dutiful scholar, after a lifetime studying a literary classic, realizes that he will never master it authentically; the culmination of his career will be to reproduce the text word for word. The point of the story is that the reception of a classic is always a matter of reappropriation, of adaptation and transformation by different circumstances and, often, different materials. The would-be classicizer draws on a repertory of received forms and arranges them anew in a reconstruction that may be regarded as a fall, a recovery, or a rival, but is never *the* original.[23]

Now Mantegna's vaulting can be seen not only as a reflection of the artifice of producing a classicizing work but also as a model of the disciplined artificiality of such a production. For one thing, it is painted; the garlands, stonework, stucco, metal, and mosaic are a calculated fiction from the start. Then too, the elaborate details, rich surfaces, and learned references testify to long study and hard work by the painter, and prescribe more of the same for the viewer; the sheer workmanship is an index of fabrication, of an artifact made and made up by Mantegna and his viewer-accomplice. Moreover, the repertory or vocabulary of motifs is quite limited, and the structure or syntax of their arrangement is, if not exactly simple, then quite regular and methodical. Depending on the count, only five or six motifs are recycled throughout—the medallion, the swag, the ribbon, the figures-in-relief, the wave pattern on the architectural ribs—and all these elements are consistently arranged and controlled. Critics like to praise Mantegna's inventiveness, but they do not have to experience all the stupefying tedium that actually painting the vault must have entailed. There is more slogging than *sprezzatura* here. Even the little variation here

23. Thomas M. Greene, *The Light in Troy: Imitation and Discovery in Renaissance Poetry* (New Haven, Conn., 1982), and David Quint, *Origin and Originality in Renaissance Literature: Versions of the Source* (New Haven, Conn., 1983), are especially valuable here. I read the Borges story translated into Italian as "Pierre Menard, l'autore del Chiscotte," in *Finzioni*, trans. Franco Lucentini (Turin, 1967), pp. 34–45.

and there plays off a schematic rigidity that anchors the pattern firmly enough to allow the fillip—a kind of pictorial acrobatics or wit—without loosening hold on the scheme.

Citation from a limited formal repertory, repetition of pre-ferred motifs, and codification of regular elements in overarch-ing patterns—these are, then, the organizing principles of the self-conscious classicism that we see at work in the painting of the vault, and that work on us, propelling the scanning eye through the design. The pictorial routine establishes in turn the field and the boundaries of an iconographic discipline cued to classical texts and images, one more case in which the specific "contents" of the vault correspond to the "forms" in which they are delivered. We can go farther to say that the vault func-tions as a mnemonic device that calls up classical references and assigns them a place in a formal pictorial order, from the first eight Caesars, Julius to Otho, in the ring of medallions to the episodes of Orpheus, Hercules, and Arion in the various compartments of the ceiling. The ideal operator of this peda-gogical machinery would have memorized the relevant texts so that they could be recalled when he saw the appropriate image. Novices or the absent-minded could turn to the library for texts, concordances, or thematic indices. In the course of these operations, the viewer would have summoned up a kind of mental file, with rubrics for various classes of information.[24]

First impressions of the portrait medallions would not neces-sarily go beyond registering the generic look of *Romanitas* based on ancient prototypes, the medal or coin and the portrait bust. Taken as a whole, the sequence is a kind of Suetonius's *Lives of the Caesars* in pictures. But any particular figure, at some resting place of the eye, might call forth something like the following outline:

TIBERIUS (fig. 7)

Looks

   Reportedly handsome, with large eyes
   Broad chest and shoulders
   Hair long, covering the nape of the neck

---

24. The major sources are actually assembled in the guise of interpretation by Signorini, *Hoc Opus Tenue*, pp. 214–28; for mnemonic functions, see the memorable work by Frances Yates, *The Art of Memory* (Chicago, 1966).

7. Tiberius, northeast corner of the vault of the Camera degli Sposi. Photograph courtesy of the Gabinetto Fotografico Nazionale, Rome.

Quotables
"Let them hate me, provided they obey my will."
Inspecting the prisons, T. replied to a man who begged for a speedy death, "I have not yet become your friend."

Lessons, Moral and Political (mostly cautionary)
There's no changing a corrupt nature
Tyrants are dissimulators (early T. as defender of constitution, plain speaker, budget trimmer, and disciplinarian)
Tyrannical appetites will come out despite efforts to conceal them (T. at Capri)

The tyrant is enemy to everybody, including himself—it was
   not fun to be T.

Et cetera: a large category where T.'s vices are concerned [25]

As for the mythological scenes, what distinguishes them
from the historical Caesars is not that one is fact and the other
fiction. The most conspicuous differences are that the myths
are represented as pictorial narratives and that they are meant
to be seen as part of the vaulting in feigned mosaic-and-relief.
Scanning across the triangular "sails" of the vaulting—say, on
the east wall—we see the three tableaux that relate the myth of
Arion. (I use this example only because the story is less familiar
than the legends of Hercules and Orpheus.) The northeast tri-
angle shows, *all'antica,* a lute player on the waves of a golden
sea, a boat with three passengers, and a dolphin surfacing in
the foreground—cues to the tale of Arion, the rich and famous
singer of Corinth who was robbed at sea and forced to throw
himself overboard after singing a song that was more pleasing
to a passing dolphin than the thieves. We see Arion traveling
on the back of the dolphin, so much faster, according to the
story, than the scheduled transportation that he arrived in port
before the thieves (fig. 8). In the third scene an enthroned ruler
or judge presides over three kneeling figures—this would be
Periander of Corinth condemning the malefactors.

It is easy to supply a moral, too easy for the pictures to be
given a univocal meaning. So, for example:

The power of music and of musicians, or, more generally, of art
   and artists

Virtue and nature itself come to the defense of art

Justice triumphs in the end

Fame and fortune are dangerous in a world where men are less
   humane than the beasts

In the face of so many perfectly acceptable interpretations, the
connoisseur's questions, quite indifferent or even positively

25. The texts for this exercise include, in addition to Suetonius, Velleus
Paterculus's *Historiae* 2.94–131, Tacitus's *Annals* 1–6, and references in the
Jewish writers Philo and Josephus (*Oxford Classical Dictionary,* 2d ed., ed.
N. G. L. Hammond and H. H. Scullard [Oxford, 1970], s.v. Tiberius).

8. Arion on a dolphin, north-central section of the vault of the Camera degli Sposi. Photograph courtesy of the Gabinetto Fotografico Nazionale, Rome.

hostile to meanings and messages in art, come as sheer relief: does the man-on-a-dolphin motif come from an ancient sarcophagus? A coin or gem? A mosaic?[26]

I do not mean to trivialize, though that would be preferable to the deadpan seriousness of so many iconographic readings of art. It is worth remembering that the court school of Mantua was called Casa Giocosa, "Happy House"; the humanist schoolmaster Vittorino da Feltre was famous for making learning into a game to get his lessons across.[27] In any case, far from being

26. Signorini (*Hoc Opus Tenue*, p. 216) uses Herodotus's *History* 1.24, Pliny the Elder's *Natural History* 9.9, and Aulus Gellius's *Noctes Atticae* 16.19 for his account.

27. The basic texts on Vittorino are in Eugenio Garin, ed., *Il pensiero pedagogico dello umanesimo* (Florence, 1958), pp. 504–718.

trivial, the responses I have sketched out are fundamental to the learning and reproduction of a classicizing culture. Whether Renaissance humanism advanced a coherent philosophy or view of the world is one of the ritual debates of Renaissance scholarship, but whatever the ideas of the humanists, it is clear that they were technicians of the classical effect. Recent studies have called attention to their notebooks filled with topical rubrics and lists of favorite classical exempla and texts for each topic; through these devices a treasury of references and a glaze of classical polish could be produced on demand for the oration, the letter, the essay, and indeed the role of a living classic, which supposedly justified all the effort.[28] We know too that images were used as cues to remembering appropriate texts for the elaboration of a given theme; that, for example, an image of Hercules could be used to bring to the mind's eye a set of phrases on, say, fortitude or the other major Herculean attributes, mental agility or, however implausibly for such a troublemaker, wisdom. It is suggestive, to say the least, that in scanning Mantegna's ceiling we are ourselves reminded that one of the standard techniques for remembering an oration was to envisage the text to be delivered as a series of images built into the architecture of a room where the speech was to be given.[29]

Another aspect of this technology of classicism on the vault can be mentioned only briefly here.[30] To preserve and defend the allegedly perennial value of the classic, time must somehow be arrested. Yet for the classics to seem relevant here and now there must also be some principle linking past and present. The archaeology of Mantegna's ceiling, however eclectic or fanciful,

28. See, for example, the important essay by A. T. Grafton and L. Jardine, "Humanism and the School of Guarino: A Problem of Evaluation," *Past and Present* 96 (1982): 51–80; reprinted in Grafton and Jardine, *From Humanism to the Humanities* (Cambridge, Mass., 1986), pp. 1–28.

29. Yates, *Art of Memory*, pp. 82–128.

30. I have found particularly helpful leads for thinking about this issue in Frank Kermode, *The Classic: Literary Images of Permanence and Change* (Cambridge, Mass., 1983); W. J. T. Mitchell, *Iconology: Image, Text, Ideology* (Chicago, 1986), pp. 95–115; Anthony Grafton, "Renaissance Readers and Ancient Texts: Some Comments on Some Commentaries," *Renaissance Quarterly* 38 (1985): 615–49; and Stephen Orgel, "The Royal Theater and the Role of the King," in *Patronage in the Renaissance*, ed. Guy Fitch Lytle and Stephen Orgel (Princeton, 1982), pp. 261–79.

is a model of a classic fixed in time in part because its antique references *are* fixed on the surface of the vault. Even so, the myths and the Caesars also represent continuity and succession—for example, from myth to history, from the age of gods and heroes to the founding of the Roman empire, and so by implication from the Roman emperors to the dynasty of the Gonzaga patrons. We could trace similar operations across the wide range of humanist culture. Nevertheless, they would not lead us very deep. Like the scan that initiates it, the technique of the classicizing effect calls not so much for depth of interpretation as for schematization, variation on assigned themes, the dutiful recitation of a litany of conventional responses.

Imagine once again the prince in the room painted for his eyes. Scanning the expanse of vaulting, he orients himself to the pattern, letting his eyes follow the design, pausing here and there to survey a simulated antique detail. Looking down for a moment, he notices the double of the ceiling pattern outlined, like a map or marching orders, on the pavement beneath his feet; as he raises his eyes again, his attention is drawn by the composition from one *topos*—"place" *and* "topic"—to another. Because he must move around the room to take in the ceiling, the prince becomes an active participant and instrument of the design, and what he sees in it—those emblematic figures calling to mind any amount of lore and learning from ancient myth and history—invites further participation. A learned member of the court stands by to prompt if necessary; a party of guests look and listen attentively as someone occasionally points to a detail or elaborates on some theme prompted by the pictures.

The references of the images and of the talk are "classical" not simply because of their antiquity or their authority as a class but also because they are tokens of the shared culture that defines this class of cognoscenti. As a patron, the prince takes great satisfaction in seeing the culture he has cultivated for years confirmed in pictures. The privileges of wealth and power are conveniently assimilated or disguised as the rewards of study and learning in the classicism of the vault. Here the prince finds both a distraction from the cares of rule and a high-minded justification for them. His old teacher, Vittorino da Feltre, had called him Hercules at school, and as an emblem of fortitude and wisdom that name would still do nicely for a prince; Orpheus and Arion stand for the powers of music, his court being famous for its musicians.[31] The ring of emperors crowns the ensemble. The prince basks in the aura of authority and legitimacy that runs, at least in art, from the age of heroes through the Roman emperors to his own time. One obliging guest exclaims, as if on cue: "*O Mantua felix*, this new Rome!"

By way of conclusion, I can hardly pretend to have given a full account even of the ceiling, let alone of the whole Camera degli Sposi. I have introduced no documents. I have no new iconographical sources to propose or "program" to assign, if we mean by that, as art historians generally do, a presumed master plan or group of texts that the pictures illustrate. Nor have I had much to say about Mantegna's style or actual intentions. In short, documentary research, iconography, and connoisseurship, the prevailing art-historical paradigms, have entered only marginally into the analysis. So have some of the more familiar approaches to art by cultural historians who supply and share the documents or the iconographic texts in their own efforts to find what they already know confirmed in art. The omissions are, of course, quite deliberate. They are meant to clear the way for a full and searching range of responses to the formal demands of art, not only because art is a matter of forms, but also because the forms of art shape and are shaped by historical configurations of culture, power, and authority. I am aware that many loose ends and missing links remain to be considered even in the case of Mantegna's ceiling, that much more needs to be said, for example about the interrelationship and ideological functions (or dysfunctions) of the three modes of seeing I have distinguished in Mantegna's pictures. At this point, however, it may be enough to have explored the proposition that what you see is what you get so far as cultural history is concerned.

31. Signorini, *Hoc Opus Tenue*, pp. 214–23; Stephen Orgel, "The Example of Hercules," in *Mythographie der frühen Neuzeit: Ihre Anwendung in den Künsten*, ed. Walther Killy, *Wolfenbütteler Forschungen* 27 (Wiesbaden, 1984), pp. 25–47.

Contributors

Aletta Biersack is an associate professor of anthropology at the University of Oregon. Her current research combines her training in anthropology and history through an investigation of structure/event and politics/culture over the last two hundred years of Tongan history. She is presently completing a book on gender, religion, and the organization of time in a Papua New Guinea community, under an award from the National Endowment for the Humanities.

Roger Chartier, Directeur d'Etudes at the Ecole des Hautes Etudes en Sciences Sociales in Paris, has taught at Princeton University, Yale University, the University of California, Berkeley, and Cornell University. He has published numerous books in both French and English and is now working on *The Cultural Origins of the French Revolution*.

Suzanne Desan is an assistant professor of history at the University of Wisconsin, Madison. Her work centers on religion and politics during the French Revolution.

Lynn Hunt is a professor of history at the University of Pennsylvania. She is the author of *Revolution and Urban Politics in Provincial France* (1978) and *Politics, Culture, and Class in the French Revolution* (1984) and is co-editor of the California series Studies on the History of Society and Culture.

Lloyd S. Kramer is an assistant professor of history at the University of North Carolina, Chapel Hill. His research focuses on European intellectual history, with particular attention to modern France and the processes of cross-cultural intellectual exchange. He is the author of *Threshold of a New World: Intellectuals and the Exile Experience in Paris, 1830–1848* (1988).

Thomas Laqueur, a professor of history at the University of California, Berkeley, is the author of *Religion and Respectability: Sunday Schools and Working Class Culture 1780–1850* (1976) and co-editor of *The Making of the Modern Body* (1987). In 1980–81 Laqueur attended medical school on a grant from the American Council of Learned Societies.

Patricia O'Brien is an associate professor of history at the University of California, Irvine. She is the author of *The Promise of Punishment: Prisons in Nineteenth-Century France* (1982), which has recently been translated into French as *Correction ou châtiment* (1988). She is currently working on a book on French policing and a project on professional formation in France during the period 1850–1914.

Mary Ryan is director of the Women's Studies Program and a professor of history at the University of California, Berkeley. Author of *Cradle of the Middle Class* (1981), *The Empire of the Mother* (1982), and *Womanhood in America* (1983), she is now examining public life in nineteenth-century U.S. cities, with special attention to the imprint of gender on space, politics, and ceremony.

Randolph Starn is a professor of history at the University of California, Berkeley. He is the author of *Contrary Commonwealth: The Theme of Exile in Medieval and Renaissance Italy* (1982) and co-author of *A Renaissance Likeness: Art and Culture in Raphael's "Julius II"* (1979). His essay in this volume forms part of a larger study he is writing with Loren Partridge on art and politics in medieval and Renaissance Italy.

Index

Abolitionism, in humanitarian narrative, 178, 179
Action: Bourdieu and, 90; Geertz on, 76. *See also* Event
Admission Day parades, 132
Advertising, in parades, 141
Aesthetics, 21; "reception," 156–57. *See also* Art history
Alberti, Leon Battista, 211, 218, 224–25
Allegorizing, 15
Althusser, Louis, 51, 54 n, 90
Anderson, Perry, 51
Androcentrism, in anthropology, 81
Anglo-Saxons, and parades, 146–47, 153
Annales, 2, 6, 8 n, 26, 34
Annales d'histoire économique et sociale, 2
Annales school, 1–4, 6–8, 11, 25–26, 49; Braudel and, 2, 3, 8 n, 26, 34, 72–73, 84; paradigm of, 2–3, 6–7, 26, 38, 72. See also *Annales*
Anthropology, 10–13, 16, 22, 84, 206; Biersack on, 13, 72–74, 93, 94–96; Davis and, 11, 52–53, 64–65, 68, 76–77, 95; and Geertz, 12–13, 15, 72, 74–84, 91, 92, 94–95; historical, 73, 74, 84–85, 96, 170; and "the other," 94; reflexive model in, 73, 95; Sahlins and, 13, 15, 64, 72–73, 74, 84–85, 93, 96; structural, 73, 84–85, 96; symbolic, 52–54, 64–65; Thompson and, 53–54; and world system, 82–84
Antimethod, 8, 39, 41
Appropriation, cultural, 12–13, 171–73
Archaeology of Knowledge (Foucault), 32, 33

"Archaeology of knowledge," Foucault's, 110
Architecture, in Camera degli Sposi, 208, 222
Ariès, Philippe, 34
Arion, in Camera degli Sposi, 228–29, 232
Arnheim, Rudolf, 218
Art history, 16–17, 20, 22, 205–32. *See also* Camera degli Sposi
Artisans, in parades, 139–41
Arts and Humanities Citation Index, 28
Asad, Talal, 79
Atlantic cable, parade celebrating, 132, 146–47
Augustine, 202 n
Austen, Jane, 181 n, 202
Author-izing, 94–95
Authors, of parades, 133
Autopsy reports, 17, 19–20, 177, 181–84, 195–97

Badinter, Robert, 44
Bakhtin, Mikhail, 15, 95, 108, 113–14, 120
Balinese cockfight, 82
Barbin, Herculine, 40–41
Barthes, Roland, 18
Battle of New Orleans parades, 132
Beauty, in art, 216
Benjamin, Walter, 178
Berkeley, Bishop, 211
Bias, 21
Bibliothèque bleue (French chapbooks), 163–65, 170
Biersack, Aletta, 13, 72–96, 233

235

Compositor: G&S Typesetters, Inc.
Text: 11/13 Palatino
Display: Palatino
Printer: Maple-Vail Book Mfg. Group
Binder: Maple-Vail Book Mfg. Group